THE REMINISCENCES OF
Rear Admiral Almon C. Wilson
Medical Corps
U.S. Navy (Retired)

INTERVIEWED BY
Paul Stillwell

U.S. Naval Institute • Annapolis, Maryland

Copyright © 2002

Preface

In the memoir that follows, Admiral Wilson summarizes his naval service by dividing it into three distinct phases: duty as a shipboard line officer during World War II in the 1940s; care provided as a clinical physician in the 1950s and 1960s; and his work as an administrator and planner from the 1960s through the 1980s. He made valuable contributions in all three areas. The oral history is a further contribution, because it is one of the few in the Naval Institute collection that presents the perspectives of an officer in the Medical Corps. Certainly part of the value is in the candor with which Admiral Wilson discusses a myriad of subjects.

Without question, Wilson's service as a line officer and the knowledge gained when he was a student at the Naval War College served him well in bridging the too-frequent gap between the operating Navy and the various staff corps that support it. As he makes clear, a number of his fellow doctors have viewed the Navy's Medical Department as an entity unto itself rather than as part of a larger whole that must work together to be its most effective. A fine example of this synergistic relationship came in Dr. Wilson's planning for the fleet hospital program that put medical support in place in the Persian Gulf region as part of the 1990-91 American efforts there during the liberation of Kuwait. Fortunately, U.S. casualty levels were low in the Gulf War, so the preparations provided excess medical capacity. That was a far better outcome than would have been the case if the casualties had been many and the preparations few.

The oral history is also rich in details of clinical treatment of patients. Sometimes it was in a ward that served retired senior officers, whose greatest therapeutic need was a drink of whiskey and a willing listener for sea stories. Sometimes it was in the Philippines, where the treatment might be for sailors injured while fighting on liberty, or it might be trying to save the life of a Filipino who was injured or ill. Sometimes it was just providing the daily bread-and-butter treatment, as Wilson calls it, that keeps sailors and their families healthy so they can do their jobs productively. And, most dramatically, sometimes it was in South Vietnam, where Wilson established medical facilities to treat the Marines who were wounded in action while fighting in that faraway land. Doubtless, many of those once-young Marines are still alive today because of the timely, effective medical treatment they received after being hit.

There is yet another story in this memoir, and it has to do with the law of unintended consequences. In the early 1970s, Admiral Elmo Zumwalt, the Chief of Naval Operations, set out to improve race relations in the United States Navy. One of his tools was the introduction of training seminars that compelled Navy people, both uniformed and civilian, to confront their prejudices. Admiral Wilson describes a case study from Great Lakes, Illinois, where the program went awry and produced the sort of unpleasantness it was designed to avoid.

In the course of moving from the raw transcript to this final version, Admiral Wilson made a number of changes and additions to the original. I have done some further editing in the interests of accuracy, smoothness, and clarity. In a few cases the editing involved moving portions of text from one place to another in order to improve the continuity of the chronological presentation. In addition, I have inserted footnotes to provide further information for readers who use the volume.

I am grateful to Geoffrey Wilson, himself a retired naval officer, for the original suggestion of his father as a suitable candidate for an oral history. Thanks go also to Ms. Ann Hassinger of the Naval Institute's history division. She has made a significant contribution through her diligence in the overall process of printing, proofreading, and overseeing the binding of the completed volumes.

                                                            Paul Stillwell
                                                            Director, History Division
                                                            U.S. Naval Institute
                                                            March 2002

REAR ADMIRAL ALMON CHAPMAN WILSON, MEDICAL CORPS, UNITED STATES NAVY (RETIRED)

Personal Data

Born: 13 July 1924, Hudson Falls, New York

Married: 24 January 1945 to Sofia "Kit" Bogdons

Child: Geoffrey Wilson, born 15 October 1946, Schenectady, New York

Education and Training

Union College, Schenectady, New York, 1946, Bachelor of Arts (History and Economics)

Albany Medical College, Albany, New York, 1952, Doctor of Medicine

George Washington University, Washington, D.C., 1969, Master's Degree (International Affairs)

Dates of Rate and Rank

Apprentice Seaman: 1 July 1943
Midshipman: 20 May 1944
Ensign: 22 September 1944
Lieutenant (junior grade): 1 June 1946
Transfer from line to Medical Corps: June 1952
Lieutenant: 1 April 1955
Lieutenant Commander: 1 December 1959
Commander: 1 August 1963
Captain: 2 August 1968
Rear Admiral (Lower Half): 1 July 1976
Rear Admiral (Upper Half): 1 July 1979

Chronological Transcript of Service

January 1945-April 1946	USS Liddle APD-60)
Month 1946-August 1946	Naval Supply Depot, Scotia, New York
August 1946-June 1952	Inactive duty in the Naval Reserve (This period spent at Union College for refresher and at Albany Medical College)

June 1952-June 1953	Intern, U.S. Naval Hospital, Bremerton, Washington
August 1953-July 1954	Medical Officer, Mine Squadron Three
August 1954-January 1959	Inactive duty in the Naval Reserve
January 1959-May 1959	U.S. Naval Hospital, Oakland, California
June 1959-July 1961	Chief of Surgery, U.S. Naval Hospital, Subic Bay, Philippines
October 1961-July 1964	Staff Surgeon, U.S. Naval Hospital, San Diego, California
August 1964-June 1965	Assistant Chief of Surgery, U.S. Naval Hospital, Chelsea, Massachusetts
July 1965-June 1966	Commanding Officer, Third Medical Battalion, Danang, Republic of Vietnam
June 1966-July 1968	Chief of Surgery, U.S. Naval Hospital, Yokosuka, Japan
August 1968-July 1969	Student, Naval War College, Newport, Rhode Island
July 1969-June 1971	Fleet Medical Officer/Staff CinCUSNavEur, Senior Medical Officer, Naval Activities, United Kingdom, London, England
July 1971-May 1974	Deputy Director/Director, Planning Division, Bureau of Medicine and Surgery, Washington, D.C.
August 1971-June 1973	Additional duty as Medical Advisor to the Deputy Chief of Naval Operations (Logistics)
June 1972-June 1974	Additional duty as personal physician to the Chairman of the Joint Chiefs of Staff
June 1974-July 1976	Commanding Officer, U.S. Naval Hospital, Great Lakes, Illinois
July 1976-July 1979	Assistant Chief for Material Resources, Bureau of Medicine and Surgery, Washington, D.C. Additional duty as Fleet Hospital Program Manager

July 1979-August 1980	Commanding Officer, Naval Health Science Education and Training Command, Bethesda, Maryland
August 1980-July 1981	Medical Officer, U.S. Marine Corps/Special Assistant to the Surgeon General for the Fleet Hospital and Hospital Ships
July 1981-December 1982	Project Manager, Fleet Hospital Project
December 1982-August 1983	Director, Resources Division, Office of the Director of Naval Medicine (OpNav)/Special Assistant to the Surgeon General for the Fleet Hospital and Hospital Ships
August 1983-October 1984	Deputy Director Naval Medicine, Office of the Director of Naval Medicine (OpNav)
October 1984	Retired from active duty.

Awards

Legion of Merit with gold "V" and two stars
Meritorious Service Medal with one star
Joint Service Commendation Medal
Presidential Unit Citation
Navy Unit Commendation with one star
China Service Medal
American Campaign Medal
Asiatic-Pacific Campaign Medal with one star
World War II Victory Medal
Navy Occupational Service Medal with bronze "A"
National Defense Service Medal with bronze star
Korean Service Medal
Vietnam Service Medal with two bronze stars and Fleet Marine Force Combat Insignia
Naval Reserve Medal
Philippine Presidential Unit Citation
Republic of Vietnam Meritorious Unit Citation with Gallantry Cross of Valor
Philippine Liberation Ribbon with one bronze star
United Nations Service Medal
Republic of Vietnam Campaign Ribbon with clasp

Civilian Career

1924-42	Born and raised in Hudson Falls, New York; all secondary education in local schools; extracurricular activities included band, orchestra, choir, and drama
1937-42	Worked part-time for an undertaking firm while attending school
September 1942-1 July 1943	Full-time student at Union College; no breaks because of the accelerated wartime curriculum
1 July 1943	Began active duty in the V-12 program
August 1946	Released to inactive duty, returned to Union College for refresher and continuing education
August 1947-June 1952	Attended Albany Medical College and held a part-time Job at Ludlum Steel Company
June 1952-August 1954	Active duty with the Navy
August 1954-9 January 1959	Resident in surgery at the Veterans Administration Hospital, Salt Lake City, Utah
1955-1959	Participated in Naval Reserve Unit with drills and annual training.
1 November 1984	Retired from active duty.
1988-1993	Worked part-time as a consultant to a high-tech firm with a government contract

Authorization

The U.S. Naval Institute is hereby authorized to make available to individuals, libraries, and other repositories of its choosing the transcripts of six oral history interviews concerning the life and career of the undersigned. The interviews were recorded on 18 May 1988, 15 February 1989, 16 February 1989, 16 September 1992, 17 September 1992, and 7 June 1993 in collaboration with Paul Stillwell for the U.S. Naval Institute.

The undersigned does hereby release and assign to the U.S. Naval Institute all right, title, restrictions, and interest in the interviews. The copyright in both the oral and transcribed versions shall be the sole property of the U.S. Naval Institute. The tape recordings of the interviews are and will remain the property of the U.S. Naval Institute.

Signed and sealed this 11th day of November 1999.

Almon C. Wilson
Rear Admiral, Medical Corps, USN (Ret.)

Interview Number 1 with Rear Admiral Almon C. Wilson, Medical Corps, U.S. Navy (Retired)

Place: Naval Medical Command in Washington, D.C.

Date: Wednesday, 18 May 1988

Interviewer: Paul Stillwell

Paul Stillwell: Admiral, to begin at the beginning, could you tell me when and where you were born, something about your parents, and your early life?

Admiral Wilson: Yes. I was born on the 13th of July 1924 in Hudson Falls, New York, which was a little paper town on the Hudson River, about 50 miles north of Albany, New York. I spent my entire boyhood in this little town, went to the public school system there, and graduated from the Hudson Falls High School in June of 1942. My boyhood was a quite simplistic one. Living that far north we enjoyed all the summer sports: swimming, hiking, and mountain climbing. In the winter there was always tobogganing, skating, and skiing. It was an ideal place to grow up.

My father was a funeral director. He worked for an old established funeral-directing firm. From the age of about 13 until I left home at the age of 18, I gradually became more and more involved in the funeral business. My first job was washing and changing the oil in the vehicles associated with the funeral business. As I grew older and could drive, I started driving various vehicles—cars, hearse, and truck—associated with the conduct of funerals.

My mother was a lady who, at the age of about 45, went back to school and became a licensed practical nurse. I have two older sisters, one of whom is a banker, and the other of whom is a nurse and married to a lawyer.

At the age of 18 I left home and entered Union College in Schenectady, New York, as a premedical student.

Paul Stillwell: What had gotten you interested in medicine?

Admiral Wilson: I really can't say, because my earliest recollection of an occupational choice was always medicine. I suppose it had to do with role models among the physicians with whom I had contact as a child in my hometown. In those days physicians were very well thought of and respected. Unfortunately, that doesn't pertain today as much as it did then. But I suspect that the role model of the local practitioner was the inception of it.

Fortunately for me, my parents were very much interested in education. They encouraged and supported us and always made it appear that anything was possible if you wanted to work hard enough to do it, so I went into medicine. Curiously enough, I had also developed a parallel interest in joining the Navy, for which I have no adequate explanation. It just always appeared to me that it might be great fun to be in the Navy.

Paul Stillwell: Had you gotten any exposure to the fleet at all?

Admiral Wilson: Never. I was 15 years old before I got as far as New York City, which is only 200 miles away. Certainly I had never seen the ocean until that day, and I had never seen a naval vessel. I had very minimal association with anyone who was in the Navy. I met one local fellow who was a seaman during the Depression, and I had heard about a young man from our community who was a midshipman at the Naval Academy.

At any rate, the Navy held out a great attraction for me. At the time I went to Union College in September of 1942, World War II was well under way, of course. In October the Navy opened up the V-12 program.* On the 23rd of October 1942, I enlisted in the Navy as an apprentice seaman, assigned to the V-12 program. I remained in college as a premed student in a civilian status until the first of July 1943, when the V-12 program officially started. We simply donned white Navy uniforms and continued our same classes. I was living in the Delta Phi fraternity house on the campus at Union College, and my sole physical residence change was to move from one floor of the fraternity house to the next. It was certainly an easy transition in terms of residence.

---

* V-12 was a Naval Reserve officer training program in which individuals received naval instruction at the same time they worked toward bachelor's degrees. The program, which was held at civilian colleges and universities, took about two years. See James G. Schneider, The Navy V-12 Program: Leadership for a Lifetime (Boston: Houghton Mifflin, 1987).

Paul Stillwell: Had the Navy been making an aggressive recruiting pitch to try to get people into the program?

Admiral Wilson: Yes, it had. Literally scores of the students at the college at the time signed up for the V-12 program. We had a typical sailor's day at school, except that our duty was to go to college rather than do other things associated with fleet and fleet support activities. We arose early in the morning, about 5:45, did calisthenics, ran around the track, and marched to chow. We did not march to class. We had strict study hours, and the academic requirements were such that if you didn't succeed academically you were sent to the fleet as an enlisted man.

By and large, it was a very good program. The V-12 seamen were paid $50.00 a month. Of course, there was discipline, and discipline was something that every young man needs. This was my first taste of it in the formal sense, and I found it very tolerable. I enjoyed the prospect of belonging to an organization where there were ground rules. You knew the boundaries and knew that if you overstepped those boundaries you were subject to punishment. I found it a very comfortable environment in which to work.

The nature of the timing of my education was such that we went to classes all year in an accelerated course. By March of 1944, I had completed approximately two and a half years of premedical studies. At the time there were insufficient spaces in the medical schools to take all the premed students. I was one of those who were offered the option of either going to boot camp to become a pharmacist's mate or the opportunity to go to what was then known as a midshipman school, the equivalent of the modern day Officer Candidate School.*

There was also a backlog of students to enter the midshipman school, which was the option I chose, so in March of 1944 I was sent to Asbury Park, New Jersey, where a naval station was established by putting a high board fence around two adjacent hotels. Originally this compound had been used as a billeting area for British ships' crews who were in this country waiting to pick up newly constructed naval vessels. As they moved out, we moved in. It was merely a place to mark time until there were spaces available in

---

* Pharmacist's mate was the title of an enlisted rating that worked in the medical field; on 2 April 1948 the rating became hospital corpsman, its present title.

the midshipman schools, but we did learn some things. We did an awful lot of marching, and by the time we got to midshipman school we could drill with the best of them.

Paul Stillwell: How much did you learn about the Navy while you were still at Union?

Admiral Wilson: Not very much, actually. The curriculum at Union was centered around the college curriculum rather than around the Navy. We learned some Navy lore from the fellows who were there from the fleet, but we had only a minimum of training in Navy organization or fleet activities. At the pre-midshipman school at the naval station we learned a little bit more. For example, there were whaleboats in which we learned to pull an oar and to be coxswains, but not very much more.

I did have one very interesting experience there. I was very much interested in marlinspike seamanship, having been a Boy Scout.[*] It happened that one gentleman there was a second class boatswain's mate who had had 56 years' service in the Navy. He had been recalled in World War II and was the brig watch. There was rarely anyone in the brig, but he was there serving his time anyway. He had gone to sea and had been a ship's tailor in the late 1880s. He spent all of his first 30 years, before going into the fleet reserve, as a ship's tailor, as a first-class seaman. He never got above first-class seaman in 30 years, because there was no such thing as a ship's serviceman rating and no way to recognize a man who spent full time being a tailor. As I understand naval history, such men did receive extra pay for being the ship's tailor, but it was not formalized in the sense of being Navy pay. Their pay was on a ship-to-ship basis. He went into the fleet reserve after 30 years' active service and had a job making eye splices for tent ropes before being recalled to active duty.

Paul Stillwell: Did you absorb lore and traditions from this fellow?

Admiral Wilson: Oh indeed, yes. He told me great sea stories about being on a battleship that towed another battleship that had broken down at sea, but mostly I learned marlinspike

---

[*] Marlinspike seamanship deals with the use of rope and line.

seamanship. He taught me how to splice and do many things with line that served me in good stead later on.

He was an interesting man. He was short—about five feet, two inches tall—and he had made his own peacoat, which came down nearly to his knees. He had built into that peacoat a series of inner pockets in which he could carry half-pint bottles of whiskey because he enjoyed his toddies. [Laughter] While there, I watched him make a seabag that looked like any other seabag except that it had a cover that came all the way down over the top, quite like a hat. It was secured by a series of lanyards around the periphery of the seabag.

Finally, in May of 1944, space became available at Northwestern University.* A large group of us were sent out there by troop train to start training in the midshipman school. We lived in a building near the university, but off the campus, that had been the Women's Tower Athletic Club. It was taken over by the Navy during the war for use as a barracks for midshipmen. There were two classes in session at all times, spaced at two-month intervals. The other portion of the group stayed at Abbot Hall, which was a new residence building built on campus by the university. The midshipman school at Northwestern University was always referred to as Abbot Hall.

We had a very strict indoctrination in the Navy there, and we did learn a lot. We took courses in seamanship, gunnery, navigation, communications, etc. We had a lot of physical education and training, marched back and forth to classes, and had strict study hours. Again, if you didn't measure up academically, you went to the fleet. Some did. But the level of interest in succeeding there was exceedingly high. The instructors—not in all cases, but by and large—were men who had had experience at sea and had returned to the midshipman school as instructors.

Paul Stillwell: Were they officers, petty officers, or what?

Admiral Wilson: These were commissioned officers. I remember one in particular, a gentleman named Perloff who had served in the USS Glennon, a destroyer in the Atlantic

---

* Northwestern University in Evanston, Illinois, was one of several sites for midshipman schools.

in the early part of the war.* He taught seamanship and was a superb gentleman. Another one was a Lieutenant Sullavan, who, by the way, was the brother of the actress Margaret Sullavan. These were talented men—all reservists who had had seagoing experience and came back to share it with us.

Paul Stillwell: Could you draw any generalizations about your cohorts in this program, what walks of life they came from, how well educated, how well motivated?

Admiral Wilson: Most of the fellows had come from college programs. I can't recall the specifics, but I believe one had to have at least two years of college to qualify for midshipman school. They were all very highly motivated, some of them so highly that they worried and developed ulcer symptoms—all signs of stress. Their backgrounds varied as widely as you can imagine. They all had college in the past or came from college programs. That provided some natural selection in the sense that they had the capacity to do college-level work. Many of them came from homes like mine that weren't exactly wealthy. They were all very intelligent young men, and they were a joy to be with because they were smart, motivated, and vigorous. It was a tough course, but it was a valuable one, worthwhile and pleasant.

Paul Stillwell: Tough in what sense?

Admiral Wilson: Tough in the sense that the volume of material that one had to learn in that 120-day period was enormous. A great deal of it was so foreign that it took a lot of time and effort to develop a mind-set that allowed you to absorb information in a strange field like ordnance, for example.† Who talks about trajectory, muzzle velocity, and translational velocities in ordinary life? You just don't do it. Navigation, of course, was an exercise in trigonometry in a kind of cookbook system. Seamanship was foreign to

---

* Lieutenant Milton M. Perloff, USNR.
† To get an idea of the ordnance material covered in the midshipman school at Columbia University, see Herman Wouk's classic novel of World War II, The Caine Mutiny, published by Doubleday & Company in 1951.

most who hadn't lived on the coasts of the United States. It was sometimes difficult to develop a positive attitude and an interest in subjects so foreign.

However, the interest levels were so high that people worked very hard. Midshipmen who had difficulty with mathematics frequently failed the navigation and ordnance examinations, which were mathematically oriented. Those fellows had a tough time, and some of them were bilged out for that reason. Students helped each other a great deal.

Paul Stillwell: How would you compare this school on an academic level with the college work you had been doing?

Admiral Wilson: It was at least as advanced in terms of difficulty—much more concentrated but otherwise equivalent.

Paul Stillwell: Did the school foster a sense of competition as a motivator?

Admiral Wilson: Not interpersonal competition. Competition was against a standard of excellence. The motivation was already there in these men. They didn't have to have a sense of competition among themselves, because the competition for excellence was the standard. The carrot at the end of the stick was a commission—the single stripe on your shoulder or sleeve—and that held great appeal.

Paul Stillwell: Was there any practical training to go along with the textbook instruction?

Admiral Wilson: Yes. The practical exercises we performed included marlinspike seamanship, the Morse code signal light, and semaphore signaling with flags. In the ordnance course we served in various positions on a gun crew to learn how they worked.

Paul Stillwell: Were there things to prepare you for the shipboard way of life? There's the right way, the wrong way, and the Navy way. Did you get the Navy way at this school?

Admiral Wilson: Yes, they gave us instruction on shipboard etiquette: saluting the colors in port, of course, of saluting the CO and OOD.* They taught us how to properly board a ship and how to properly leave a ship. They taught us wardroom etiquette. They taught us some shipboard organization—how a ship was functionally oriented and organized, the duties of various divisions and departments, etc. When we were at the pre-midshipman school in Asbury Park, we had been taken to New York City, where we toured a couple of naval vessels. We visited an LCI and an LST.†

At midshipman school we did another couple of interesting things. The Navy had an old Great Lakes vessel that was used as a seagoing school. We used to go out overnight on it and do navigational exercises and gun-crew exercises. We learned to holy-stone decks.‡ We also had the use of a group of YPs known colloquially as the Yippie boats.§ They were World War I antisubmarine warfare vessels. They were old, but they were perfectly adequate for navigation exercises and gunnery practice and that sort of thing.

We also went to the Great Lakes Naval Training Station and did some work with whaleboats. I mentioned before that we had done some rowing in Asbury Park, so those of us who had been there were adept at not only pulling an oar but also acting as the coxswain giving the orders. We had exercises such as getting away from the side of a sinking vessel in a lifeboat, how to safely clear the vessel, and how to get the boat under way with oars. Those were practical exercises carried out along with the academic work.

Paul Stillwell: Did you get a sense of how to conduct yourself as an officer who is a leader of men, how to relate to enlisted men?

Admiral Wilson: Yes, we did. In those days fraternization was frowned upon most severely. We had some leadership training. The most significant thing I remember about the leadership course is that in some respects it was boring when you just listened to it.

---

* CO—commanding officer; OOD—officer of the deck.
† LCI—landing craft infantry; LST—tank landing ship.
‡ Holy-stoning refers to the practice of scrubbing wooden decks by scraping them with bricks pushed back and forth across the planks by means of wooden handles. It is a laborious operation.
§ YP—yard patrol craft.

We learned a more practical approach from the commanding officer of the midshipman school. He was Captain Wygant, and for some strange reason his nickname was "Bicycle Benny."* He was a small, somewhat sturdy gentleman with silver-gray hair and a silver-gray mustache. He had a chest full of ribbons, and he was a most impressive role model. When we graduated, his really masterful statement on leadership was, "Gentlemen, you are going out to the fleet. Enlisted people are going to be working for you and looking to you. In time of crisis, say something. Don't just stand there and do nothing, because a bad order is better than no order." His statement epitomized the ultimate leadership problem.

Paul Stillwell: I remember an experience from my own time in Officer Candidate School. A chief petty officer said, "Always give a quick answer when asked a question. That impresses the senior. If you find out your quick answer is wrong, you go look it up and get the correct answer. Then the senior is impressed that you are very conscientious in addition to being quick."

Admiral Wilson: There's merit in that.

Paul Stillwell: What did you virile young American men do as far as liberty from Northwestern?

Admiral Wilson: Chicago at that time was one of the best liberty cities in the world. For example, you could ride anywhere in the city on the public transportation system free of charge. The people were most gracious and wholly supportive. If you went into a bar on the weekends, it was quite likely that you wouldn't be able to pay for a drink, particularly if you were in one of the more sophisticated places like the cocktail lounges in hotels. Chicago at the time was a bustling place. There were all kinds of things to do, even though we didn't have much money. We were paid only $50.00 a month, and about $40.00 was held back to support us in reporting to our first duty stations. Other than that, we had to

---

* Captain Benyaurd B. Wygant, USN (Ret.).

pay for our laundry, so I think we ended up with about $6.00 a month for liberty. That didn't go very far, but we had fun.

Paul Stillwell: That was where the free drinks came in handy.

Admiral Wilson: Yes, indeed. [Laughter] The city and its people were awfully good to the military people.

Paul Stillwell: I have heard that the Navy sent some of the best-known names from each of the specialized groups such as aviation, submarines, PT boats, and what have you to recruit the future officers. Did you have that kind of a pitch in your school?

Admiral Wilson: I don't recall having been exposed to that kind of recruiting. It's been quite a while now, and I can't remember all the details, but I recall that there were people on the staff with experience in various segments of the Navy, PT boats being one of them. The destroyer Navy was very appealing to everyone. The amphibs had a sort of checkered reputation at the time; they were thought to be a cut below the rest of the fleet.[*] The glamour ships were the cruisers, the destroyers, battlewagons; those contained the highly desirable billets.

Paul Stillwell: How much control did you have over your own destiny in getting a first assignment?

Admiral Wilson: We had absolutely none. When our group was commissioned on the 14th of September 1944, some of the fellows went to ships immediately. I was sent to the naval training center in Miami, Florida, for further training. It turned out that the training at Miami was largely a repeat of midshipman school. It was interesting at the time that there was a radar installation on the compound at the naval training center in Miami. When we asked about it, we were told it was too highly classified for anyone to discuss it with us. We certainly never saw the gear, even though everybody who went from there to

---

[*] Amphibs—ships and landing craft of the amphibious forces.

sea had to deal with radar. I have a little story about that later on. It was a paradox: here was a brand-new instrument of great importance, and nobody was allowed to learn about it.

After the naval training center experience, I had a brief period of leave. In early December of 1944, I reported for duty as a student at the antisubmarine warfare school in Key West, Florida, a five-week course. The school ships were interesting. One of them was a four-stack destroyer from World War I, the USS Goff. The other ships were PCEs, 135-foot, metal-hulled, high-forecastle patrol vessels which were very uncomfortable when you had to lie in the trough between runs on submarines.

The target submarines were mostly R-boats and S-boats from World War I. Occasionally we would get a new fleet submarine fresh from the yard in Groton, Connecticut.* The fleet subs did part of their shakedown up off the Connecticut coast, then sailed down the Atlantic coast to Key West to finish their shakedown training. While there, they acted as target ships for the school vessels, then loaded out with torpedoes and sailed through the Panama Canal for war patrols in the Pacific. For the uninitiated it was a dramatic series of events.

Each student was allowed to go on a submarine for a day during the period of time we were in school. I spent a day on the USS Hackleback, one of the new fleet submarines. I have to confess to you that after eight hours under water I was very pleased to surface and get out of that stale atmosphere. While on board the submarine, I had nothing to do except watch. So I inspected the vessel, and all along the bulkhead were gauges, knobs, dials, valves, pipes, wires, etc. As I was traveling along the bulkhead looking at all these things, I suddenly came upon a one-armed bandit, a gambling slot machine tucked in with all the other gear. That was probably the only recreational space in that incredibly cramped submarine.

We managed to survive the ASW school. I remember my great success on the USS Goff was to make a direct hit on a target submarine. The hit was identified by dropping a yellow dye marker in the water in the center of the simulated depth-charge pattern. When the "center" charge was dropped, a signal was sent to the sub, and it blew out a large burst

---

* Groton, Connecticut, was the site of the Electric Boat Company, one of the nation's principal submarine builders in World War II.

of air, thus signifying the success or failure of the attack. Those old four-stacker destroyers were built in such fashion that to turn them quickly one had to stop the inboard engine and put the helm hard over. They were terribly clumsy. It was the only triumph I ever remember in ASW. [Laughter]

The students from ASW school then went back to Miami to await orders. In January 1945 I received orders to the USS Liddle, the APD-60, in San Francisco.[*] I was given nine days to get there: five days' travel time and four days' proceed time. So I took the train to Schenectady, New York, where my fiancée lived.[†] I arrived there on Monday, and we were married on Wednesday. We enjoyed a brief but cold honeymoon at Lake Placid, New York, where it was 35 degrees below zero.

Just after midnight on Saturday, the 27th of January, I boarded a United Airlines plane for San Francisco. An aircraft ferry pilot had bumped me from a TWA flight I was scheduled for, so I was put on this United flight.[‡] The TWA flight crashed in Texas, and everyone was killed. The United Airlines flight to San Francisco took 22 hours, including a refueling stop in North Platte, Nebraska. We descended into what was seemingly a wheat field and landed on a small airstrip. People came out from sheds carrying square five-gallon cans of gasoline to fill the wing tanks. It was quite like the scene from Lost Horizon, a recent movie at the time.[§]

At any rate, I reported aboard the USS Liddle at pier 32 on the Embarcadero in San Francisco on Monday morning. The ship was in the yard for repairs after having been hit by a kamikaze aircraft at the Battle of Ormoc Bay in the Philippines.[**] The remaining crew had managed to keep the vessel afloat and jury-rig it sufficiently to get it back to the United States. The ship carried 14 officers and about 235 men, and 9 of the officers and 29 members of the crew were killed.

---

[*] USS Liddle (DE-206) was commissioned 6 December 1943 as a destroyer escort. She was subsequently converted to a high-speed transport and redesignated on 5 July 1944 as APD-60. She had a standard displacement of 1,315 tons, was 306 feet long, and 36 feet, 10 inches in the beam. Her top speed was 23 knots. She was armed with one 5-inch gun, six 40-mm, and carried four LCVP landing craft on davits.
[†] Her maiden name was Sofia "Kit" Bogdons.
[‡] TWA—Transcontinental and Western Airlines, later Trans World Airlines.
[§] Lost Horizon was a 1937 movie adapted from the James Hilton novel of the same name. It told the story of a group of travelers whose airplane crash-landed at Shangri-La, a mythical Tibetan paradise.
[**] The Liddle was hit by the kamikaze on 7 December 1944; 38 of her crew members were killed.

The aircraft hit the ship in the flying bridge on the conning station. The Zero carried a 500-pound bomb under each wing. It cleared off three levels of the superstructure, including the conning station, the pilothouse, the radio shack, the captain's cabin, and CIC, and it destroyed the mast.[*] When the ship reached Pearl Harbor, the shipyard there estimated it would take six months to make repairs, so they sent it on back to the West Coast, where the Matson Steamship Line said they could do it in six weeks and did so.[†]

Paul Stillwell: Did Matson have its own yard there?

Admiral Wilson: Yes, they did. They were under contract to the Navy to provide repair services for fleet vessels. When I first saw the Liddle, my heart just plummeted. It looked like a hulk. There was no mast and no forward superstructure. The landing boats which had been in Welin davits on the boat deck were absent. There were shell fragment holes all over the ship. The ship was filthy dirty, because it was a crawling mass of workmen with the welding torches and various kinds of wires, air lines, and other equipment they needed. I thought to myself at the time, "Boy, you're really in a whole lot of trouble getting into something like this." But in a few days the nature of things began to change. In the meantime, the crew was living on a barracks barge on the other side of pier 32. We were cramped but had wardrobe space, and we lived handily. Everyone was participating in getting the ship ready for sea again.

I was appointed to be the assistant first lieutenant, as a fresh ensign right out of school. My boss was Lieutenant (j.g.) Fred Stunt, who had been with the ship before it had been converted from a destroyer escort to an APD. He was to go on leave, because his wife was about to have another child. Before he left, he said, "Make sure that the yard workers get this ship put back together right."

Paul Stillwell: As if you knew.

---

[*] CIC—combat information center.
[†] The Liddle reached San Francisco for repairs on 16 January 1945.

Admiral Wilson: Right! [Laughter] I said, "I'm not really sure I know quite how to do that. Can you give me a few pointers?"

He said, "It's no problem. In the locker in my stateroom there are blueprints of all the systems in the ship. All you have to do is read them." I spent a lot of days and nights poring over those blueprints. In the meantime, the yard delivered an entire new superstructure to the ship. They brought it down from the fabricating shops on a flatcar, hoisted it aboard, and set it in position. Then the welders went along the edges of it and welded it in place. Immediately they connected the wiring and the other necessary utilities. Right behind the new superstructure came a brand-new mast, which was stepped in a matter of minutes.

Suddenly, a hulk began to look like a ship again. After a flurry to finish work in plumbing, wiring systems, and painting, we went into the dry dock and all that sort of stuff. Finally, the ship was ready for sea trials. I had studied those ship's plans so thoroughly that I really knew the ship very well. The knowledge was to stand us in good stead later on, because we had some non-hostile damage, which led to flooding in several compartments. I was able to go into those darkened compartments and turn the correct valves to stop the flooding, simply because I knew where they all were.

Paul Stillwell: That knowledge would be especially valuable for someone in the first lieutenant's department, because damage control came under that also.

Admiral Wilson: Absolutely. I felt that I had had a marvelous exposure early on in the game to help with something for which I would be responsible later on.

Paul Stillwell: How did you adjust to being a married man with no wife? That would be a difficult situation.

Admiral Wilson: In modern terms, with great difficulty. [Laughter] The ship was destined to be at sea until New Year's of 1946, which was approximately a year after we were married. As I mentioned, we had a three-day honeymoon; then I was off to sea for a year.

Fortunately, I married a magnificent woman, so it wasn't a problem. We have gotten along happily ever since.

Paul Stillwell: Where had you met her, at the college?

Admiral Wilson: I met her at the Ellis Hospital in Schenectady, New York. My future wife was a student nurse. When I entered college, I went to work there as an orderly. Just to give you a comparison of wage scales, I worked from 7:00 at night till 7:00 in the morning for three nights a week and received a salary of $7.50. If I got really ambitious and worked five nights a week, my pay suddenly went to $20.00 for 60 hours' work. At any rate, we met in the hospital and began going together. We had been going together steadily for two and half years by the time we were married. It's been a very happy marriage. As of the date of this interview, we've been married over 43 years, and I still think marriage is a great institution.

Paul Stillwell: Good.

Admiral Wilson: When the ship was ready for sea, we took it out on sea trials. We went out under the Golden Gate Bridge and out beyond the Farallon Islands off the San Francisco Bay. There I was introduced to radar.

I was one of several junior officers, and we were all inexperienced, so the commanding officer assigned us four-on and eight-off watches: four hours on, eight hours off. The junior officers alternated their watches between the conning station with the OOD and in the combat information center. I happened to be in the combat information center on the day we were doing the sea trials. The OOD called down and said, "Give me a range and bearing on the Farallon Islands."

Well, the radar had been operating only a few days, and I had never seen the thing really run except to see a screen and see the cursor go around it. I didn't know how to find out what the range and bearing were. All of the radarmen were very inexperienced, and they didn't really give me much information. So I stepped out on the adjacent wing of the bridge and used a stadimeter, a device for measuring the range to another ship if you know the height of its mast. Using the stadimeter and estimating the bearing, I passed the information to the bridge and they allowed as how that was pretty close. So I got off the hook for being totally ignorant of radar operation. [Laughter]

By the time we returned to the United States some 11 months later and after 120,000 miles, we were all expert radar users. We became especially adept at radar piloting, because a great deal of our work as an assault landing ship obviously had to do with going inshore. We ultimately felt somewhat exonerated after that inauspicious start.

As a young ensign fresh out of the hills of northern New York and probably one of the least cosmopolitan people in the world, going to San Francisco was an experience by itself, and to be there in time of war was magic. It's impossible to describe the level of activity that was all over the city, and particularly on the waterfronts. There were naval vessels all over the place undergoing repair. There were cargo vessels coming and going. It was a time in history that probably has not seen a parallel. This war had lasted long enough by that time so the country was fully mobilized. The mountains and mountains of supplies and material evident on the piers were just awesome.

The war situation at that time was such that we were pretty well into recapturing the lost islands out in the Pacific. There was a very great deal of experience in naval operations at the time. When I entered the war, it was really at a time when the war-making systems were sophisticated and there had been a lot of experience. A lot of tragic things had happened getting that experience, but by early 1945 the systems were well oiled and smoothly operating.

Still, some funny things happened. Before we sailed, the supply officer ordered 120 cases of toilet paper. We received 1,200 cases, so we had toilet paper all over the place. Of course, we couldn't take 1,200 cases and had to leave a lot of it on the pier. Things like that happened. It was indicative of the times that an oversupply of things was available rather than a paucity of things.

I remember seeing the USS Iowa in dry dock, and I thought it was the biggest ship that had ever been built on the face of the earth.[*] It's interesting that they've recently been

---

[*] The battleship Iowa (BB-61) arrived at San Francisco 15 January 1945 for overhaul at Hunters Point shipyard. She was 887 feet long and displaced approximately 58,000 tons at full load.

brought back into commission because of their basic utility.* At any rate, we sailed for the Western Pacific sometime in late February in convoy of a couple of cargo vessels.

Paul Stillwell: What do you remember about your first skipper and his indoctrination of you as a seagoing officer?

Admiral Wilson: I remember a very great deal about him. I tell people that I went to sea a boy and came back a man. My commanding officer was a man named William Dewitt Kennedy, a graduate of the Naval Academy in 1928.† He was not commissioned at the time because he had injured his shoulder while wrestling.‡ In that particular period in history, any excuse was a good one not to commission somebody because of severe budgetary constraints. He got a job with the Navy Department writing sailing directions.

In 1940, when our participation in the war was much more likely, he was recalled to active duty and reported as XO on a PC, a small patrol craft on the East Coast.§ He eventually became the commanding officer of the PC and then became the executive officer on a destroyer escort. His DE was one of the ships converted along with the Liddle and served as part of Transport Division 103. He was executive officer in the USS Kephart. When the Liddle was hit by the kamikaze airplane, the Liddle's executive officer and commanding officer were killed. At the time, Lieutenant Commander Kennedy was transferred to the Liddle as commanding officer. When I went aboard the ship, he was the skipper.

A little bit of history about the organization. The USS Liddle was one of five APDs operating as TransDiv 103. The division consisted of the USS Newman (APD-59); the USS Liddle (APD-60); the USS Kephart (APD-61); USS Cofer (APD-62); the USS Lloyd (APD-63), the flagship. The rest of the division had remained out in the Western Pacific when the Liddle had to come back for repairs. The Cofer was detached for a

---

* The Iowa was recommissioned in 1984, then decommissioned again in 1990, after this interview. Her three sister ships were also recommissioned in the 1980s and decommissioned in the 1990s.
† Lieutenant Commander William D. Kennedy, USNR.
‡ Kennedy resigned from the service on 14 June 1928, a week after his class graduated from the Naval Academy.
§ Kennedy returned to active duty as a lieutenant (junior grade), USNR, on 15 September 1940. XO—executive officer.

protracted period for special operations, inshore minesweeping, and the USS Diachenko (APD-123) was assigned to keep the division at five ships.

We sailed out to WestPac by way of Eniwetok.[*] Then we went to Ulithi, where we went on liberty on a small island called Mog Mog, which was nothing but a coral atoll. There we saw concrete barges used as fuel tanks. We sailed on into Leyte Gulf, refueled, and went on to Subic Bay. We arrived in Subic Bay sometime in March, about a week after the Japanese had been driven out of the area. We sailed in through the channel, past Grande Island, and anchored at short stay in Subic Bay.[†] We maintained war cruising watches at short stay during the time we were there.

The perceived threat was from midget submarines, and we kept a gunner's mate on deck with a rifle to deal with them. I have no idea to this day what good a rifle would do against a midget submarine, but anyway that was the dictum at the time. It was interesting to be at Subic Bay at the time, because later on I went back to Subic Bay for shore duty. There was a Zero or the remains of a Zero on Grande Island.[‡] If you remember, Grande Island was fortified at the end of the 19th century. It had huge coastal guns emplaced there. We retrieved parts of the Zero for souvenirs.

There had been a U.S. submarine base at Subic for some years prior to World War II. There was a nose of land that came down into the bay on the south side of the bay near Grande Island. At the foot of that nose of land on the beach the construction crews were already building an officers' club out of bamboo—one week after the Japanese had left. Later on, that nose of land was to become Naval Air Station Cubi Point, also known as Radford's folly.[§] Admiral Radford, being CinCPac at the time, thought that nose of land would be an excellent place for an airstrip, so they cut the nose down, flattened it out, and made it into an airstrip that's still in existence.[**]

We sailed from Subic Bay down south of Manila Bay to Balayan Bay on the southwestern side of Luzon. There we picked up Army troops on the beach as they

---

[*] WestPac—Western Pacific.
[†] Short stay refers to an anchor that has been heaved in to a point just short of breaking ground. In other words, the ship is ready to get under way on short notice.
[‡] The Mitsubishi-built A6M Zero was the best-known fighter plane in the Japanese Navy in World War II.
[§] Admiral Arthur W. Radford, USN, served as Commander in Chief Pacific/Commander in Chief U.S. Pacific Fleet, from 30 April 1949 to 10 July 1953.
[**] The U.S. armed forces eventually pulled out of the Philippines in the early 1990s.

stepped out of the jungle, having marched south from beyond Manila.* They were filthy dirty and sweaty. When we took them aboard, they dropped their clothes on the fantail, went through the showers, and were issued clean clothing on the other end.

The troops were loaded onto the five vessels of the division, and we sailed around the southern end of Luzon through the San Bernardino Strait. On Easter Sunday in April of 1945 we made an assault landing at the port of Legaspi at the inner end of Albay Gulf. This was a very interesting event to us for a number of reasons. First of all the Cofer, the APD-62, had put ashore its four LCVP assault landing boats and had taken aboard four different LCVPs equipped for inshore minesweeping.† The Cofer went into this long, narrow gulf about midnight, and the minesweeping boats swept the shore. Larger minesweepers had swept the channel into the gulf, and the rest of the division went in just before first light and anchored.

There were other landing vessels there, particularly an LSM with tanks aboard.‡ In the morning, at roughly 7:00 o'clock, we landed our troops. About the time we got the first waves ashore, the Japanese shore batteries opened up on us. We were anchored perhaps 600 or 700 yards offshore, and on our port bow was a destroyer providing gunfire support. As the Japanese shore batteries got their range, they started walking up on this destroyer. It had to back down to get out of the way.

One tragic event sticks in my mind. The LSM with tanks aboard sailed in and beached. They dropped their ramp and off-loaded the first tank. Quite unbeknownst to them, they had beached on a sandbar just off shore, and behind that sandbar was deep water. They dropped a tank into the depression behind the sandbar, and the whole crew drowned. It was a sad occasion. The rest of the landing went well. Some Army Mitchell bombers came in and knocked out the shore batteries, so no damage was sustained by the assault force from those batteries.§ We were interested to learn later on that there were some additional Japanese shore batteries immediately on our port beam, as well as those

---

* These soldiers were members of the 158th Regimental Combat Team.
† LCVP—landing craft vehicle and personnel.
‡ LSM—landing ship medium.
§ The B-25 Mitchell was an Army Air Forces twin-engine, twin-tail bomber used throughout World War II. It was named for Brigadier General William Mitchell, a bombing proponent of the 1920s. B-25s were flown from the carrier Hornet (CV-8) for the Doolittle raid on Tokyo in April 1942.

that were dead ahead of us or slightly off the port bow. The shore batteries on our port beam had plenty of ammunition. They were simply never served. Had they been served, those weapons could have blown our entire landing force out of the water. It's another one of those enigmas that dot the history of World War II.

Paul Stillwell: You had two groups of crew members on board at that time: the survivors from the kamikaze and the new people. How did the two groups react once you got into combat?

Admiral Wilson: That fact was one the things that concerned us as we went into this first combat operation. We thought the older crew members, who had been in the ship when it was damaged, might be a little jittery. Certainly the new crew members might be a little jittery, so we went in with some reservations about how the crew might react. The crew settled into their general quarters stations, and there was not one single solitary bit of evidence that anything untoward came about. I think that was in large measure due to several of the senior officers.

The commanding officer was in his 30s.* The senior watch officer/gunnery officer and the first lieutenant were very mature young men. They weren't very old—25 or 26 at the time—but they'd had a lot of time at sea, and they had strong but gentle personalities. They were stable and logical and had a very calming effect on the crew. I give them credit for strong leadership at the time when things could have unraveled rather handily.

Paul Stillwell: How would you assess Captain Kennedy's leadership?

Admiral Wilson: He was a superb leader, a thoroughgoing professional naval officer. He knew his business and, among other things, was an expert navigator. Not only that, he was a superb seaman. He always amazed the signalmen, because he could read light and semaphore as rapidly as they could. If they gave him a message that he had already read and it wasn't right, they knew it. He had a sixth sense when it came to weather. His

---

* Lieutenant Commander Kennedy, the commanding officer, was born in 1907.

ability to predict weather trends was uncanny. He was tough and in some ways unjust through the eyes of a new ensign, but through the eyes of an old admiral, he was right.

Paul Stillwell: Can you give some examples to illustrate that?

Admiral Wilson: His favorite phrase for junior officers was "Goddamn JOs." Nobody who was an ensign or a jaygee was worth much in his eyes, and only by the grace of God were they allowed to stay on earth. In his wardroom they were of the lowest priority you can imagine. He was a perfectionist, a very demanding man. He expected you to know, and if you didn't know he expected you to ask. If you didn't do things correctly, you really got chewed out. If you did things correctly, nothing was said, because that is what he expected. He was a little bit two-faced. He didn't tolerate the crew's gambling on the ship, and yet he and the chief engineer would gamble in his cabin. [Laughter]

I have a marvelous story about him. He loved to drink. He didn't drink at sea, but when he was on the beach he did considerable. He and the chief engineer went ashore on an island with a couple of cases of beer and couple bottles of booze and came back late at night. I happened to have the watch as OOD in port. When he came back there was quite a heavy chop running—three- or four-foot swells—and the fantail did not have all that much freeboard, maybe six or seven feet.

As the LCVP came alongside and was heaving on the swells, the skipper stood up on the gunwale and made a lunge for the Jacob's ladder. He missed. Seeing that he was not quite steady, I had squatted down. As the boat sheared away and he lost his balance, I grabbed him by the arm and literally heaved him aboard. He wasn't a very big man, probably didn't weigh more than 130 pounds. He was three sheets to the wind and the fourth flapping, and he landed in a heap at my feet. He picked himself up, shook himself a little bit, straightened up, straightened up his uniform, looked me right in the eye, and said, "Mr. Wilson, don't you know enough to keep your goddamn hands off your commanding officer?" [Laughter]

I said, "Yes, sir." [Laughter] That was typical of him. Nothing was ever said about it again, and that was the way it was.

Paul Stillwell: How was he tactically and operationally?

Admiral Wilson: Very adept. He had as his gunnery officer a man named David Deits.*

He had another superb man as operations officer, so the Liddle always met its commitments on time and in a very seamanlike fashion. Kennedy was indeed a fine officer in most all respects. Even if you didn't like him, you had to respect him, and you somewhat feared him. His actions led one to think that he emulated the person who motivated Machiavelli to say, "It is far better to be feared than loved, because people can fall out of love with you." He ran the ship and he ran it well.

After the landing at Legaspi we picked up troops at Mangarin Bay, Mindoro, in mid-April and took them past Zamboanga and eastward across Moro Gulf, to land them at Polloc Harbor on the island of Mindanao.† On this particular occasion we had cruiser gunfire support. This was a relatively heavily defended beach, and we had not had such large-ship gunfire support before. It was really quite an experience to see those big old ships lob shells onto the beach for seemingly hours before the troops went ashore. The troops went ashore without much difficulty on that landing; then we made another supply run into Polloc Harbor.

Next the Liddle went down to the Halmahera Islands north and west of New Guinea, the staging area for the invasion of Borneo. We went there in early May and stayed the whole month. It was tremendously hot. The troops staging there were Australian, commanded by General Wootten.‡ These Australian soldiers had been away from home nearly five years. They had fought through all the North African campaigns, then sailed around from North Africa and were within 70 miles of Darwin, Australia. They never got to go ashore in Australia before they were put on the southern tip of New Guinea to fight their way up that island. Then they moved over to Morotai Island, which is one of the Halmahera Islands group.

We anchored in Wajebola Roads and stayed there while the Australians were getting their act together. We eventually boarded them about a week before we sailed.

---

* Lieutenant David S. Deits, USNR.
† The landing was on 17 April 1945.
‡ Brigadier George F. Wootten, 18th Australian Infantry Brigade.

They were tough, tough soldiers. They were typical Australians: tall, raw-boned, and lanky. Their officers were really of high quality. We spent lots of nights ashore drinking beer in the local officers' club and they had the best repertoire of rugger songs and dirty limericks you could imagine. We had a wonderful social time singing.

At any rate, early in June we sailed for Brunei Bay on the northwest corner of Borneo and landed these troops. During that assault, we had a group of rocket ships, LCIs armed with rockets.* They started a shore bombardment of the beach from about 500 yards out in the water. The LCI(R)s walked those rockets from 100 yards offshore toward the beach at 10- to 20-yard intervals for a quarter to a half mile onshore before we landed the troops. Our ship was held in reserve, so we didn't put our troops ashore immediately. Standing on the fantail and watching other troops cross the beach, we could see them cut down by machine gun fire coming from various hardened defensive positions that the Japanese had built underground and had withstood the rocket bombardment. I believe our destroyers and other gunfire support ships took them on as targets, and eventually the troops were safely landed.

We were inside the bay and then were ordered to go out of the bay and speed down the coast a bit to land our troops in support of an assault landing there. We landed our troops without difficulty. There was a threat from small boats the Japanese were operating. They were small speedboats armed with machine guns and carrying heavy explosive charges in the bow. They were designed to strafe and ram ships. For the two nights we remained there we had a patrol sector that took us from the five-fathom line inshore straight offshore for a half mile. All night long, we steamed in and out from that beach, turning on the five-fathom curve.

One interesting thing did occur. We picked up an enemy aircraft on radar, and it was the first time we had seen a U.S. night fighter in operation. All we saw was the bogey on radar, then the flaming wreckage as the P-38 came in and shot it down.† We were very grateful for that P-38.

---

* LCI—landing craft infantry.
† Bogey is the designation for an unidentified air contact. The P-38 Lightning was an Army Air Forces fighter plane.

Paul Stillwell: Did we stand deck watches?

Admiral Wilson: Yes, I stood deck watches as the junior officer of the deck and alternated in the CIC. The routine was four hours on and eight hours off.

We went back to Morotai, picked up another load of troops, and sailed through Makasar Strait, across the equator to Balikpapan, Borneo, and put our troops ashore there the morning of 1 July 1945. After landing our troops, we lay offshore until about 1400, when we were ordered back to Morotai in escort of three Australian LSIs, which are infantry landing ships, equivalent to American APAs.[*] We went back north through the Makasar Strait and across the equator again.

At sunset on the first day the tactical commander ordered the convoy to stop for a burial at sea. These LSIs had taken aboard a group of wounded men. Some of them had passed away, so the ships stopped for a burial at sea service. I shall never forget the scene. It was at sundown. The water was like a mirror. The sun was casting a golden glow on the water. We stopped the engines, and the silence was deafening. When they played taps for the men being buried, the sound wafted over the waters like something out of the movie. It was a most moving experience. I'll never forget it.

After that, we sailed on to Morotai and made a resupply run back to Balikpapan with cargo and more troops. We were then ordered to Leyte Gulf for a brief period of repairs. Then they sent us back to Legaspi, where—under fire—we had landed the 158th Regimental Combat Team, an Army group, as I described earlier. The Army commanders wanted their troops retrained for amphibious assault in the planned invasion of Japan. It was mid-July when we went back to Legaspi and finally got to know the troops we had landed. We had a couple of very interesting experiences.

One of the officers in that regimental combat team was an Army captain named Carlson. He was in a ship west of Pearl Harbor when Pearl Harbor was attacked. From December 1941 to the time we're talking about, July of 1945, he had been continuously in combat. To say the least, he was edgy. He wore two pistols, and when you said, "Good morning," you were never sure whether he'd answer or shoot you.

---

[*] APA—attack transport, a ship perhaps 500 feet long and displacing more than 10,000 tons.

A lot of those men were married, and they hadn't been home, hadn't seen their kids. We invited them out to the ship for a hot shower and served them some frozen food, which they'd never had. We had an ice cream machine, so we invited the officers into the wardroom and the enlisted men into the galley, and we fed them all ice cream. Those men ate heaping soup plates full of ice cream with tears running down their faces. This was a piece of home.

Then we started planning for the assault landing training, which we did over the next two or three weeks. About the time we completed it, it was August, and all of the sudden the Japanese-American War was over.[*] Of course, there was great rejoicing. During the time that we had been down in Borneo and up in the Philippines, the Okinawa campaign had gone on. That had been a terrible trial for the Navy with all the kamikaze activity. We were really fortunate not to have been involved in that action.

Paul Stillwell: Did you have any antiair actions at all?

Admiral Wilson: We had a few antiair scares. We had some occasional bogeys that came close. But by that time we had pretty much 95% control of the air in the areas where we were operating. We had all kinds of carriers out there at that time, as you can well imagine. We had secured the Luzon and most of the rest of the Philippines.

Paul Stillwell: The small ships generally had more crew unity and camaraderie than the big ones. What did you experience in the Liddle?

Admiral Wilson: Well, of course, with a small crew like ours, everybody knew everybody, and you soon got to know their personalities. Some were good and some weren't. They came from every walk of life. We had a physician who was an obstetrician. One of his pharmacist's mates, Mr. Deale, was indeed a pharmacist from Herkimer, New York. The only medical action we had was that one of the Australians developed acute appendicitis a couple of days before the landing in Brunei Bay, Borneo. They used the wardroom table as an operating table and did an appendectomy. It was a big deal at the time.

---

[*] Hostilities ceased on 15 August 1945 after the Japanese agreed to Allied terms.

Paul Stillwell: Did you get called upon to assist?

Admiral Wilson: No, I was not a physician and had no medical experience except that as an orderly. The pharmacist's mates helped the doctor.

After the war was over, we were ordered to Okinawa to pick up some 100 service troops to be transported to Inchon, Korea. We were part of a very large convoy—over 200 ships. At the time I never thought much about it, although I knew that 200 was a lot of ships. In later years, the Navy dwindled down and the ship numbers became very much smaller. It was a marvelous experience to be part of a huge convoy like that one. Since we had ASW gear, deck guns, and antiaircraft guns, we were always used as part of the defensive escort.

Some weeks before this all happened, minesweepers had cut a hole in mine line seven, the Japanese minefield sown across the mouth of the Yellow Sea as a defensive measure. During the period of that sweep, hundreds of the mines were cut loose but not destroyed because of a storm. They remained floating in the North China Sea and Western Pacific.

When a ship spotted a floating mine, it notified the convoy commander. The convoy was moved out of the way, and the ship stayed in the local area to destroy the mine. That was an interesting threat and hazard. Free-floating mines caused a lot of trouble later on during the typhoon. I will tell you about that later. Anyway, we transported these service troops from Okinawa, which, incidentally, was a battered hulk of land, to Inchon, Korea. I don't think that in the time that we spent at Okinawa I saw one piece of land that hadn't been devastated in one way or another by gunfire, shellfire, bomb, or bulldozer.

Paul Stillwell: What kind of shape were the people in?

Admiral Wilson: We never saw any of the people. I don't know where they were, but they weren't around where we picked up anybody. We sailed to Inchon, through the channel and across the outer and inner lagoons. Inchon has a tremendous tidal variation, about 35 feet. We sailed into the tidal basin at the flood tide and moored and unloaded the ship.

The commander of our transport division was a captain, a splendid gentleman named Parsons.* Moored at one end of this tidal basin was a captured Japanese midget submarine. As soon as the work was over, all the off-duty crew grabbed wrenches and anything they could get hold of to go over and get a souvenir from this midget submarine. One of the crewmen managed to detach the helm. About the time he did, Captain Parsons, the division commander, came down the ladder and said to this fellow, "Gee, son, that's a fine souvenir. Would you consider selling it?"

The kid said, "Yeah, I guess so."

He said, "How much do you think it's worth?"

They settled on $25.00. So Captain Parsons peeled off $25.00 and handed it to the lad. The lad shoved off, but when Captain Parsons tried to leave he couldn't get the souvenir helm out through the conning tower. [Laughter] It was the laugh of the day for the crew.

Paul Stillwell: Wouldn't it fit through the hatch?

Admiral Wilson: It wouldn't fit through the scuttle.

We stayed in Inchon for a little while, and among other things we did something that is current today. We did interdiction of small fishing vessels thought to be transporting Japanese soldiers and/or arms. We had a boarding crew and went out into the outer lagoons. There the boarding crew jumped aboard these little Korean vessels, only to find some poor farmer hauling a sack of rice. We never found anything of significance.

Then we got an assignment to go up to Port Arthur in escort of some APAs to pick up prisoners of war who had been released. By this time, the Russians had control of that portion of China, Manchuria. There's a very long channel from Inchon Harbor to the Yellow Sea. It's dotted with islands and quite torturous, so it's quite a feat of seamanship

---

* Captain William Seavey Parsons, USN. He is not to be confused with Captain William Sterling Parsons, USN, who was the weaponeer on the mission that dropped the atomic bomb on Hiroshima, Japan, in August 1945.

to navigate it safely. We sailed out through the channel fine, but then we had a fire on the ship. It was a small fire that didn't cause any major difficulty. As we entered the Yellow Sea, we had what we thought was a submarine contact. We sailed into Port Arthur and anchored. We had the hook on the bottom only a few minutes when the Russians ordered us to sail, leaving one of the three APAs, the USS Colbert.

We returned to Inchon and on the way discovered and sank a floating mine. When we arrived at the mouth of the channel, there was a dense fog. When we went up the channel, we passed through the middle of an outbound convoy with radar ranges down to 25 and 50 yards and never saw a ship! It was a hair-raiser.

Paul Stillwell: What are the experiences you recall from riding with the weather in the Liddle?

Admiral Wilson: The nature of the vessel's construction—with these four landing boats up at the boat deck level—was such that it made the vessel very top-heavy in a heavy seaway. It had a slow roll, but in the heavy seas it would roll far enough so the boats would tend to roll uphill on the davits. So we had to wedge the davit wheels with wedges and then pound those wedges back into place every hour or so to make sure that they didn't come loose. It was a very trying trip in heavy weather.

We actually experienced two typhoons, both of which were frightening experiences. The one I remember best occurred in September, when we were escorting several ships from Inchon to Okinawa. As we cleared the mouth of the Yellow Sea, the typhoon warnings became more frequent and more alarming. The farther south we proceeded, the worse the seas became. The tactical officer in command finally broke up the convoy, and the Liddle reversed course to run back into the Yellow Sea, hopefully to find the lee of an island.

After a few hours of turning up about seven knots—because we could not handle the seas over the bow at any greater speed—we learned that the typhoon center was moving to catch up with us at a speed of about 10 knots. Due to the ship's top-heavy nature, we would be unable to survive the severe winds close to the center of the typhoon. At that point we were headed directly north into the mouth of the Yellow Sea. The typhoon was catching up to us from the southeast. We couldn't turn to the east, so we had no choice but to turn to the west. Being as far west as we were, we really had to go southwest, which was far and away the safest course to follow. However, a complication was that the southwesterly course would take us through a known mine field. At this time the seas were running about 20 to 25 feet high, the wind was blowing about 50 knots, and things were beginning to get pretty uncomfortable.

The commanding officer conferred with his senior watch standers and decided that he would bring the ship about and head it southwesterly. So we called all hands on deck in life jackets at midnight. The commanding officer turned to his two senior OODs and said, "When I think we have the smallest sea that we will get out of any series, I'm going to give the order to come about. If either of you think that that's not the time to do it, countermand the order." He relayed this information to the helmsman. Well, the skipper was the best seaman aboard. He picked the appropriate time, and we did indeed come about. We pitched and rolled and tossed a good bit, but we came around safely and that put the seas behind us.

Over the next 24 to 36 hours the storm intensified. The seas became about 50 feet high. The wind velocity went up to 65 or 70 knots, and we were turning up something like 17 knots on the screw shafts and with the following seas were making 22 knots over the ground. The difficult part was the fact that as a small ship, only 300 feet long, we were prey to the seas—the following seas in particular. The following sea would crash over the fantail and bury it in six or seven feet of green water, and the ship would be driving forward and would bury the bow in the oncoming wave. At any given time, the ship might have six or eight feet of green water on deck. Then it would blow itself to the surface through its innate buoyancy.

The brakes would hit the screw shafts and the ship would start down the far side of the sea to go through the same gyration hour after hour, time after time. Keeping the vessel at right angles to the seas was a difficult task at best. Sometimes the rudder was ineffective, and the OOD had to steer the ship with the engines. It was an almost intolerable environment. The conning station was an open flying bridge, and the wind velocity coming from dead ahead was of such magnitude that the spindrift off the top of the seas was actually painful and sometimes on some occasions drew blood on the faces of the top deck watch standers.

It was during this period that we had a radio message in the night that the USS Colbert had taken a drifting mine in its only engine room and was adrift without power. This was the one APA that we had left at Port Arthur, and it was loaded with POWs picked up there. We later learned that the ship not only survived but it was taken back to the United States. On our return voyage we met the USS Butte coming back out to WestPac.

Some very interesting personality traits emerged during this stressful time of the typhoons. On every ship there is a braggart, a tough guy who is in the midst of all the altercations. In our particular case this was one of the cooks. When we were in the dire straits, people were having to hang on for dear life to keep from being thrown about and injured. This rough, tough fellow was perched in the passageway aft of the galley. He was on his knees, praying for the Lord God to let the ship come up one more time from one of its deep rolls. Other members of the crew who were thought to be perhaps not quite as intelligent were the ones who went about their business, did their jobs, said nothing, and were really the stalwarts and the bulwark of the crew's mastery of the storm at sea.

One of the LCVPs broke the strongback which supported it, and it began to swing with the ship's roll. We would have gladly have jettisoned the boat but could not, because the boat would probably have punched a hole in the side of the vessel. We could do nothing but try to secure it. We were able to get a heavy line outboard of the LCVP and trice it in, due to the heroic efforts of the first lieutenant, who dangled out over the side of the boat deck with green water coming up under him to catch a messenger line to take in a cable with which we could secure the boat. Everybody felt that this was a very clear and close brush with our maker.

The interesting thing about typhoons is that they cause such an enormous disturbance in the oceanic water mass that it takes several days for the seas to settle down. Even after we made port at Naha in Okinawa, we were unable to leave the ship for two to three days while the seas calmed down to a point where we could launch boats and start shore traffic.

Paul Stillwell: Did you have any close encounters with mines?

Admiral Wilson: We did pick up a total of about a half dozen over the period of several months. We didn't really have close encounters. We obviously couldn't see how close we came at night, but we certainly didn't blow up any. In the daytime we had an augmented watch on deck to look for them, and we developed a technique as everyone else did. When you spotted a mine, you signaled any accompanying ships to stand clear and then you fired at the mine with 20 or 40 millimeters until you detonated it or sank it. Most of the time we could detonate the mines with gunfire.

Paul Stillwell: What about when you were in this minefield during the typhoon?

Admiral Wilson: We had no difficulty at all. Our information was that they were moored mines, and the size of the seas would certainly keep us well above them so long as we didn't drop on one in the trough. That, of course, was a hazard but no more so than the hazard of rolling the stacks underwater near the eye of the storm or on the back side of the storm. So we just crossed our fingers, gritted our teeth, and prayed a little harder, and we came through. It was really a position of being between a rock and a hard place and picking the softer of the two.

Later in September, the Navy sent us over to Taku Bar, which is off the mouth of the Hai River and downstream from Tientsin, over past Chefoo. Mind you, the silt that comes out of that river is of such character that it colors the Yellow Sea, and that's why it has the name. It has created such a delta that we anchored 15 miles offshore in 15 fathoms of water. We were there ostensibly as the port director's ship. We never really assumed that duty, because there were other vessels there more senior to us that had stayed there longer and were to stay longer. But we were there nominally as port director's ship.

We stayed there 30 days, and it was very interesting, because we had the opportunity to get to Tientsin, China, on a couple of occasions for an overnight stay. China at that time was reeling under the effects of years and years of war, either at the hands of the warlords or the hands of the Japanese or—at that time—the hands of the Chinese Communists, who were getting more and more vigorous. China was really on its uppers.

Of course, as a young man, 21 years old, I was fascinated by China, the sampan families dwelling along the river's edge; old people were found dead in doorways every morning; and a monetary exchange rate of 2,100 to 1. But the most interesting feature was the international settlement of Tientsin. There were settlements representing the major European nations—Italy, Britain, France, Germany, and the United States.

Paul Stillwell: Undoubtedly holdovers from way back.

Admiral Wilson: Yes. You could buy durable goods there. You could buy things that you hadn't seen in the United States all during the war. I remember buying a harmonica, for example, that you couldn't find during the war. I always wanted to buy one so I would have something to use at sea. You could find them there. In the Italian section there was a large hai alai fronton, and we went there. They served any kind of whiskey that you wanted—whiskey that you couldn't buy in the United States at the time because of rationing of various kinds. I remember going to a luncheon at the very formal British Victoria Café, complete with a three-piece string ensemble, potted palms, and uniformed waiters. I remember buying a bottle of Chablis '29, a 16-year-old bottle of wine, and I think it cost a dollar and a quarter. Well, such things are impressive to young men.

At any rate, we stayed in North China until mid-November, when we were ordered home to the Brooklyn Navy Yard.[*] We refueled in Buckner Bay, Okinawa, and picked up about 100 Seabees to transport to Pearl Harbor. Prior to the return voyage, we lost all of our senior officers, who got out on the point system just before we sailed from North China.[†] They had become increasingly dissatisfied with the CO, who instituted some very irksome programs, such as a course in maneuvering-board exercises—after the war was over.[‡]

---

[*] The official name was New York Naval Shipyard.
[†] For the demobilization of the U.S. armed forces after World War II, the services had a point system to determine individual priorities for leaving the service. Points were awarded for length of service, overseas service, battle stars, decorations, and dependent children. Those with the highest number of points were the earliest discharged.
[‡] A maneuvering board is a sheet of paper containing a compass rose, concentric circles, and logarithmic scales. It is used for working out relative motion problems for ships that are maneuvering.

Paul Stillwell: What did that make you when they left?

Admiral Wilson: That made me the first lieutenant and an OOD, so we all stood watches.

Paul Stillwell: What memories do you have of the trip from the Western Pacific back to the United States?

Admiral Wilson: Only that the trip home was a terribly long one. We had long days at sea and long distances. From China we went to Okinawa, then sailed a great-circle route to Pearl Harbor, which, of course, is a tremendous distance. Standing watches during long transits like that is tedious. Going the same course and same speed for day after day after day really became a monotonous bore. We were glad to get back to Pearl Harbor, where we could get some fresh vegetables and have an overnight rest while we refueled and re-provisioned the ship. While in Pearl Harbor, our very unpopular (for good reason) XO was detached and given command of another ship. When he went over the side minutes before we sailed, there was a great cheer from the crew. I am sure the departing XO misinterpreted the crew's sentiment.

Of course, a couple of thousand miles to San Diego was a breeze compared to the long haul from Okinawa. On arrival in San Diego the city—the Navy in particular—was very well set up to receive homecoming ships. There were bands and committees of welcome and banners flying. You felt as though you were really home when you reached San Diego. We stayed there just overnight, long enough to refuel and re-provision the ship, call home, and then sail down the west coast of Mexico, through the Panama Canal, and out to the Atlantic across the Caribbean Sea.

When we cleared the Windward Passage just south of Cuba, we came into the teeth of a Nor'easter, a heavy storm that lasted all the way up the Atlantic coast to New York City. When we entered New York Harbor on New Year's Day, it was zero degrees Fahrenheit. Having just come from the tropics, everyone was absolutely frozen stiff in those temperatures. Fortunately, the warming trend began when we pulled up at a pier, and many of our families and friends were there to meet us, and from then on it was old home week. It was a delightful occasion. Of course for me, the new bridegroom when I sailed, it was especially grand.

We spent 30 days in Brooklyn, having the ship repaired, getting it ready to be mothballed down in the St. Johns River south of Jacksonville, Florida, at Green Cove Springs.* We had an uneventful time sailing down the coast and getting into the Green Cove Springs area. I left the ship some few months later in April.

Paul Stillwell: What do you remember about the mothballing process?

Admiral Wilson: Well, the mothballing process really didn't amount to much when we went there, for the reason that they had not yet built up an activity to actually mothball the ships. What we did was Chinese-moor out in the stream. They did not have mooring buoys, and on one occasion when a strong west wind came up it all but swept the whole nest onto the lee shore. One vessel anchored singly did drag down and stuck its screws in a mudbank. It had to go out under emergency power.

What we did do was to fill out the inventory of the ship's allowance list. We got aboard all this gear that the ship was supposed to have. Most of the stuff that we got aboard would never in God's world ever be used.

Paul Stillwell: Such as?

Admiral Wilson: Oh, towing bridles, huge, great big wire cables which we never would use. All kinds of damage control equipment that we really needed out in the WestPac but didn't ever have. [Laughter] It was that sort of thing. It was kind of waiting for things to happen, waiting for the preservation activity to develop, waiting for the big mooring buoys that would be the permanent anchorage for the vessels. Of course, we began to lose people, and we got new people. The commanding officer and I left in the same boat. The boat officer became the commanding officer. It was quite an evolution.

I had the good fortune to receive orders to the Scotia Naval Supply Depot, in Scotia, New York, directly across the Mohawk River from Schenectady, where my wife

---

* The ship was decommissioned at Green Cove Springs on 18 June 1946.

was residing. As a young line officer with basically a year at sea, I went there on a special arrangement that the Bureau of Personnel had offered. When I went there, I was made the assistant storage officer. Now, that sounds like a highfalutin title, but you must remember that in those days virtually all the people who did anything of significance in these depots were civilian workers. They knew what was going on and really took the responsibility for making things happen. At any rate, I was given the nominal title of assistant storage officer and the nominal responsibility for six buildings of what were then called BuShips equipment.*

In this depot, in these 200- by 600-foot warehouses, they had what amounted to entire ships, except for the hulls, radios, and guns. They had the engines, the big reduction gears, the turbines, all of the furnishings, all of the equipments. No ammunition but everything else that the ships needed was there.

Paul Stillwell: What kinds of ships are you speaking of?

Admiral Wilson: All kinds, all the way from destroyers to battlewagons. We had replacement reduction gears for battleships, cruisers, and destroyers, and we had the turbine engines to go with them. The people who had been there a long time and had served there during the war told me stories of cases where they had emergent requirements to provide new engines or turbines for damaged vessels.

On one memorable occasion the requirement came through at midnight on New Year's Eve, and they had to move a lot of other heavy equipment and heavy machinery to get to the proper turbine. They finally got it, put it on a flatbed trailer, gave it a police escort and they went from Scotia, New York, down to New York City in time to get the engine there by 8:00 o'clock in the morning. When they arrived at the pier, the shipyard had already removed a part of the deck sufficient to allow the new engine to be dropped in place. It was dropped into place, pins were put in the corners to align it properly, and the vessel shoved off to sea. That kind of supply support during the war was very common and certainly kept the war effort going.

---

* BuShips—Bureau of Ships.

Paul Stillwell: Why Scotia, New York, for this kind of facility?

Admiral Wilson: I suppose because it had good transportation access by road and rail. And it was inland; there was certainly adequate land for it. It's like why put a naval ammunition depot in Crane, Indiana? The logic is not always clear.

Paul Stillwell: There is a ships' parts center in Mechanicsburg, Pennsylvania. Is this a successor to the Scotia facility?

Admiral Wilson: I expect so, although SPCC Mechanicsburg operates on a very different basis than Scotia did.* Scotia had automotive repair parts at one point for all the vehicles in the Navy. Mechanicsburg now operates on the COSAL system, coordinated ships allowance list, where it stocks the spares for ships at sea.

My recollection of Scotia is that it was more of a bulk supply depot dealing with general merchandise and perhaps less with finely specific spare parts for specific vessels. It's my recollection that supply depots, particularly those in Navy yards on the coasts, were much more oriented toward ships' parts than were places like Scotia. Scotia had warehouses full of things like undershirts, underwear, blankets, silverware, galley equipment, and things of rather general nature, rather than tubes for radios and that sort of thing, except, of course, for the spare parts for the major machinery in the vessel.

Another interesting thing was happening at that time. The World War II fleet was being drawn down. Some of its ships were being dismantled, and all of the seemingly useful equipments in those ships were being removed. A great deal of it was sent to Scotia. Every day we used to receive whole railroad gondolas full of parts from ships: everything from electrical distribution panels and electric motors to pumps and evaporators and refrigerators and galley equipment.

There was an entire staff of inspectors whose job it was to identify the piece to see what it was, determine its characteristics, and make some gross appraisal of its salvageability. Then there were the other people, the preservers, who went through a very formalized, very complicated process of cleaning and repairing and preserving these pieces

---

* SSPC—Ships' Parts Control Center.

for whatever subsequent use could be found for them. The variety was almost infinite and went all the way from small hand-sized or pocket-sized equipment all the way to cherry pickers and other types of small cranes, bulldozers, trucks, road graders, and all kinds of equipment brought in from the islands. Some of the vehicles still had coral stone in the recesses.

At this point I was promoted to lieutenant (junior grade) in the line, and in August of that year, 1946, I went to inactive duty in the Naval Reserve to return to college and on to medical school.

Paul Stillwell: What became of the facility at Scotia after you left?

Admiral Wilson: It rather dwindled away as a major material base. At one point it became the automotive center, providing spare parts and tires for the Navy's vehicles. Ultimately it became the center for the correspondence courses for the Navy. Its latest and most recent mission has been to be an administrative support center for the nuclear power school at Milton, New York. The school has a contract nuclear reactor provided by the General Electric Corporation to train people for nuclear power operations on ships and submarines. This is about 15 miles up the road from Scotia. To the best of my knowledge, it's still fulfilling that role as an administrative support center. The supply center at Scotia was there a long time and did a lot of good things for the Navy during the war and after, but it's dwindled away like a lot of other bases.

Subsequent to my release from active duty to inactive duty, I returned to Union College. There I took some refresher courses and continued my studies toward a degree.

Paul Stillwell: How did you feel about the Navy at that point? You were certainly in a far different position than when you had been there before. Did you see the Navy in your future?

Admiral Wilson: I really did not at that time. I think you could imagine the multitude of feelings, including perhaps the relief at having survived the war and now looking beyond the present into the future.

The college, of course, had grown by leaps and bounds because so many veterans wanted to go to school after the war. When I attended earlier in the '40s, the student body was about 700 or 800. When I returned there in the fall of 1946, it had jumped to about 2,000. At that time they had erected some family housing, which were essentially old Army barracks. They were wooden frame structures set on wooden pilings. They were cold and hard to heat. I remember that we drove thermos bottle corks in the knotholes in the floor to keep the wind from blowing up through. We bought a cheap woolen carpet, and for an underlayment, we used multiple layers of newspapers to provide some insulation on the floors. But for all of that we were young and vigorous and interested and glad to be back together and really had a marvelous time with our brand-newborn son.[*]

After some college work, I entered Albany Medical College as a student and graduated in 1952. During this time I held a reserve line commission but did not actively participate in reserve affairs. The units really didn't have billets for people like me, and I was so busy at med school that I really didn't have time for the reserve anyway. Medical school, of course, was a grueling experience at that time. The year that I matriculated, there were 2,000 applicants for 50 seats. Just to get into medical school was a triumph in itself, to say nothing about staying there.

Paul Stillwell: Why such a disparity between supply and demand?

Admiral Wilson: Well, there were so many people who had programmed themselves into medical school and either were drafted or enlisted in the various services that there was this tremendous backlog of people who wanted to become physicians. It was like so many other things. It involved the very nature of the college support for the vast numbers who wanted to go to school. You can well remember how colleges doubled and trebled and quadrupled their enrollments and new colleges sprang up all over the country.

The GI Bill, of course, was the big driver in that.[†] It meant that people who had previously been unable to afford the cost of an education now had the opportunity, so the

---

[*] Geoffrey Peter Wilson was born 15 October 1946.
[†] The GI Bill, officially the Servicemen's Readjustment Act of 1944, provided educational assistance and other benefits to all veterans honorably discharged with six or more months of active service after 16 September 1940.

market for educational institutions was enormously strong. Med schools, being as restricted in numbers as they were, just felt that competition more keenly than other schools.

At any rate, after long, grueling, and hard struggle we graduated from medical school. At that time there came into being a matching program. The basic mechanism of it was that the medical student signed up with a preference for internships. I requested a Navy internship, because I was so broke that I needed a job that paid some money to help support my family. I requested Chelsea Navy Hospital at Boston and Newport, Rhode Island, Hospital, because the Navy said that you should request those installations closest to your med school for the sake of economy.

I couldn't think of any other place that I really wanted to go, so I put down Bremerton, Washington, as the third choice, simply because we had never been out West. Lo and behold, we were cross-matched with Bremerton, Washington. So we duly marched across the country and set up residence there. I became an intern there for the academic year 1 July '52 to 1 July '53.

During that time the Korean War was winding down. We were receiving patients from Korea. These were wounded men who were coming back for convalescence, but there were also a lot of ill patients. We saw a lot of malaria patients and even as interns became quite adept at diagnosing malaria. The hospital staff was composed of a few regular officers and a large number of reserve officers. The reserve officers were of superb clinical standing. They were men who subsequently have become some of the leaders in various specialty fields. I remember one name, Dr. Ray Casterline, an internist who was since become quite well known in medical circles nationwide.[*] He's from Medford, Oregon. There were others.

Paul Stillwell: How do account for that phenomenon, that high level of talent in the reserve officers?

Admiral Wilson: I think because it took a cross-section of the country. A great many of these people were interested in academic medicine, having little innate interest in the

---

[*] Lieutenant Ray L. Casterline, MC, USNR.

military service. When they were drafted, the Navy benefited by their presence. Subsequently, as I had a medical career, I concluded that one of the best things that happens to the Navy is to have a strong reserve component on active duty, even if for brief periods of time, two to three years. It injects a different viewpoint on common problems. It brings a new set of talents. I think it is a very healthy thing for the medical department.

At any rate we had a good experience there. We got a lot of experience. The teaching staff was good; there was adequate clinical material. I was interested in surgery, and I got a good basis in surgical techniques from a variety of people.

Then I was ordered to duty in Sasebo, Japan, as the squadron medical officer for Mine Squadron Three. MineRon 3 had been sent to Korea right at the outset of the war. The landing forces were off the east coast of Korea, ready to land at Wonsan, and they found that the harbor was mined. They flew a man named Lieutenant Commander Don DeForest from Mine Force Atlantic out to Wonsan on a very hurry-up basis.* He had his own special plane from Charleston to San Diego to Pearl Harbor to Tokyo to Itizuki Air Force Base, which is on Kyushu Island just north of Sasebo. They had a sedan waiting for him at Itizuki base. They took him to Sasebo, and he went to see the flag officer in the USS Dixie.† The admiral told him that there was a destroyer with steam up waiting for him, and the net tender was standing by at the antisubmarine nets. So he was virtually whisked to Wonsan Harbor almost overnight to take charge of the minesweeping operations.‡

At that time MineRon 3 consisted of two groups of ships: a dozen wooden-hulled AMSs that were 135 feet long and had high forecastles, and a complementary group of six to eight metal-hulled minesweepers. Most of them came from MineRon 7 at Long Beach. During the subsequent minesweeping operations that took place prior to my arrival, the Pirate and the Pledge—both of them minesweepers—struck mines and were sunk. The minesweeping operations were successful at Wonsan; they did get the landing force ashore.§ The rest is history.

---

* Lieutenant Commander Don C. DeForest, USN, a former enlisted man.
† The flag officer was Rear Admiral Allan E. Smith, USN, Commander Task Force 95.
‡ For details on DeForest's work, see Malcolm W. Cagle and Frank A. Manson, The Sea War in Korea (Annapolis: U.S. Naval Institute, 1957).
§ Elements of the First Marine Division landed at Wonsan on 26 October 1950.

By the time I arrived at Sasebo, the Korean War had wound down. The MineRon had been given an assignment of patrolling the east and southeast coast of Korea from the DMZ down to the more or less southernmost tip of Korea.* The ships would be out on patrol two or three weeks at a time. The mother ship was the tender, and the staff headquarters was in an LST. The LST was based in Sasebo and acted as a kind of floating storage depot for the specialized equipment for resupply of the minesweepers. The LST sailed to Korea every month to make an income tax run. In those days an income tax advantage accrued to you if you served at least one day a month in Korea. We went up there to resupply the ships on patrol and occasionally to carry out minesweeping exercises to keep the crews sharp.

During the tour in Japan with that squadron, the skippers and other officers of the minesweepers soon learned that I had been a line officer. They used to razz me about how they were going to get me to stand watches in their ships. We had a good laugh over it in the club every once in a while. I said, "No, I can't do that anymore. I'm a healer now; I'm not a warrior. You know, the Geneva Convention prevents me from doing that warrior work."

Well, that fall—in November, I believe—the LST went up to Korea to resupply the ships on patrol and to conduct a minesweeping drill on the same occasion. Since I'd never had any at-sea experience with the minesweepers, I asked the commodore if I might ride one of the sweeps that were to be engaged in the exercise. He agreed, so I duly went aboard. The skipper of the ship was a bachelor and a wild Irishman who had a marvelous sense of humor.

One time we were off the coast for exercise minesweeping in very, very cold weather. It was a gray, overcast day with a sharp wind blowing, and the temperature was in the upper 20s. After watching operations from the flying bridge, I went down to the wardroom to have a cup of coffee. While I was there, I was piped to the bridge over the 1MC.† When I arrived there, the skipper said, "The course is such and such; the speed is such and such; there's a drill mine half a mile off the port bow. You've got the conn. Go pick it up."

---

* DMZ—demilitarized zone.
† 1MC—the ship's general announcing system.

Obviously, they were calling me out to see if I really had any line experience. So I saluted and said, "Aye, aye, sir. I have the conn. Full speed ahead." I conned the ship into a wide, sweeping turn to port, brought it downwind from the mine, and stopped it. The mine drifted down toward the side of the ship, and the deck crew stuck a pelican hook in the mine and lifted it aboard. I got the ship under way, turned to the captain, and said, "What's the next evolution, Captain?"

He said, "That'll be all, you son of a bitch."

After that, en route to Sasebo, I met a very interesting man named Vance Gordon.[*] He's a tombstone admiral, a submariner during the major portion of his career.[†] As a commander he was sent out to Pusan to be the executive officer of the U.S. Naval Advisory Group to the Republic of Korea Navy. At the end of World War II the United States Navy had given the Koreans a number of amphibious vessels, particularly LCIs and LSMs. These ships provided the backbone of the Korean Navy at the time.

He told me a very interesting story after he had been there a few months. He indicated that to operate these vessels that had been given to them by the United States, the U.S. provided the South Koreans with a half million gallons of diesel fuel a month. He said about 100,000 gallons of that was disappearing.

I said, "What do you think of that?"

He said, "Well, first of all you have to know that Korean Marines make furniture and sell it. The Korean Army transports goods, and the Korean Navy builds and repairs fishing boats. They do this to fund the retirement pay for their military people. So all the services are in business. Well, we could very easily detect and derive that the diesel oil that was disappearing was going into the fishing fleet"

I said, "Can't you stop it?"

He gave me one of the most politically astute answers that I can ever remember. He said, "It is far cheaper to let them steal it from themselves than it is to set up an agency to give it to them." [Laughter]

---

[*] Commander Charles Vance Gordon, USN.
[†] In the years after World War II, officers who had received combat decorations received a one-grade honorary promotion widely referred to as a "tombstone promotion." Although the individual still received the retired pay of his actual rank, he was authorized to assume the title of the higher grade. Gordon, who reached the rank of captain on active duty, retired as a rear admiral in 1958.

Paul Stillwell: Sort of your automatic distribution system.

Admiral Wilson: That's right. I thought it was quite interesting at the time and have always remembered it. Later on, during my early flag years, his son came to work for me, an interesting follow-on.

Paul Stillwell: What was life like in Japan for your family?

Admiral Wilson: I did not take my family. I had to leave them in Seattle. This was an unaccompanied tour. I lived in a Quonset hut on the beach.* I had a bunk in the LST, but those small ships really had very inadequate medical facilities. They had no laboratory, no X-ray, and in one case an LST had no sterilizer. So with the agreement of the squadron commander, Captain George Phillips, I lived in a Quonset hut ashore and saw the squadron patients in the local dispensary.† I shared the workload in the dispensary by taking night watches, so it worked out as an equitable arrangement. I got service and used their facilities, and our people got good care.

At that time, 1954, Japan was still recovering from the devastation of World War II. It had been only nine years since the war ended. The main streets of Sasebo were unpaved, essentially gravel roads. There were some cars but not too many. Prices were very low. A beautiful string of cultured Mikimoto pearls cost $50.00. Now they cost $300.00. Most of the things you wanted to buy as souvenirs to send home were dirt cheap. A whole set of dishes was $10.00 or $12.00, sometimes less. The Japanese people were very accommodating.

Sasebo as a base was very well put together. It had been one of the Japanese Navy's biggest naval shipyards. They had graving docks that would take the largest of our ships including the carriers, dry-docking facilities, machine shops, ammunition depots. Repair facilities of all kinds were there, and the base did a magnificent job of supporting the fleet operating around Korea.

---

* A Quonset hut is a semi-cylindrical metal building that can be shipped to an advance base area and erected quickly.
† Captain George L. Phillips, USN.

We had to treat a few of the usual accident-type things in the ships. One sailor was struck on the head when a hatch cover was dropped on him as it was being removed. It knocked him unconscious for a few hours, but it didn't cause permanent damage.

Paul Stillwell: How much of a preventive medicine program did you have?

Admiral Wilson: There was a preventive medicine unit ashore that took care of that aspect of the medical things. The water supply was adequate. There was good sewage disposal for the base, at least where I lived. The community water supply was okay. Community sewage was still the benjo ditch, as many people from that era will remember. There were some good hotels. There were some favorite nightclubs, which were very good. I don't recall anybody getting sick from the food out in town.

I remember on one occasion we had a food poisoning problem on our mother ship, the LST. As I recall, it related to some custard pies that had been left out and not properly refrigerated. All of a sudden we had 100 sick men with nausea, diarrhea, unable to work. At the same time, the commodore had been receiving word that some of his patrol ships were having to put into Pusan to deliver people who were ill. He said to me, "There's something going on up there, and I don't like it. I want you to go up there and see about it."

I said, "Commodore, I'd love to go, but I've got 100 men down on this ship alone."

He said, "Get the doctor from the next ship to take care of them. Didn't you hear me? You're going to Korea in the morning."

I said, "Yes, sir." So I contacted the physician from the ship next door. He took care of the remnants of the problem, which fortunately was short-lived. So I went to Korea.

I went up to Korea on the USS Mainstay, one of the metal-hulled 170-foot minesweepers. We arrived on station off Pusan late one afternoon and almost immediately had a call from one of the ships on the southern sector saying they had a patient whom they thought had appendicitis. We reversed course and steamed at flank speed south. The AMS steamed north, and we rendezvoused in a little bay.

I looked at the patient, and, sure enough, he did have appendicitis. So we took him aboard the <u>Mainstay</u> and went at flank speed to Pusan, where we put him in the Army hospital for surgery. We went back on station, and within 12 hours the same thing happened again. Within a matter of three or four days, we hauled three acute appendicitis patients to the hospital with just a few hours' interval between the notifications. It was almost as though the commodore had set it up.

Paul Stillwell: An epidemic.

Admiral Wilson: An epidemic, yes. [Laughter] An epidemic of appendicitis. That didn't last forever, of course, so I went back to Sasebo and resumed my duties there.

Paul Stillwell: What can you say about the overall health of the Navy people you were dealing with. You had a generally young population.

Admiral Wilson: Oh, they were in good health. The average enlisted man was a young, strong, healthy man who had been well screened before ever coming into the Navy, and his health had been maintained by the medical facilities wherever he went. We had no really difficult problems.

I remember we had one chap who was a latent homosexual, and he was triggered into what's known as a homosexual panic state. That state precipitated a fully blown paranoid schizophrenic reaction, wherein he was convinced that some of the crew members were out to kill him. We happened to be on port visit in Kagoshima, at the southern tip of Kyushu. As we steamed back north, as soon as we were in helicopter range we transferred him ashore and sent him on up to the naval hospital at Yokosuka.

We didn't have very many problems, because the crew and officers we had were very healthy. It was good tour for a young medical officer in the sense I didn't have any major severe problems to really beat me down. I had an excellent general practice, and so it was one year's experience before I went into formal surgery training. That duty stood me in good stead, because surgical patients also have other things wrong with them. To be able to diagnose the other things at the same time is important. So, all in all, it was a good year.

Then it was time to march on. So in July of 1954, having been there since early August of 1953, I boarded the USS Bryce Canyon, a destroyer tender, and sailed back to Pearl Harbor. There I transferred to an airplane and flew on back to Seattle to be released to inactive duty once more in August of 1954.

From there we went to Salt Lake City, where I became a resident surgeon in the VA Hospital associated with the University of Utah.[*] We were there four and half years. During that time I was trained to do all kinds of surgery, from neurosurgery to urology to ear, nose, and throat as well as general surgery and some orthopedics. I must say that it was a very good program for turning out practical surgeons who could go to work when they left.

During this time we had made some contacts in northern Montana. I had surgery friends in Kalispell, Montana, which is about 700 miles north of Salt Lake City. We became really close friends, and one individual in particular wanted me to join him as an associate. The local bank was ready to fund us, and the community seemed receptive. But as I went through the last few months of my residency in late 1958, the nation was in a recession. Montana led the nation in unemployment, and Kalispell led Montana. It was almost as if the gods were speaking to me. [Laughter] It wasn't the right time to do what we thought we ought to.

Paul Stillwell: How had you picked that particular place in the first place.

Admiral Wilson: Well, interesting story. The man who was the commanding officer of one of the tender ships for the mine squadron was a fellow named Bill Gaffney.[†] He was an old Idaho cowboy who was smart as a whip and had a master's degree in forestry from Yale University. Just as a parallel thought, he has three children, and all of them are

---

[*] VA—Veterans Administration.
[†] Lieutenant Commander William S. Gaffney, USNR, who was promoted to commander in 1957 and retired in that rank in 1967.

Ph.D.'s, and very, very bright wife as well—very brilliant family. He had been a forest ranger in the area around Kalispell. [Laughter]

One of the things that he had done was to go way out in the primitive wilderness in the wintertime. He stayed out in the wilderness all winter with a fellow named Norm Schappacher to track the elk herds in the area of the south fork of the Flathead River. Now, that's about as remote as you can get. But he's the fellow who referred me to Kalispell, because he thought it was a nice small town where I'd be happy, and that's what I told him I wanted to do. Well, we made friends with Norm Schappacher, and to this day we still visit them, and that's 30 years ago. That's how we got tangled up in Kalispell.

During this recession, though, we elected to return to the service. At the time we lived in Salt Lake City, and I started wearing western clothes, and I remember I wore a Stetson hat and a brand-new brown suit. I came back to Washington, to the Bureau of Medicine and Surgery, to talk to the leader of the professional division, Frank Norris.[*] I asked him about available assignments and what to expect. I recall that the conversation revolved more around my hat than it did about what we were going to do, but in due time we received an assignment to Subic Bay.

Paul Stillwell: You enumerated all those different specialties. Was it common for somebody to have that many surgical areas?

Admiral Wilson: In those days general surgeons were much, much more general than they are now.

Paul Stillwell: I see.

Admiral Wilson: Those specialties now have become very, very narrow fields, and general surgeons don't do them anymore. But back then we were trained to do the ordinary, straightforward operations in all those fields. It was a good thing because I had to work in most of them when I went out to the Philippines.

---

[*] Captain Frank T. Norris, MC, USN, later a rear admiral.

I went to Oakland in January of 1959 to spend a few months waiting for our son to finish his school year. Then we went on out to the Philippine Islands, where I was the chief of surgery in a little station hospital at Subic Bay. I was not only the chief surgeon, I was the only surgeon, so it made it very easy. That, of course, brought back a lot of memories from the days that we sailed in there in 1945 in the <u>Liddle</u>.

The nose of land that I had referred to had been scraped away, and now there was an airstrip. The village of Olongapo was a group of nipa huts on the shoreline in 1945. Now there was a very well developed base, and Olongapo had been set back from the beach about half a mile. The Navy at that time owned the town of Olongapo. It was within the Navy compound, and the naval reservation extended for several miles along the Subic Bay coastline.

Paul Stillwell: Was it as raunchy then as it was, say, in the late 1960s?

Admiral Wilson: Not really, for one good reason. The mayor of Olongapo was a Navy commander. [Laughter] The little hospital in Olongapo was operated with Navy support by Filipino physicians. The prostitution was there, but the sanitation and the control of prostitutes' health was much more stringent than it was in later years, when the town was turned back to the Philippines community. That happened while we were there, by the way. The effect was immediate. You could see it happening as all the hustlers and the entrepreneurs flooded into town. It gradually took on a much more tawdry, raunchy tone than it had been while under Navy control.

It was quite an experience out there. We did a lot of trauma surgery. The sailors were always fighting with the Marines; Marines were fighting with the Filipinos; the Filipinos were fighting with the sailors. Then there were automobile accidents and particularly scooter accidents. We had a lot of surgical work to do for the fleet.

When an aircraft carrier came in, for example, the ship's senior medical officer would come up to my office immediately on arrival in port and bring with him all the patients who had surgical problems. We would stop all business to see those patients. We admitted those who needed surgery and treated as out-patients those who did not. At the same time, we cleared the operating room schedule for the following day, whatever day it was: Saturday, Sunday, Monday, whatever. We operated on all those patients who needed surgery from that ship. Most of them were ordinary things: hernias, hemorrhoids, pilonidal cysts—bread-and-butter, simple, straightforward general surgery.

Very few patients had any complications. For those who were doing well, ambulatory and eating, we could send them back to the ship by the time it sailed five or six days later. That provided the dual advantage that the ship did not lose its men, and the hospital cleared the beds. It worked out very nicely. There were competent medical officers in the carriers to provide the post-operative care for these patients. So it was a comfortable arrangement for me professionally. I didn't feel the patients were being abandoned or neglected.

So we had an enormously busy time there. Being the only surgeon, I was on call 24 hours a day, every day, and a lot of this trauma work went on at night. In fact, about a third of the major surgery that we did there was at night. It seemed like weekends were busy. I remember doing six appendectomies in one weekend. It just fell that way. So it was a good tour in many ways, because I got an awful lot of experience doing a lot of things. We had a lot of head injuries. I opened a lot of heads. I had to take care of a lot of gunshot wounds of the head. We had a big trade in cheekbone fractures and broken jaws from sailors and Marines fighting one another. Dentists wired the jaws of those with fractures. So we had a good, broad clinical practice that supported the fleet, and it was a good learning experience for me at the outset of a surgical career.

Paul Stillwell: How was the relationship between the medical officers there and the line officers?

Admiral Wilson: At that time the line officer commanding the base, Captain P. D. Quirk, "owned" the hospital.[*] There was a station hospital funded by the base command. The senior medical officer of the hospital was exactly that—the senior medical officer, not the commanding officer. We had enormously good rapport with the line command. They felt well supported, and we broke our necks to make sure that they were. We felt the same way about the fleet. So we had a good rapport with both the shoreside line and with the

---

[*] Captain Philip D. Quirk, USN.

seagoing line, because we took care of them. We always had money enough to get the essential things we needed. We didn't have to go to Washington to get authorization and money to buy a new suction pump; we could get the funding right there. So it was a very happy arrangement.

Paul Stillwell: Did you have any major catastrophes to deal with in that time?

Admiral Wilson: We had one. A group of us were down at the club one night, having had dinner and dancing a little bit. The OOD's desk at the hospital called to see if any of the staff was there. Somebody said, "Of course, about half of them." It seemed that someone had thrown a homemade bomb into a fiesta crowd in a little Filipino village about 20 miles north of Subic Bay. The town sent 13 casualties to us. Of the 13, one died almost immediately, because he had such massive head injuries that there was no way to save him. Of the others, five or six had minor wounds. One of them had sort of intermediate wounds, and three of them had abdominal wounds. So we explored three patients' abdomens that night.

The injured mostly had fine pebbles blown into their abdomens with perforations of their intestinal tracts. That involved opening the abdomens, finding the holes, and closing them up. It is not technically difficult if you're trained in abdominal surgery, but it's just time consuming. In the middle of the night, it is extremely fatiguing.

The last patient was a young man who had multiple puncture wounds on his abdomen. I started operating on him about 11:30 the following morning to explore his abdomen. Just before putting him under anesthesia, I re-examined his chest to make sure it was clear. It was. I had him put under anesthesia, operated on him, and plugged up the holes in his gut. I was applying the dressing on him when he stopped breathing. In those days instead of doing external CPR as we now do it, it was the practice to open the chest and massage the heart.* He was still under anesthesia, fortunately.

We opened his chest, and, lo and behold, there was a lot of blood in it. And we had just listened to him and looked at the X-rays. What had happened was that a little piece of gravel had pierced his chest wall. It had hit a small artery that supported a little fat pad on

---

* CPR—cardio-pulmonary resuscitation.

the top of the sac that surrounds the heart, the pericardium. That little bit of fat is called the pericardial fat pad, and there is a little vessel that supports it. That vessel had been severed, and it bled partly into the pericardium and partly into the chest. It caused what is known as a cardiac tamponade. With the heart trying to beat with a sac full of blood around it, it could not do so. We simply slit the pericardium, dumped the blood out, and the heart started immediately. We sutured the bleeding vessel, cleaned out the chest, closed him up and took him back to the ward. He never turned a hair and left the hospital in ten days.

Paul Stillwell: CPR wouldn't have dealt with that, would it?

Admiral Wilson: No, it would not. Had it been five minutes later, when we were taking him down the passageway to his bed or having put him in bed, he would have arrested, and we would never have known why until we did a post-mortem exam on him. It was just a fortuitous circumstance.

Another time we were there, the senior medical officer called me in my office one day and said, "The Midway is down at the pier, and it's on fire. I want you to rig for taking burn casualties." So we did that immediately. In those days what you did was sterilize whole rolls of Vaseline-soaked gauze, because it was easy to do, and we had the materials. We did it in record time.

The ship had had a fire in a fuel-oil transfer pump room. They extinguished the fire and closed the hatch. The fire rekindled and blew the hatch open. That happened a half a dozen times. They had an awful time putting it out, but they finally did. We had no burn casualties, just the threat thereof. We did get a young man who wrenched his knee trying to help in the fire fighting. I guess you call that a burn-related casualty.

Paul Stillwell: Did you get to travel in the Philippines?

Admiral Wilson: Yes, we did some. We got to go up to Baguio for a weekend.[*]

---

[*] Baguio is the site a summer resort about 130 miles north of Manila on the island of Luzon in the Philippines.

During the time that we were in the PI, the hospital took six directors of Philippine provincial hospitals and brought them to the hospital at Subic Bay for a refresher course. All of these physicians had graduated from medical schools in the Philippines, and most of them had been out of med school for some time. We brought them in and essentially gave them a three-month internship to bring them up to speed on various treatment modalities and methods of diagnosis. They were very receptive people.

We had a formal lecture program for them. I remember one day I was lecturing to them about how to manage chest wounds. I went through the litany of all the things I knew to tell them, and I said, "Are there any questions?"

This young-looking physician raised his hand and said, "How do you treat spear wounds?" [Laughter]

I said, "Doctor, where I come from, spear wounds are not very common." I said, "From the tone of your question it appears to me that you have treated some, so why don't you tell us."

Well, the story that evolved went something like this. There was a bus running from the high mountains up in the Benguet Bontoc range area north of Baguio. It is a very, very remote area, part of which is still inhabited by Igorots and Ifugaos, some of whom are said to be headhunters. Anyway, this Filipino bus was caroming down a narrow road where you could see over the side and spit 5,000 feet.

Lo and behold, in the middle of the road there was somebody lying with a spear sticking in him. Not knowing whether he was dead or alive, they picked him up, threw him on the floorboard between the seats, and drove on. When they got to Baguio, the fellow was still alive, so they took him into the little provincial hospital. This doctor said, "The first thing you do is cut the handle off the spear, because it usually won't go through the door." [Laughter] I said that sounded like pretty common sense to me.

The upshot of the thing was really quite remarkable. That spear had barbs on it like fishhooks. They dissected the spear out of that man's chest without damaging any of the major blood vessels, and it went up pretty deep into his chest. He survived until he got a massive infection and died of infection. But the simple act of saving the man's life by getting that spear point out of him without hemorrhaging to death is to me an accomplishment.

Well, as a result of having had two or three groups of these people there for refresher training, we were invited by the Philippine health department to go and look at some of the provincial hospitals. The administrative officer and I went out on the road for about a week to visit various provincial hospitals.

We arrived at one of them, which was operated by a young lady, a Filipino physician who had two years of pediatrics training in the United States. She had just completed a caesarean section and a hysterectomy on a woman under local anesthesia and had a living baby and a living mother. I thought that was great performance under considerable adversity, because these hospitals were so simplistic. Most of them looked like a camp that you might have at a lake. There was open framework on the inside and no inside plumbing. Their linens were washed in the local stream a good bit of the time, very primitive. Some of the others were more sophisticated.

We walked into one hospital and were invited to go to the operating room where they were doing an abdominal surgical procedure. There was a child who looked to be about seven years old running around the operating room in cap and a mask. I said to the anesthesiologist, "Who is this young man?"

He said, "Oh, that's my son, he's learning the business." [Laughter]

Of course, we went to Manila occasionally. It's an 85-mile drive from Subic and not the most pleasant and rapid drive. But we used to get there once in a while for some special occasion.

Paul Stillwell: Were there any other really unusual and interesting cases that you can relate, comparable to the spear story?

Admiral Wilson: Let me think a minute. Well, as most people know, the Philippines has a group of individuals known as Negritos. They are short, black people with Negroid features such as thick lips and tightly curled hair. Actually, they are Ieta tribesmen. They are from the same ethnic origin as the Australian aborigines, the Lomboks of the Dutch East Indies, and the Phnoms of Cambodia. They were extremely good to our people in the Philippines during World War II and were responsible for rescuing and harboring many downed aviators. When we went to their village and met them and talked with them, we bought their homemade spears and bows and arrows. They told that some of the fliers from World War II were still sending them care packages.

At any rate, they were very simplistic people and very poor. Most of them were destitute and ill because of the parasitic diseases that are rife in the Philippines. Malaria in particular is a bad problem. The hospital medical officers put together a small traveling clinic. They'd take a cracker-box ambulance and go out to the Negrito village once or twice a month to hold a clinic for these folks.

On one occasion they discovered a 24-year-old woman who had a huge spleen. A spleen is ordinarily the size of a large man's fist. Hers filled three-quarters of her abdomen. So they got permission from the senior medical officer and admitted her to the naval hospital to see what could be done for her. After due consideration, it was decided that she should have her spleen removed. Now, they are still very tribal, and for her to be admitted and especially for her to be operated on, we had to have the permission of her husband, the tribal council, and the tribal chief. Mind you, the Negritos still used bows and arrows, spears, and poison-tipped blowgun darts.

Eventually we got all set to operate on this young woman. The morning of her surgery, in marched the tribesmen in breechcloths. They were carrying spears and blowguns and bows and arrows. They sat in the lobby with an interpreter. We operated on this lady, removed her spleen and for a variety of technical physiological reasons that I won't go into, she immediately went into deep shock. We did all of the emergency things that were possible, and she actually rallied around and acted like she might recover.

When things were stabilized somewhat, I went out the operating room suite door to the lobby. Through the interpreter, I told the family and the tribesmen that we were having difficulties. I said that she was a severely ill woman, as we had told them before surgery, but that we were having such difficulty that she could very possibly die on the operating table, and that we were doing the best we could to keep her alive. I told them, and they all nodded their heads.

Well, about an hour later she did indeed die. We found out later that she simply had an undernourished heart. The wall of her heart was about a centimeter thick. Ordinarily it's about four or five centimeters. So she just had a bad start in life and had a malnourished heart that failed. So I then went back out to the lobby to explain to the family and the tribesmen that she had passed away. The interpreter went over to the group and said what I had asked him to say. He came back, and it seemed to me like it was an hour—even though it couldn't have been more than a couple or three minutes. He said, "The patient's father, the patient's mother, the patient's husband, the tribal council, and the tribal chief want you to know that they understand that you did the best you could and that the tribesmen will not be after you with their bows and arrows and spears and blowguns." [Laughter] So I felt a great sigh of relief, because in all truth had they decided otherwise I would have probably lost my life. They were that simplistic.

Paul Stillwell: How do you react emotionally, either to the loss of a patient or saving one under difficult circumstances?

Admiral Wilson: The loss of a patient in the operating room is always a very bad emotional experience for a surgeon, because you constantly have to ask yourself, "Does this patient need to be operated on? If so, am I planning the right procedure? If so, have I done the right procedure? Have I made all the proper diagnostic tests? Have I done all the necessary preparation on the patient? Have we done our homework, really?" If you lose a patient on the table, even after having done all of that to the best of your ability, it makes you feel terrible.

Sometimes you're dealing with patients who have very, very severe trauma, and I lost a couple on the table for that reason in the Philippines as well. A common patient lost is someone with a ruptured liver. The liver can practically explode from blunt trauma, and the individual bleeds to death. It makes you feel terrible because there is nothing you can do about it. Emotionally that gets to you. From the success side you are happy because you may have brought somebody back from the brink. But that emotion is not as strong as the one where you lose somebody.

Paul Stillwell: Because that is what you expected to do with the person you succeeded on.

Admiral Wilson: Sure. You have had some dramatic things happen, I don't know what you know about ruptured spleens, but ruptured spleens can cause a patient to bleed into the abdomen to the point of dying in a matter of hours, sometimes minutes. We did a number of splenectomies for that reason. Most of the time they occur because people are in accidents at various times, and they hit their abdomen on something very hard. A classic case was the handlebars on a scooter out there. So you get all the blood cross-matched and all that sort of stuff. Then you open the abdomen, and there is a geyser of blood that comes out all over the place. Then you get into the abdomen, get the bleeding under control and do all the right things to suture: ligate the vessels, get the spleen out, clean up the abdomen, transfuse the patient, see the blood pressure come up and stabilize, and see the pulse come down and stabilize. All those things are great indicators of success, but you'd feel terrible if you didn't win. That's the kind of thing where you should win, and if you don't then is the time you really would be torn up because you lost.

Paul Stillwell: What sort of business did you do in venereal disease cases when you were in the Philippines?

Admiral Wilson: We did not handle those at the hospital per se unless there were some complications. We had a preventive medicine unit and a unit that dealt with the population in town. I mentioned the Filipino hospital supported by the Navy. They held a clinic for the prostitutes in particular and treated them. Now, the enlisted people or anyone else who went out in town and became infected—they were dealt with by their own medical department people, in the ships principally. We had some of our own problems on the hospital staff, and we took care of those.

We were not in the business of venereal disease epidemiology. That was a different matter, and it was not only the preventive medicine people, but it was also the research people. At that time a penicillin-resistant gonorrhea was emerging. It became quite a problem and still is. I didn't have to get involved with it much basically, because I was a surgeon and we didn't have all that much in our own staff.

Paul Stillwell: You mentioned the Midway case, which seems like an exceptional instance. Did have much interaction with ships?

Admiral Wilson: Yes, we dealt with the ships' medical officers all the time. They came to us with a variety of problems. They had clinical problems where they needed consultation by specialty people such internists; surgeons; orthopedicists; ear, nose, throat, and eye specialists; whomever. And they came to us with supply problems and administrative problems. So we had a good interaction with them from the medical department side of the house. We didn't necessarily have to have any interface with the commands as such except through the medical department. Occasionally some commanding officer would come up and see his people and want to know what was going to happen to them and that sort of thing. But it was always a very pleasant relationship, because, as I say, we bent over backward to support them. That was our business.

Paul Stillwell: Did you find yourself growing as a physician during that period?

Admiral Wilson: Oh, very much so. When you finish a training program, you then have to develop confidence in your abilities, and you have to refine your manual technical skills. That certainly was an opportunity for me to do that, and I like to think it happened.

From there we went back to San Diego hospital, where I went on and got some further experience at a more sophisticated level. But that duty in the Philippines was a marvelous first step out of training into practice. I have always appreciated that opportunity.

Paul Stillwell: There are the technical skills certainly but also the personal relationships. Did you find yourself growing in that area also?

Admiral Wilson: Yes, you have to exert some kind of leadership, because there is always somebody working for you. In this particular instance I ran the surgery department. I had a couple or three medical officers working directly for me all the time, and we interfaced with the other departments. I had a whole crew of enlisted people who were rounders personally, but they were as competent as anybody could be in their technical skills, in their specialties.

You can't help but grow. You have to learn administration as well as clinical things. You have to know how to get supplies. You have to know how to get rid of patients as well as get them. Patients have to be discharged in various ways, either sent back to duty or evacuated or transferred to some other service or some other facility. So you have to learn the internal workings of the patient-affairs system. As you take on more responsibility, you can't help but grow. As time passed, I felt more confident in my ability to deal with problems as they arose than I did when I first went there. That's what growth is all about.

Paul Stillwell: Experience and confidence.

Admiral Wilson: Right. I went out there as a two-stripe reservist. I had missed the last promotion board to lieutenant commander, so I went out there as a lieutenant. The next selection board I was selected for lieutenant commander and then backdated a couple of years to make it equitable in comparison with my other counterparts. My application to augment into the regular Navy came through, and I went regular on that tour. So that was the inception of the rest of my career as a more senior medical officer. Subic was an ideal place to do it.

Paul Stillwell: So you then went from there to San Diego then.

Admiral Wilson: I went to San Diego. I spent three years there, the last two of which I ran the SOQ. Sick officers' quarters no longer exist, because the great powerhouse says that everybody is equal to everybody else, and to segregate patients is not right. So we don't have SOQs anymore. But at that time we did, and I had a 30-bed general surgery ward at San Diego. All of the patients were officers, active and retired. About probably 85% of our practice at that time was retired military. We had some of the great people from World War II still left over, particularly flag officers living in Coronado. I think at the time there were something like 94 admirals over on the island.

One individual that I remember was Admiral Standley.* He was quite elderly at that time, but he was invited to all the functions and very much respected and revered.† Still quite sharp. We had people like Felix Gygax, who ran the coastal defense activities off of Manila Bay when the Japanese had attacked.‡ An old captain who came in there had been recalled and made a convoy commodore. He was the commodore for convoys that ran from the West Coast to Australia. When he came to the hospital, he was an elderly gentleman and had terrible arthritis in his fingers that made it difficult for him to hold on to silverware while he was eating. He used to like to sit on the edge of his bed and eat from the over-bed table. When he dropped his silverware, you could hear him swear from one end of the hall to the other.

These old gentlemen from the island had a behavior pattern that was virtually standard. Those who could get up went out on the golf course. Everybody stopped at sundown and had a cocktail. It was just as much a ritual as the British tea ceremonies, if you could imagine. In those days we were permitted to have whiskey in the pharmacy. Whiskey is legitimately prescribed at times as a stimulant for patients. So I legitimately prescribed a shot of whiskey for all those who were able at cocktail hour. [Laughter] They used to look forward to an ounce of whiskey before their dinner. They'd all smile and lick their chops and had a wonderful time over it. I felt it was one of those little things that didn't hurt them and probably gave them a little lift. We had a great good time.

Paul Stillwell: Were these men inclined to sea stories?

Admiral Wilson: Oh, absolutely! One of my patients was a wonderful gentleman, General Walter Greatsinger Farrell.§ He was a pioneer in three areas. He helped develop the rubber assault boat, he was one of the early scuba divers, and he was one of the early pilots in the Marine Corps. He used to fly these old single-engine scout planes. He was also an

---

* Admiral William H. Standley, USN (Ret.). He had served as Chief of Naval Operations from 1 July 1933 to 1 January 1937.
† Admiral Standley died in October 1963 at the age of 91.
‡ Rear Admiral Felix X. Gygax, USN (Ret.).
§ Farrell received a tombstone promotion to major general at the time of his retirement from the Marine Corps in 1946.

Olympic-class swimmer. At the time I knew him, he was something like 67 years old.* He was doing 50 push-ups and 50 sit-ups every morning. He was wiry and strong, played tennis and swam.

He told the story about flying one of his floatplanes off the coast of San Diego. He said the engine went out on him, and he had to put it down at sea about 15 miles offshore. So he waited around to see if anybody missed him. Nobody came looking for him, so he dove over the side and swam ashore, 15 miles. When he got to shore, he said, "I must be out of shape. I'm puffing." [Laughter]

He came in to see me because he had a hernia to be repaired. We discussed it thoroughly, and he wanted to know how soon he could resume his physical fitness activities. I said, "General, it's going to take six to eight weeks before you can go back to doing exercises. You have to give yourself time to heal."

So he said, "That long?"

I said, "Yes. There's no way that I can hurry it, nor can you. If you're not going to have the same thing happen all over again, you are just really going to have to believe me."

He said, "All right" very reluctantly. I discharged him in a week, which was normal for that time. (Now they discharge them after two or three days.) He called me every single solitary day from the day he was released until the day I told him he could go back to doing his exercises. Never a day went by that he didn't call. At that time he also had joined the Sierra Club and was doing rock climbing and very well at 67. An enormously interesting man.

He subsequently used to call in for appointments in the surgery clinic. He used to call in for an appointment, and I made it a point not to ask people over the telephone why they were coming in, because that's embarrassing. But I often wondered why he came in. Finally it dawned on me. He had nothing wrong with him, but he just wanted to come in and visit. So I'd block out 30 minutes for him, and he'd come in and we would sit down and tell sea stories, and laugh and scratch. He just loved it and so did I. Wonderful people, parts of history.

Paul Stillwell: Well, not only that, but medicine is more than pills and cutting.

---

*Farrell was born in 1897.

Admiral Wilson: Absolutely—a little psychological support was indicated there. A man of his caliber and experience and activity level probably didn't have many people to talk to who were interested in what he had to say anymore. That's a sad thing about older retired people. I know, because I'm in that position myself now. It's always stimulating to have someone come by to whom you can speak about professional things, Navy or medicine.

Paul Stillwell: What did you do as far as training younger physicians?

Admiral Wilson: There was a very large residency program at San Diego at the time. We had interns and surgical residents and residents in all the specialties. Some were in fellowships beyond the residency level. Most of the time I had a resident whom I taught surgical things. We did a lot of colon surgery, for example, more than any other service in the hospital. That was largely because we had an older age group in whom the colon problems were prevalent. So I trained an awful lot of residents in colon surgery, which happened to be one of my favorites. We did a lot of training. We had a lot of tumors, a lot of cancer. We treated a lot of patients at the outset, in the middle, and at the end. It was in the days before intensive care units, and so our wards were filled with patients in various stages of demise—as well as survival, I hope. So it was a busy time, a gratifying one.

Paul Stillwell: How much did you spend with dependents, as opposed to active duty personnel?

Admiral Wilson: I spent one year with them when I first went to San Diego, because I was on a dependent surgical service. After that, when I went to this SOQ job, I did not deal with dependents at all. It was strictly an active duty, retired male officer ward. But I saw a lot of dependents in my day. Women are marvelous surgical patients. They are better patients than men.

Paul Stillwell: Why do you say that?

Admiral Wilson: Well, they are better motivated to get out of the hospital in the first place. They feel very strongly their responsibilities to get home to run the household and to take care of the children. By and large, they have pain thresholds that are higher than men's. You can do a hernia repair on a woman and send her home in a day or two. Try to do that to a man in those days and he'd balk. So they are good patients. They're motivated to help themselves get better and are very strong.

Paul Stillwell: Well, Admiral, we are right near the end of this tape. Do you have any final thoughts for this session?

Admiral Wilson: I might make a note here that we had pretty much covered our service up through the end of the tour in San Diego, at which time we'll march off to the Chelsea Naval Hospital and on to Vietnam.

Paul Stillwell: It was a pleasure to meet you for the first time today, Admiral. I think we got off to a good start. Thank you.

Admiral Wilson: We certainly did, and it's a pleasure to meet you, Mr. Stillwell. Thank you very much and we look forward to the next session.

Paul Stillwell: Great.

Interview Number 2 with Rear Admiral Almon C. Wilson, Medical Corps, U.S. Navy (Retired)

Place: U.S. Naval Institute, Annapolis, Maryland

Date: Wednesday, 15 February 1989

Interviewer: Paul Stillwell

Paul Stillwell: Admiral, I'm happy to see you again. We're in a different location this time. Just to review briefly, when we finished the last time we concluded your tour of duty at San Diego in 1964. Now we're ready to move to the Naval Hospital in Chelsea, Massachusetts, which obviously was a quite different environment for you.

Admiral Wilson: Well, indeed it was. During the summer of 1964 we were transferred to Chelsea Naval Hospital, at my request, for a variety of personal reasons. We made the trek across the country in two automobiles and arrived sometime in August.

Chelsea, Massachusetts, is a city on the north side of the Mystic River, next to Boston. It is directly across from a junkyard in which there is a huge magnet, and they load scrap iron 24 hours a day. Either the junkyard or some other industrial entity in the area apparently uses a coal-fired boiler, because there is soot all over the place all the time. The classic thing about the Chelsea Naval Hospital is the fact that it was soot covered 24 hours a day, seven days a week. It never changed, and it could never be cleaned up. You could go along a window sill anywhere, anytime and wipe up soot.

Chelsea Naval Hospital had had a fine reputation and still did have when I arrived. It had been in business a very long time, of course. The original hospital—the oldest one in the system—was still there. It was built in the 1830s.[*] It was down on the river bank, and it was old enough so it still had dungeons and iron rings in the walls to chain up prisoners. The brig hadn't been used for any purpose at all in many, many years, but it was an interesting historical place. The commanding officer's quarters used to be an inn for the travelers crossing the river by boat, and it's a lovely old set of quarters.

---

[*] The Chelsea hospital opened in 1836.

In its heyday, the hospital itself had very close relationships to the medical schools in Boston and to the medical community in general. It was a very well-respected hospital for its affiliations, for its staff, and for the quality of the people who were trained at Chelsea. I went there as the assistant chief of the surgical service at a time when the hospital was not terribly busy. Mind you, I had just come from San Diego, where it was excruciatingly busy, so it was quite a change to go to Chelsea where things were so different.

Paul Stillwell: How would you account for that difference in the workload?

Admiral Wilson: Well, Chelsea was a smaller hospital in the first place. It was there basically for the shipyard, and Charlestown Shipyard wasn't all that busy.* So there wasn't the pressure of all that many uniformed people and their families on that medical institution.

Paul Stillwell: Did it draw on the Newport naval community at all?

Admiral Wilson: Only for specialty referral on occasion. Newport is about 65 miles south of Boston, and it had more of a community-type hospital with perhaps fewer specialists. We used to get some work from them. We also got some from the Portsmouth, New Hampshire, hospital and from the shipyard and the ships there. Quonset Point patients were funneled through Newport.† Anyway, we did have a few interesting clinical problems.

One interesting little feature came up. During that year the Bureau of Medicine and Surgery started to program a new hospital for Chelsea. Mind you, Chelsea was a very old place. It was on land that belonged to the city, and under the terms of the city granting the Navy the use of it, the property was to be returned to the city upon the completion of the Navy's utilization of it.

---

* The Boston Naval Shipyard was in an area of the city known as Charlestown. The shipyard closed on 1 May 1974.
† Quonset Point, Rhode Island, was the site of a naval air station near Newport. The station closed in June 1974.

At any rate, the bureau called and said they wanted a space program for a new hospital. They wanted it, of course, two days ago, which was usual in most of these administrative efforts. Harley Heaton was a very talented Medical Service Corps officer on the staff, and the two of us sat down to figure out a space program for this hospital.[*]

Paul Stillwell: Why you?

Admiral Wilson: I was interested in it. I had always been interested in planning and facilities. I'm a sort of frustrated engineer, I suppose.

It turned out that one of the prior executive officers had been the director of the planning division at the Bureau of Medicine and Surgery. His name was Captain Evan Stone.[†] He was a very compulsive fellow, and he had done virtually a whole space study for the Chelsea Hospital. So it was quite easy for us to take his work and bring the space requirements up the standards of the Bureau of the Budget, which was in existence then. Incidentally, BuBud, as it was known in those days, was a very unpopular portion of the government, somewhat like the Office of Management and Budget and the General Accounting Office are today. They seemed to have a great bent for reducing everything from budgets to space allocations. They like to reduce anything you can name that can be quantified. At any rate, we finally did put together the space program.

Paul Stillwell: Did this envision doing something on the same site or at a different location?

Admiral Wilson: They never got to the point of making that decision. However, the prospects were most likely that it would go on the same site. It was to be a part of history that that project never came to fruition. As a matter of interest, $10 million was appropriated for that purpose. That money was subsequently taken from the Naval Hospital Chelsea project and put into the Naval Hospital Oakland Project. Oakland got a new hospital that was commissioned in 1968. Chelsea Naval Hospital was destined to be

---

[*] Lieutenant Harley L. Heaton, MSC, USN.
[†] Captain Evan C. Stone, MC, USN.

closed in the early '70s as a part of a general drawdown on the number of facilities that the medical department operated at the time.* Others included such places as St. Albans Hospital in New York and Portsmouth, New Hampshire, which came down to clinic status.

Paul Stillwell: It is wise in retrospect that it turned out the way it did.

Admiral Wilson: Yes, it was good judgment. Because the shipyard in Charlestown, of course, is now civilian, and we have really no major uniformed presence in the Boston area. With the medical evacuation team as it is now, it's thoroughly feasible to move Navy patients down to Bethesda or Newport or wherever is necessary.

Paul Stillwell: Ten million dollars doesn't sound like very much to build a hospital.

Admiral Wilson: Well, in 1964 dollars, it was quite a lot of money. If you can remember back what you could buy things for in 1964, it's quite interesting. Automobiles didn't sell for $12,00 and $15,000 and $18,000. They sold for $7,000 or $8,000 or $9,000 at the most, and some of them a lot less than that.

Paul Stillwell: That's right—candy bars for a nickel or a dime.

Admiral Wilson: So everything is relative. The naval hospital at Oakland, for example, turned out to cost $24 million. That was quite a bargain for a hospital the size of Oakland.

Paul Stillwell: What do you recall of your medical practice at Chelsea?

Admiral Wilson: It was a sort of bread-and-butter practice, really. I started off taking care of some patients who had what was known in those days as dirty surgery. There really isn't anything like dirty surgery, but it had patients who had ano-rectal problems—hemorrhoids, pilonidal cysts, etc. It was a small service. I was put on that service because the chief of surgery didn't really know me nor know my capacities and talents. Eventually,

---

* The Chelsea hospital closed in 1974 because of the closing of the naval shipyard that it had served.

I took over my old job as being officer surgeon in the sick officers' quarters, and I ran that service until I left in May of 1965.

Paul Stillwell: Did you get any industrial-type injuries or accidents from the shipyard?

Admiral Wilson: I can't really recall any industrial accidents. What I do recall is that we used to get patients in a most unusual fashion. We would get calls from politicians. Some of the patients would call their local ward politician, the priest, and then their doctor before they came to us. Boston at that time—and still is, I suppose—a very political city. It was interesting that people would start with the politician and go to the priest before they went to the doctor to grease the skids to get in the hospital, which wasn't necessary if they were ill anyway. [Laughter] So it's a little bit of the local Boston lore that persisted and pertained at the time.

Paul Stillwell: How did your family adjust to this much different culture than San Diego?

Admiral Wilson: Well, it was interesting. Mrs. Wilson was a nurse when we were married, and she had long wanted to be a historian, so she had returned to college. She attended Harvard while we were there, and she enjoyed it immensely. We together enjoyed the Harvard Square area of Cambridge immensely because of the bookstores, and they had a couple of theaters there that played vintage movies which were of considerable interest to us.

Our son Geoff, who had been in Bullis prep school in Washington, had become ill. We brought him up from Washington, and for a number of months he was a patient in the hospital off and on. He had a most thorough workup at the hospital. Part of his disease pattern caused him to be terribly fatigued, and so he required a great deal of rest. However, he did recover quite handily and attended school.

We lived in Belmont, an interesting place which is a suburb of Boston just out from Cambridge. It had been there a long time. It was populated by people, many of whom were retired, but most of them wealthy. We rented the only rental property in town. Belmont had had the same city manager for 40 years, and during our year's stay there the city manager died. When he passed away, the community had a million-dollar surplus in the community treasury. They did such things as buy high-voltage electricity from Consolidated Edison and then distributed it through a community-owned electrical distribution system. They had done that forever.

To show you the difference in how people react, the Northeasterners—and the New Englanders in particular—have the reputation for being somewhat clannish. The lady next door to us, very shortly after our arrival, came to my wife and said, "You have three strikes against you in this community, you know."

My wife said, "Yes? What could they possibly be?"

She said, "Well, first of all, you're in the military. Secondly, you're renting. And thirdly, you have California license plates."

Kit said, "Well, I'll remember that." We lived there for ten months, and during that time not one single, solitary local citizen crossed our threshold. Fortunately, we understood that, because I'm a native of northern New York, quite close to the Vermont border, and my forebears are all New Englanders. Mrs. Wilson also was raised in Schenectady, which isn't all that far from New England, and she understood them. So we were not as perhaps devastated by this lack of warmth as some other folks might have been.

Paul Stillwell: Did you make any attempt to cultivate the locals?

Admiral Wilson: Yes, we tried to be nice to them. For example, across the way was the home of a widowed lady, and one time we had a quite a severe snowstorm. So I went out and shoveled the sidewalks and the driveway in our home. Then I went and shoveled hers, just as a matter of neighborliness. It was several weeks before she got around to saying anything to me, and then she gave me a very, very begrudging thank you. I would rather she had not said anything, frankly. [Laughter]

Paul Stillwell: Well, at least you knew where you stood.

Admiral Wilson: Yes, yes, no question about that.

Paul Stillwell: Do civilians in that kind of situation ever try to impose on the fact that you're a doctor?

Admiral Wilson: No, they never made any suggestion or request or anything. Of course, in that community they're all wealthy enough, they're all older, maturer families. I'm sure they all had family doctors or family specialists and, of course, wouldn't stoop to ask a military person.

Paul Stillwell: Especially one from California.

Admiral Wilson: Yes, that's right. [Laughter] In a rented home.

Paul Stillwell: It sounds as if you found that a satisfying tour.

Admiral Wilson: It was not really a satisfying tour in the professional sense.

Paul Stillwell: More the ancillary things.

Admiral Wilson: Yes. I did however use it as a transition period. I began to become interested in administrative things. I was a commander at the time, so there was no opportunity for me to be a full-time administrator in a hospital. So I needed to go on in the clinical world. But I also was interested in learning some of these peripheral matters that we call administration.

Paul Stillwell: How did you go from there to Vietnam?

Admiral Wilson: We didn't know it in the early '60s, of course, and it wasn't being noised about very loudly, but the U.S. had had a presence in Vietnam for several years. Small groups of people were doing quiet things in Vietnam, and then in 1964, after the Gulf of

Tonkin, the decision had been made.* In March of 1965, the Marines moved into Danang to protect the airstrip. They also moved into Chu Lai, which is some 50 miles south of Danang. Then the third place was at Phu Bai, about 40 miles north, where there was another airfield near the city of Hue. The Marines were to go in there to protect those airfields. They went in with a small unit; I think it was the 9th Marine Expeditionary Brigade.†

At the time the U.S. presence in Vietnam was being started, it occurred to me that we were going to have some sort of major involvement there. I concluded that this might be as good a time as any for me to break and go and get involved in that work early on in the game. The opportunity to do your own thing—to make adjustments in the standard systems—occur only during the early and confusing days of a new conflict. I had been long interested in Marine support. As a matter of fact, a year or so before I had spent some time at Pendleton, going on some surgical team exercises as an observer to see how the Marines supported themselves during a landing.‡ It turned out to be very valuable experience.

Well, the upshot of all this was that I went down to the Bureau of Medicine and Surgery and saw Captain Herb Stoecklein, who later became a flag officer.§ He was commanding officer at the hospital in San Diego when he retired. At the time Captain Stoecklein was the detailer, and he and I struck a bargain that I would go to Vietnam for one year as the commanding officer of the Third Medical Battalion for the Third Marine Division. After that I would go to the U.S. Naval Hospital in Yokosuka as the chief of surgery. So, armed with that information, I went home to make the announcement to my family.

In June 1965 our son graduated from high school. As I mentioned, his mother had gone back to college to be a historian. She also had an interest in art. When she found out

---

* On 2 August 1964, North Vietnamese patrol boats in the Tonkin Gulf attacked the destroyer Maddox (DD-731) in international waters. On the night of 4 August the Maddox and the destroyer Turner Joy (DD-951) reported being attacked by North Vietnamese craft. The question of whether the second attack occurred has never been completely resolved. The reports of the two attacks led to the congressional Gulf of Tonkin Resolution, which provided the legal basis for the commitment of U.S. armed forces in Vietnam.
† On 8 March 1965, the first of 3,500 Marines landed on the beaches near Danang, South Vietnam, to assume responsibility for the security of the Air Force base there. The 9th Marine Expeditionary Brigade was commanded by Brigadier General Frederick J. Karch, USMC.
‡ Camp Pendleton is a large Marine Corps base near Oceanside in southern California.
§ Captain Herbert G. Stoecklein, MC, USN.

that I was to go to Vietnam on an unaccompanied tour, she strongly considered going to Mexico City to study art while I was away. Our son said to her, "Since Dad's going to go to Yokosuka next year, why don't we go to Japan, for I may not have another chance to go out there?"

So Kit said to him, "It doesn't really make that much difference to me. I can go to Japan and study Japanese and Chinese art." So with that we started a round of activities which ultimately culminated in their going to Japan by themselves on a Japanese freighter on student visas. While I was in Vietnam, they lived in a suburb of Yokohama, in a Japanese house and on the Japanese economy. They were both full-time university students, and they had a marvelous experience. Our son was going to stay but one year, two at the most. He wound up staying four years, completing his undergraduate college work there at Sophia University.

Sophia University is a well-known college in Tokyo. It's run by the West German Jesuits, and it operates a Japanese section for the Japanese nationals. It also operates an international division, which meets beginning at 4:00 o'clock in the afternoon for the English-speaking students. A great many military and civilian Americans in Japan sent their children or attended Sophia themselves. It was a well-recognized school. Its credits were transferable to other colleges, so it was a very happy circumstance in that sense.

In the meantime, I was transferred from Chelsea to the Third Marine Division and had to stop off at Camp Pendleton to attend the field medical service school for six weeks. This is a school operated at the Marine Corps base. It's operated by Navy medical people, Medical Service Corps officers, mostly corpsmen, and some physician lecturers. The idea is to give both the enlisted and officer students a look at how the Marine Corps functions in the field. They learn what the problems are for the medical department personnel; how to conduct themselves under combat conditions; how to really deal with war as a medical department person. Corpsmen are taught how to carry people on litters, how to carry them on their backs, etc. They go over the principles of first aid and that sort of thing. Field combat training is a major subject also.

Paul Stillwell: Certainly different from pilonidal cysts.

Admiral Wilson: My role as commanding officer, however, of this medical battalion was really more oriented to the administrative side of the house. How did I keep the battalion supplied with the goods that it needed? What were the channels of approach to getting things done? To whom did I speak for the solution of problems? The field medical service school was not very basic to my education as far as those things were concerned.

Paul Stillwell: Was there a conception then how big the job would be for you in Vietnam?

Admiral Wilson: No, there was not. It turned out to be a great deal more than any of us anticipated. Mind you, the first Marines went in there in March of 1965, and by the time I got out there in mid-July they were at the division level of end strength, about 25,000 men. When I finished all the schooling, I flew out to Okinawa to pass through the rear echelon of the Third Division.

Paul Stillwell: Did you get any of the SERE training along the way—survival, evasion, resistance, and escape?

Admiral Wilson: No, escape and evasion training was not part of it. It turned out that it wasn't necessary for me anyway. I never was threatened that much.

At the rear-echelon headquarters in Okinawa we learned some very interesting facts. We learned first of all that their supply activity there didn't have anything to give anybody. During the peacetime years between Korea and Vietnam, it was a sad fact that in some cases readiness inspections were passed so long as there was a requisition in the box. That does very little for people going to war who need the gear.

The Marine Corps has always been very frugal, and the Third Medical Battalion, as I recall, had an annual budget of about $200,000 to operate its internal workings and to maintain its shelf stock of supplies. You have to realize that there are lots of items in the medical world that don't have a very long shelf life, particularly in the warm areas. I'm talking mainly about rubber goods, like anesthesia masks, and rubber catheters and things, many of which have now been replaced by plastic. But in those days they were not plastic.

So when the Third Medical Battalion and the Charlie Company of the Third Medical Battalion left Okinawa and went into Vietnam, they went in with some empty supply cans. And this was after they had stripped the shelves in Okinawa of everything that was medically useful as they went. When I got out there three or four months later, the shelves were bare, and the pipeline had not yet filled up. There were a lot of people running around frantically, but nobody saw any great quantities of things arriving.

Within a matter of two or three days after arriving in Okinawa, I was shipped down to Vietnam. It turned out to be the day after my birthday. I arrived in country on the 14th of July 1965. In the airplane in which we went there were some people I was to know a lot better later on. One of them was Colonel Wilkinson, who turned out to be the G-4, the logistics boss for the Third Division, and later on the operations boss.

I took with me two brand-new MSC ensigns. One of them went on to have a very, very successful career—Captain Bob Ozment, Medical Service Corps, who recently retired.[*] We flew to Vietnam in a C-130 that was loaded with supplies and equipment.[†] We sat along the side of this airplane with our knees tucked up under our chin and our legs straddling cargo chains that were tied so tight that you could almost hear them sing if you touched them.

In the middle of July in Vietnam—at least in the northern part—it was hot, it was humid, and it was dusty. The dust was a fine red powder, and it stuck to any wet surface. If you perspired a little bit, you turned dusty red very quickly. We landed on the Danang airstrip, and as we flew in there and looked out the window to see what the terrain looked like, it was absolutely gorgeous. Danang sits on Tourane Bay, surrounded by these lush fields and tree-covered mountains in the background. We saw China Beach, the beautiful white beach and the blue water and the sunshine. Then, looking at the airstrip, one saw all the scars of ammunition dumps, refuse dumps, motor pool parks, and helicopter landing pads that kind of destroyed the landscape.

Paul Stillwell: Did you have any contact with the naval support activity in Danang?

---

[*] Ensign Bob Lee Ozment, MSC, USN, in 1965.
[†] The Lockheed C-130 Hercules began as an Air Force cargo plane; it was also adapted for a variety of uses by the other armed services.

Admiral Wilson: Oh yes. A lot later on I had a very great deal to do with the people who oversaw the construction of the Naval Support Activity hospital there, in particular the commanding officer, Captain Bruce Canaga.* He and I were good friends for a long time; he's now passed away.

Paul Stillwell: Was this at Camp Tien Sha?

Admiral Wilson: No, it was south of Tien Sha, over near China Beach. Camp Tien Sha was farther north, up toward the off-loading docks.†

Paul Stillwell: What was the command relationship between you and the Marine Corps there?

Admiral Wilson: I was a battalion commander, and my immediate boss was the deputy chief of staff for logistics. The division surgeon when I first went there was Captain Bill Wulfman, and later on it became Captain Homer Arnold.‡ Both of them were staff officers without command responsibility. They were advisers to the commanding general of the Third Division. I was commanding officer of one of the support battalions and did have command authority, including nonjudicial punishment authority.

My relationship with the division surgeon was one of professional consultation, more or less. It was professional in the medical sense and not quite so professional in the military sense. In the military world I was much more lined up with the logistics people for whom I worked. Medical support is, of course, one of the logistic support elements of a Marine division or of any functional military unit, so the command structure was such that we worked for the G-4.

The division surgeon was the general's adviser on medical things. In theory he would tell the general what he thought ought to be done, and in theory the general would

---

* Captain Bruce L. Canaga, Jr., MC, USN.
† For maps of the Danang complex, see Frank Uhlig, Jr., Vietnam: The Naval Story (Annapolis: Naval Institute Press, 1986), pages 180 and 210.
‡ Captain William A. Wulfman, MC, USN; Captain Homer S. Arnold, MC, USN.

tell me what to do, through his G-4. In the real world of how things get accomplished, the division surgeon and I worked out the problems well ahead of time and talked them over with the logisticians to make sure the functions were doable. It worked out very smoothly in the main.

When we arrived in Danang, we were met by a man whom I came to know much better. He was a black Marine private, and he was one of the most lighthearted and happy persons I have ever met in my whole life. He always had a broad smile on his face. He was a very willing, hard-working kind of fellow. He just happened to be there when we landed, and he drove us out to the camp. It might be interesting to note that the transient barracks at the time consisted of one CP tent on the edge of the airstrip.[*] It was so filthy dirty and dusty that I don't see how anybody could live in it.

At any rate, this happy young private drove us in a Mighty Mite, which is a sort of a diminutive jeep, out to the foot of the Hill 268, which had recently been a rice paddy. There I cast my eye on what was to be my home for the next year. It was a group of tents, most of which were on the ground in the former rice paddy. A few of them had been framed out. The headquarters tent had been framed out, and two operating rooms had been framed out. The operating rooms had been lined with plywood and had air-conditioners in them. That was all. These were small operating rooms. They were based on a GPM tent, a general purpose medium tent, which is 16 by 32 feet, and that is a poor dimension for an operating room. Operating rooms are much handier if they are about 20 feet square. At any rate, while there was a lot of square footage in them, they weren't as useful as the versions later developed.

The staff at Danang at the time consisted of about nine medical officers. Everybody slept in tents. Most everybody slept on a cot that was sitting on the ground. There was, of course, no air-conditioning. It was hot. It was dusty. We ate out of mess kits. We did our own laundry. The shower consisted of a 55-gallon drum with a small pipe with a valve on it in the bottom. Water ran into a large fruit juice can with holes punched in the bottom to give the effect of spray. To make this thing work, you took a five-gallon water can and carried it up the steps that were attached to the support for this

---

[*] CP—command post.

barrel, dumped the water in and went down and took a shower. We did not have hot water for nearly a year.

Food was remarkably good, considering the difficulties that the cooks faced. We had a lot of B rations, which are canned rations, as opposed to C rations which are the dry ones that nobody liked. Eventually we had a lot of A rations, which had fresh-frozen foods.

During those early days of our time in Vietnam, supplies were very, very low. For example, after having been in Vietnam about a month or a little bit longer, I went back up to Okinawa to see if I couldn't do something about our supply plight. We were having terrible difficulties getting enough supplies. When I left, there was something to the order of a day and a half of fuel for the aircraft and the motor transports. This was for the entire division. It had something like two days of food and two days of ammunition. They got to the point eventually where they were flying 105-millimeter ammunition from Okinawa down to Vietnam to keep the artillery supplied, which is, of course, a very, very wasteful use of aircraft. But things were that tenuous.

Fortunately, we didn't have a lot of casualties at the outset. The war was just starting, really. We would get an occasional group in that had been hit by some mortar fire or had been involved in an accident. One of the things that you have to remember is that when you go to war you take all the non-hostile kinds of injuries and illnesses with you. You also pick up the illnesses which are inherent in being in the field, dysentery and diarrhea in particular. But the hernias and the hemorrhoids and the common colds and the pneumonias and the sprained ankles and the automobile accidents, particularly Jeep accidents, were all there. History from earlier conflicts repeated itself. In the postwar analysis we learned that over half of the admissions to hospitals had nothing to do with combat injuries. They were non-hostile acts and injuries and illnesses.

We were going through the typical learning curve of young surgeons in a war. It has to be said that when each war comes along, there is a new population of surgeons which has to learn war surgery. Fortunately—or unfortunately, however you wish to put it—in the civilian sector there are few injuries that are true counterparts of combat injuries. That may sound funny, but it's true. True combat injuries, by and large, are due to high-velocity missiles.

Paul Stillwell: What about all the gun-shot wounds inflicted on America's mean streets?

Admiral Wilson: Most of them are due to guns with low muzzle velocities. The AK-47 and AR-15 have very high muzzle velocities, and the wounds they generate are different and worse because of the attendant blast effect. I will say that now, 20-some years after Vietnam, high-velocity bullet wounds are more common in the civilian world.

The muzzle velocity of the weaponry in use in Vietnam was so high that the individual who was hit by a bullet or a mine fragment or a mortar fragment was hit with a fragment that had moved at such a speed that he was not only injured by the missile itself but also by the blast effect of the missile passing through the tissues. So that what you might think would be a one-centimeter wound in an artery would turn out to be a three-, or four-, or five-centimeter piece of dead artery. The blast effect had destroyed the blood supply in the wall of that artery at some distance from where it was penetrated by the original fragment. I don't mean to get too technical, but the point is that there is a wartime technique of cleaning up these wounds, debriding these wounds, that simply has to be experienced or else taught very carefully during peacetime. It's difficult to teach something without doing it.

Paul Stillwell: What there any existing literature from previous wars that you could draw on?

Admiral Wilson: Oh, yes. There was all kind of experience from Korea and World War II. You can read all that material but until you experience it, it really doesn't sink in. The fellows were very much aware of the fact that wartime wounds were different. They became very expert very quickly. Their learning curve was steep but short.

Paul Stillwell: By "the fellows," do you mean the more junior surgeons?

Admiral Wilson: The surgeons in general. Most of the surgeons were lieutenant commanders. I was a commander at the time. As it turned out, I did very little surgery personally. I was much too busy with the logistics of keeping the commands running and various hospitals running. We had surgeons enough to do the job and do it well.

Paul Stillwell: How was morale in that environment?

Admiral Wilson: It was tremendous. I can never recall ever, ever having to call a surgeon or any of the physicians to go to work, or a corpsman, or a Marine. By the time the second helicopter had landed, even in the dead of night, the entire camp would be on its feet, and everybody at his duty station. The Marines would be out on the airstrip waiting to unload the helicopters, to act as stretcher bearers, or to load the medevac birds if we were shipping patients out.*

Let me tell you a little about operations and how we managed them. I have in my possession a summary of the way we were organized and the way we were deployed at this time. A brief sketch would do this. The Marine divisions are organized with three infantry regiments and an artillery regiment in a division, plus some support forces, like tanks and reconnaissance and beach party and such.

In the medical support organization there is supposed to be a collecting and clearing company for each of the infantry regiments and one at the headquarters of the division. The collecting and clearing companies are supposed to be mobile so that as the infantry regiment moves, the C&C company can move with it. In Vietnam we fought a static war, so the C&C companies didn't move. It was a good thing, because C&C companies are not designed to be definitive treatment facilities, the way they are organized, the way they are equipped, and particularly the way they are housed. To the extent that that's true, they were the wrong kind of facility to put there, but they were the only ones available. So as the collecting and clearing companies came in country, they were positioned in support of the various airfields that were being protected.

The first company, the Charlie Company, wound up in Danang. The Bravo Company wound up down at Chu Lai. The Alfa Company was at Phu Bai. The materials and the equipment for the Delta Company were retained in storage in Danang; I'll say more about that later. The way things worked, patients who were received and treated

---

* Medevac—medical evacuation.

were kept in country if they could go back to duty shortly. The theater rule was that if a man could go back to duty in 120 days, they kept him in theater. Otherwise, he was shipped back to the United States.

Paul Stillwell: Did you have any hospital ship support yet at that time?

Admiral Wilson: No. This was in the summer of 1965. The hospital ships didn't come on scene until after January 1966. Shortly after we arrived there, the decision had been made, and the gear arrived for the naval support activity hospital, the so-called G-4 hospital. Now, G-4 is a designator for a hospital of perhaps 600 beds. I can't remember now, it's 400 or 600. But the G-4 was a designator in the advance base functional component system, which was a system of providing wartime materials for facilities to be built in support of the wartime activities.

What happened was this. The G-4 hospital was in storage in depots in the U.S. They collected all the pieces and parts and shipped it out to Danang to be erected. It was to be put in Quonset huts with concrete pads. They had the principal functional units, like the X-ray, the laboratory, and the central sterile supply and the operating rooms pretty well finished when the Viet Cong raided the airfield, which is right across the road at China Beach.

This attack was late in October. The G-4 hospital was over near China Beach and right next to the Marine Air Group 16 helicopter pad. The Viet Cong started a 60-millimeter mortar bombardment and walked shells right through the Seabee camp and the hospital site, which was just inland from the helicopter pad.* They then swept both the Seabee compound and the hospital site with machine gun fire from a small rise nearby. In the meantime, a group of VC demolition men sneaked through the airfield defenses and planted satchel charges in a large number of helicopters and blew them sky high. We lost about 25 helos plus about 10 others damaged. It was a real shellacking for us.

The hospital people were able to avoid being wounded by simply hitting the deck and staying flat. The hospital suffered severe damage. There were lots of casualties among the Seabees, because the attack caught the Seabees asleep. They had about 50

---

* Seabees is the name applied to members of the Navy's mobile construction battalions (CBs).

wounded and about four dead. Fortunately, the wounded were not severely wounded, and that was attributed to the fact that they had wounds from multiple small, sharp metal fragments from a 60-millimeter mortar, which is better than an 81-millimeter mortar, which is much more lethal. It was reported that the people on the helicopter side of the road fought the VC at the doors of their tents with .38s. We killed 39 of the VC, but only after they had accomplished their mission. That attack set the Seabees' timetable back several weeks, because they had to get some replacement materials and equipments out there, which was always a problem.

In our own case we had severe problems with a variety of issues. First of all, the functional flow of the hospital was poor. So one of the first things we did was to reorient the flow of patients through the hospital. When the patient entered the system at the helicopter pad, he went one of two directions. He went immediately to the place where we did the acute care, the so-called shock and resuscitation tent, or he went to a holding area for the less severely wounded. In these locations patients were examined, evaluated, and moved to the proper area for either minor surgery or put in the priority system for major surgery, had their X-rays and laboratory studies completed, and had intravenous fluids started. Once the patients entered the system at these two portals, the flow pattern was such that they would never have to backtrack. It was forward progress all the way.

Paul Stillwell: That's after you got it squared away.

Admiral Wilson: Yes. You have to remember that every one of these patients was being manhandled from point to point, being carried by stretcher bearers. That's an enormous amount of work when you're moving large numbers of patients.

Paul Stillwell: What was the capacity of the hospital?

Admiral Wilson: We had 75 beds, but we didn't have enough people to run 75 beds. So when we got individuals who were badly hurt and couldn't go back to duty, we would keep them long enough to make sure they were stable, and then evacuate them to Clark Air Base Hospital, which was 800 miles away.[*]

As things progressed and we got busier, we very frequently had to move patients immediately after they were operated on. We had insufficient beds to keep them, and we didn't know what the next hour was going to bring. We didn't know how many more casualties we were to get. So one of our experiences was standing on the airstrip during the monsoon season, watching incoming patients being off-loaded from helicopters and those same helicopters being used to move patients down to the airstrip for evacuation. Typically, a Marine was wounded, say, one or two or three hours before we received him. Upon entering the hospital system, that wounded Marine was resuscitated, underwent a three- or four-hour operation, came out from under anesthesia, and within an hour or two could be in an airplane headed for Clark Air Base.

This was possible for several reasons. First, the Marines were tough. They were young and healthy—pretty rugged kids. Secondly, we were able to resuscitate them adequately. We had enough fluids and blood so we could restore their vital systems promptly. Thirdly, as long as they came out from anesthesia without any difficulties with their breathing, their blood pressures steady and stable, it was a golden time to send them. This was true because they would travel before they had time to develop any complications like pneumonia or atalectasis.

Our batting average for keeping patients alive was very good. Our analysis showed that if a patient got to us alive, he had a 98% chance of living—at least to get out of our shop. Now, having said that, we understood full well that we were shipping some desperately injured people. We knew that what we did was only the first stopgap measure, really. Even though it was looked upon as being definitive in the sense that the patients were operated on and the holes in their intestines were patched up, that was only part of the solution. There is always a problem of infection and other complications that can happen with patients. To the extent that that's true, we shipped a lot of potential problems, as well as some early successes. I would not like anyone reading these words to get the idea that

---

[*] Clark Air Force Base was about 50 miles north of Manila, on the island of Luzon in the Philippines. It was closed as part of the U.S. military withdrawal from the nation in the early 1990s.

we felt we had solved the entire problem in those C&C companies, which had really become hospitals.

Paul Stillwell: But you needed to do that to keep them alive.

Admiral Wilson: Yes. It was absolutely necessary. There's no question about that. There's a rule of thumb in the combat wounding world that everybody ought to be treated within 12 hours, and it is far better if they are treated within eight or fewer hours. So you simply could not let badly wounded patients drift for very long.

Paul Stillwell: One military blessing you had to support that medical team was control of the air to move the helicopters in and the transports out.

Admiral Wilson: Yes and no. We did have control of the air in general. We certainly had air superiority in terms of the fixed-wing fighters, and we had the helicopters and the VC did not.* That's all true. However, it was really no man's land out in the bush for those evac pilots going out to pick up the wounded in the "Dustoff" operations.† There were a number of them that came in shot up from having picked up patients in landing zones where they were taken under fire by the VC.

As a matter of fact there was a Marine major named Kelly, a fine red-headed gentleman who flew medevac virtually all of the time. I think he—as one pilot—probably delivered more patients to us than any other single pilot in the system at the time. We got to know a lot about helicopters, in the sense that we could identify them from afar, and on occasion we could identify the nature of the problem. It's a fact of life that the fastest way a helicopter can travel is to tip up on its nose and fly down at treetop level where the air is densest. When we heard helicopters coming in making the very characteristic noise of a high-powered, full-throttle approach at low level—and it's a very distinctive sound—we knew full well that there was somebody very critically injured aboard.

---

* VC—Viet Cong.
† Derived from the radio call sign of a medical evacuation helicopter pilot, Major James L. Kelly, who was killed in action in July 1964, "Dustoff" became the nickname for medical evacuation helicopters in Vietnam.

When helicopters landed, they were on the ground less than 20 seconds. We had people always available to take patients from the helicopters. Standard procedure was for somebody to take the stretcher under one arm and rush out to the helicopter with another stretcher bearer, get the patient out of the helicopter, put the fresh stretcher in, and move the patient into the shock and resuscitation area. The helicopter could then leave, and this was a matter of 20 seconds if just one patient was involved.

Paul Stillwell: Did you get advance warning by voice radio on what the nature of the casualty was?

Admiral Wilson: No, we did not. We did not have radio communication with the helicopters at our station at the time. So the only notification we had usually was the helicopter landing. On quite a number of occasions, we would get casualties and the division would not know that there had been an action in the field.

Because of the secure nature of things, we did some things that were probably not very effective for any professionals in the area. We used to call the staff G-2 section, the intelligence folks, and say, "A couple of friends just dropped in, and you might want to come down and have a chat." That was our way of telling them that we had casualties, and did they know and did they want to come down and interrogate them? Lots of times we had the first indication that anything was happening. It got to be more or less routine to make sure that the intelligence and operations folks knew when we had casualties. That would tell them that there were actions going on in the field.

Paul Stillwell: Did you ever get any wounded prisoners who had been captured?

Admiral Wilson: Yes, we did. We had a few VC, maybe half a dozen in a year.

Paul Stillwell: You mentioned the supply problems you faced when you got there. What were you able to do to improve that situation?

Admiral Wilson: Well, mainly we waited. There didn't seem to be much that we in the field could do specifically to improve the delivery time on things. However, some other people did some very good things for us. When we went out there, we really did not have good blood-bank refrigerators. We were keeping whole blood in food refrigerators, which is a no-no, really. One time we had a visit from Chuck Brodine from the Navy research community; he came out and saw that we were having this difficulty.[*] Lo and behold, within a matter of a month or so we had two beautiful brand-new blood-bank refrigerators for each of our three companies. So things could be made to happen, but we couldn't make the system work from out there. We were caught up in the Marine supply system, which was absolutely terrible at the time, and virtually everything was almost a special order.

At one point in history, probably between July and October 1965, we were down to only half a dozen boxes of intravenous fluids, each box containing six bottles. Now, mind you, whenever a casualty came in, he had to have intravenous infusions, because everybody was dehydrated to the tune of at least one or two liters of fluids. So that when you look at six cases of IV fluids, it was really a drop in the bucket.

So I wrote the general a letter and said, "General Walt, we have come to that critical point in medical supply where if we had a group of admissions, we would run out of medical supplies and be unable to function."[†] I also indicated that we had begged, borrowed, stolen, and otherwise used up all of our credit and goodwill with the Army and everybody in the Navy in the area. I said that I needed $20,000 to buy things that I knew I could buy in the theater, but I had to have the money to do it. Well, I had $5,000 in a matter of hours, and I had $20,000 within a matter of a couple of days.

The interesting thing was that he put those monies under control of the division surgeon, Captain Wulfman, who never released them.[‡] It was one of the real horror stories of my tour over there. Captain Wulfman was not a man of any great field experience. He was a radiologist and not attuned to the surgical world. It was a great trial to deal with

---

[*] Commander Charles E. Brodine, MC, USN.
[†] Major General Lewis W. Walt, USMC, promoted to lieutenant general in early 1966, was Commanding General, III Marine Amphibious Force/Third Marine Division, 1965-67.
[‡] Captain William A. Wulfman, MC, USN.

him, because he did not ever develop a deep understanding of how things worked clinically and logistically.

Fortunately, there was a local Vietnamese hospital that was being supplied by the U.S. Army. I went down and talked to the Army representative at that hospital and told him my plight. I said, "I am assured by our supply people that we've got tons of supplies on the way, but that doesn't do me a bit of good now." I said, "I've got a now problem, and what I'd like you to do is to let me borrow some IV fluids from you. All I can do is give you my word that we'll pay you back when our supplies come." He agreed to do that, and that's how we survived for a couple of months until our supplies did get there. We did pay back the supplies to the Army.

Paul Stillwell: I'm sure the fraternity of physicians helped in that case.

Admiral Wilson: Yes, it did. That's another point I'd like to make. There's always a lot of noise and talk around the world about inter-service rivalry. I can tell you from personal experience that nobody in the world was any better to us than the Air Force at Clark Air Base and the Army up and down the Vietnam coast, in Camp Kuwae in Okinawa, in Japan and in Honolulu—anywhere they were. They gave us magnificent support. As a matter of interest, I was to learn latter on that approximately two-thirds of the Marines who went to Japan on the way back to the United States wound up in Army hospitals and not Navy hospitals. The Air Force hospital at Clark Air Base in the Philippines did a monumentally successful job of receiving the casualties, not only from us but from the Army as well.

There was a colonel surgeon named Iggy Stein, who used to meet every inbound air-evac plane and personally go back through all the patients and reprioritize them.[*] He re-sorted them so that no mistakes were made in terms of neglecting a seriously injured patient. He was to later on suffer an early demise for some reason that is not clear to me. I attempted to trace him through the Air Force to let him know how much we appreciated his services, and I learned that he had passed away. He was one of the truly great contributors to the proper care of patients early on in the game when things were so difficult.

---

[*] Colonel Ignatius J. Stein, MC, USAF.

The supply problems in the year that I was there lessened somewhat. They never really got to the point where I was happy with them. It was just too early in the war.

Paul Stillwell: What plans did you make to try to expand the capacity there at Danang and perhaps make it more permanent?

Admiral Wilson: Our biggest needs were really in the size and the number and the sophistication of operating rooms. It's a fact of life in field medicine that when you build medical facilities you really need to create an environment in which talented people with the proper equipment can do their jobs and do them well. They need enough hospitals so they can have the time to do things for all the patients who are brought to them. This time, talent, equipment, and environment formula has been in existence forever and it's still a fact.

Paul Stillwell: Just to backtrack a bit, we've taken a break here and you've been looking at some documents that allow you to expand on some of the things you have just been mentioning.

Admiral Wilson: Yes. I have a note here that relates to an attack on one of our outposts. I'll just read some of it to put it in the record for interest sake. In late October and early November we had some outposts out around the perimeter of the Danang enclave. These were usually company outposts. On one occasion, at 5:15 in the morning, we received word that we'd receive 30 casualties. It turned out that we received 42 injured and 13 dead. A company out on the edge of the perimeter and on a hill near the deep jungle was virtually overrun by the VC. It was not a pleasant story.

The VC started the attack about 0200 by knocking out two bunkers on the west side of the company outpost perimeter and then charging with hand grenades. They breached the perimeter and ran through the compound throwing grenades. The Marines reacted with gunfire, killing a good number of them. The Marines found out the next morning that some of the dead VC were children who had been selling Cokes near their camp only a few days earlier. The kids ranged in age from 8 to 9 up to about 14 years.

The VC removed their dead and wounded to keep us from knowing how many casualties we caused, and how they removed them is a grizzly tale. There were people in the attack force whose job it was to see that their dead and wounded were retrieved. Their method of retrieval was to use bale hooks, quite like stevedores use to handle boxes on the wharf or the farmers use to handle bales of hay. They would hook a dead or wounded VC under the arms with this hook and drag him off. The Marines found a cave at Chu Lai containing 66 dead, and almost all of them had marks on their chests where they had been impaled with the hook and dragged from the battle area. That's a sad commentary on our civilization, and that is undoubtedly why we took so few prisoners.

Throughout the first three or four months in Danang, we were constantly beset by shelter problems. The tents we had were old, worn out, and decaying in the heat and the rain. It was a constant problem to get materials to improve the facilities. The technique that we employed was to take a tent that was pitched on the ground and frame it out with 2-by-4's and build a plywood deck, then put the tent back over it. When we had the screen, we put screens on the outside of them and eventually replaced the tents with corrugated tin roofs. The problem was always the availability of lumber and screen and tin roofing. We went through all sorts of gyrations to get these materials.

When we did get them, we had a very interesting system for utilization. One of the corpsmen was a second class whose name was Griffin; he was 62 years old, and everyone called him "Pappy." He was the foreman in charge of a small group of corpsmen who had the job of framing out the tents, and they became a very proficient team. They framed out virtually all of the tents on the compound under the supervision of a third class Seabee builder, who was very faithful in his attendance at the outset but who soon appeared on the scene less and less frequently. But by the time that happened, Pappy Griffin and his crew were pretty experienced and did a good job in building these tents.

About this time, probably early December, the Marines finally had enough manpower in country and the opportunity to go into the field to chase the VC and do something offensive, as opposed to sitting in their enclaves on the defensive. This, of course, was much more to their liking, so the planning started for an operation known as Harvest Moon.

As mentioned earlier, this particular conflict did not require that the collecting and clearing companies be very mobile, because the infantry regiments didn't go very far. The truth of the matter is that the terrain is such that moving a collecting and clearing company probably would have been pretty difficult. There just weren't any roads to amount to anything, and the nature of the clearing companies is that they are pretty heavy to go into the jungle.

At any rate, after thinking the problem through in consultation with my staff medical officers, we concluded that the way to support the regiment going in the field on an operation was to first of all not deplete the staffs at the fixed installations. Those staffs had to be intact to take care of the definitive surgical requirements that would be generated by any action. We therefore decided to try something new and put in the field what we called a shock and resuscitation team.

Basically, what we did was to send out into the field a super-duper emergency room. Under ordinary circumstances, one of two things happened. Either you put a C&C company out in the field and do things in the field, or you have corpsmen out there who are doing basic first aid and sending the patients back. We felt that we could do something intermediate between those two extremes if we were to provide some talented people. We selected six talented people—among them an anesthesiologist, an orthopedic surgeon, and a general surgeon.

There were six medical officers and about 25 corpsmen and some Marines on the team. We equipped these people to do effective resuscitative work. They had a blood bank, chest tubes, and tracheotomy tubes. They had sufficient sterile gear to do such things as control hemorrhage, complete amputations that were necessary, and in general to stabilize the injured patients, particularly the severely injured patients. The plan, as it was worked out, was that the patients would be funneled to this group in the field. The line Marines always managed to place the medical unit between the ammo dump and the fuel dump, which told us something. [Laughter] This particular system of doing business worked very well indeed.

The patients would be brought into this unit in the field, where they would be resuscitated with blood, IV fluids, have a chest tube inserted if necessary. After the doctors got the major bleeding controlled and applied sterile dressings, the wounded were then shipped virtually immediately by helicopter to the nearest fixed hospital. In this particular instance, Chu Lai was the nearest one to the operational area. We beefed up Chu Lai and had a shock and resuscitation team in the field. Some of the patients were brought to Danang simply as a matter of taking some of the excess load from Chu Lai.

Resupply was of interest. The unit in the field had good control over its inventory. They knew what they had with them, and, of course, they knew what they'd been using. We beefed up the supply capability at the Bravo Company down in Chu Lai and put some people on the edge of the helo pad on a 24-hour watch. So anytime a chopper came in, it might carry just a simple slip of paper from the commanding officer of the unit in the field saying that he needed more blood or more supplies of some kind. Ninety percent of the time the chopper could carry the needed resupply item back out into the field in a matter of minutes. This worked extremely well and provided no complications. A simple matter of a little foresight answered a bad problem. The concept was worthwhile, and it has eventually become a standard piece of the doctrine for the Marine Corps when it goes into the field now.

What we called the shock and resuscitation unit was called other things by my successors as CO of the Third Medical Battalion. Such terms as a light clearing company were used to describe it, but the basic idea was to provide more sophisticated support for the regiments in the field.

In early December the Marines tangled with the VC in this operation called Harvest Moon.* We took a lot of casualties. We had so many casualties that on one occasion the field unit from the Third Medical Battalion, the shock and resuscitation team, saw 94 wounded in 24 hours. Seventy of those casualties were flown into Danang. Since we were unable to get to all of them with the necessary dispatch, some of them were sent immediately to Clark Air Base.

Paul Stillwell: Was there anything in the airplanes to keep them going?

---

* U.S. and Vietnamese Army units set out on Operation Harvest Moon on 8 December 1965; the first engagement by U.S. Marines was the following day.

Admiral Wilson: Yes, they all had IV fluids, dressings, and medications. But the thing that is important is the fact that those patients were very carefully selected. We sent only patients who had been fully resuscitated and only patients with relatively minor wounds who could actually get to treatment quicker by going to Clark Air Base than they could if they were put in the queue in our own hospitals. That was the reason: we could not get to them in time.

Paul Stillwell: Who was making the decisions on who went where? Was that your job?

Admiral Wilson: Yes. One of the things that has to be learned very quickly by everybody, but particularly by the surgeons and anesthesiologists, is the concept of sorting. I'd like to make one more plea to anybody who reads this to understand the difference between triage and sorting. Triage is a term that was brought into play when the world at large began to talk about nuclear casualties which were estimated to be in the tens of thousands. In that case there are patients who are going to die, and there is nothing in the world you can do about it. There are three categories for a triage: those expected to die, the seriously wounded, and the lightly wounded.

In the methodology that supports triage, the lightly wounded and the intermediately wounded are the ones who are treated, because they are the greatest source of people who can continue to live and to help with the problem. Those who are over-radiated and cannot be expected to live will not have resources expended in their care. This is something very foreign to our nature, but this is the way the thinking is run in relation to triage.

In Vietnam we did not use triage; we sorted patients. We sorted them out and took the most seriously wounded first. By this technique we applied the immediate emergency resuscitative and therapeutic measures earliest on the most severely wounded. It's of interest that an analysis of our first experience in the field of this shock and resuscitation team revealed that the team probably saved at least seven people from certain death by their prompt resuscitation efforts.

One of these was a colonel and operations officer for the First Marine Air Wing. He was hit in the left leg by a .50-caliber bullet and brought to us. The bullet blew out four inches on his left leg, left shin, and left both arteries open. The fellows in the field put a tourniquet on him, gave him some blood and fluids, tied off his open arteries, and sent him on to the Danang hospital when he was resuscitated. He underwent amputation and even agreed to have it photographed.

Paul Stillwell: What was the purpose of the photography—as a teaching tool?

Admiral Wilson: It was apparently a war record that somebody wanted.

Paul Stillwell: In what way did Harvest Moon lead you to expand your capabilities?

Admiral Wilson: Well, it taught us several things. First of all, as I mentioned quite a lot earlier, we had only two operating rooms. It's a fact that the average operation in a war zone such as that requires between three and four hours. You cannot count on doing more than six cases in one operating room in a 24-hour period. When you consider operating time, cleanup time, and preparation time for the ORs, you are lucky to get six patients through there. Some people even use five per operating room per day for planning.

It was obvious from our Harvest Moon experience that we did not have enough ORs to keep up with the heavy casualty load. I made this clear to General Walt. Almost immediately, three Quonset huts were made available to us in Danang, and several were made available to the other units, a couple down at Chu Lai and a couple up at Phu Bai. Phu Bai was a smaller unit, and they used one of their Quonsets to incorporate two operating rooms, expanding them to three, and the other Quonset hut was used for an intensive-care ward. In Chu Lai they did essentially the same thing. In Danang we got three Quonsets; two of them were made into ORs, giving us a total of four, and the other one was made into an intensive-care ward. The addition of those Quonset huts, which were air-conditioned and plumbed, was an immense improvement in our capability. These improvements were stimulated by the Harvest Moon operation in which we were essentially overrun with casualties.

Paul Stillwell: Did you get more people, or did you need more people?

Admiral Wilson: Well, we really didn't need all that many more, although over time we did build the staff up to much more reasonable levels. The reserves began to come in sometime along about the first of the year in 1966, so within a matter of four to six months we started to get more people. A lot of the people who were out there when I arrived were out there on a TAD basis.[*] Some of them converted and stayed on for a whole year, and some went home at the end of six months or so.

Paul Stillwell: How much personal dealing did you have with General Walt?

Admiral Wilson: General Walt was always around. When I say that I mean this. In all the time I was in Vietnam, I don't think he ever missed coming to see the wounded after an action. He was down at the compound twice a week before our routine evacuations to pin Purple Hearts on people. I used to wait up for him after the actions. Later on, it was quite common for us to get casualties at the end of the day, about sundown. We might get 30 or 40 or 50 of them at the end of the day. Then by midnight or so, or maybe 1:00 or 2:00 o'clock in the morning, the fighting would have settled down. The tactical area would be secured, and the general's work would be essentially accomplished. Then he would arrive at the hospital at 2:00 or 3:00 or 4:00 o'clock in the morning to see the wounded, talk to patients, and cheer up my guys. So I got to see him very often.

He also used to invite me to have lunch with him on occasion, particularly on Sundays. I would go down to his China Beach house or up to his quarters in the bunker, and we'd have lunch and chat about things. Of course, he was always vitally interested in what was going on with us. He did a lot of things for us, by way of material things, that made it a lot easier for us to work. His influence was, of course, the important influence over there for us.

On one occasion, we were down in Chu Lai, and there were some casualties there from a local action. There were, oh, maybe 40 or 50 of them, and they were all lightly wounded. He said, "What's going to happen to these patients?"

---

[*] TAD—temporary additional duty from some other command.

I said "General, we're going to have to send them over to Clark, because we don't have the beds to put them in to keep them here long enough to heal them up and still have any beds to take care of an emergency."

He said, "How much more facility do you need to keep them in country?"

I had started work on this problem, and I said, "I can't tell you right here in the field, General, but I have the information in my office."

He said "You go get in my helicopter, and when I go back there I want you to go back with me, and I want you to come down and tell me what you need."

So I did. I went back to the office, picked up the information, took it down to him, and the very next morning there was an engineer battalion at the gate with truck loads of materiel and an engineer force. I can't remember exactly now, but it seems to me they put up about three 40-bed wards in a matter of a few days. The unfortunate part of it was that we didn't have the staffing to go with it right at the time to make all that construction useful to us in the manner he wished it could be accomplished.

Paul Stillwell: What do you remember about General Walt as a person, as a leader?

Admiral Wilson: Well, I think the most important thing about him was the fact that he was a Marine's Marine. He was a huge man, you know. He was well over six feet tall and a stocky man, so there was an awful lot of him. He was a very impressive mortal and had boundless energy. I rarely saw him ever get angry. Once is all I can ever remember. He always spoke to me in terms of his Marines as patients with the kind of attitude that made me understand that he was concerned about them. He showed some really deep personal concern about the way the men were injured and was deeply grateful to our staff for the way they treated them. At the same time, he was a Marine's Marine. He was a tough guy, and when you sat in on meetings with him, where they were talking about problems and things they had to do and situations that needed to be corrected, he was tough. He was a demanding man, and he got more out of people who didn't know they could do it than you can imagine. How do you get people to work 16 hours a day, six and a half days a week?

So my recollections of General Walt are all very positive. I met him a number of times after the Vietnam conflict. Just before his retirement, he was the Assistant Commandant of the Marine Corps and he wrote a book.*

He was greatly in favor of the people-to-people operations that were going on out there; he spent a lot of time and effort. I believe he truly thought that we could do something for those people. I'm sorry that I couldn't agree with him. I spent a lot of time out in the Far East, and I think that was an impossible battle to do much for those poor folks. It was impossible.

Paul Stillwell: We have a great deal of hindsight now that would have been useful at the time.

Admiral Wilson: Yes. There's a lot of Oriental psychology that pertained that our people never understood.

Paul Stillwell: I'm a little curious about your request. You were immediately responsive when he asked you about the expansion plans. Had you felt reluctant to submit them up the line earlier?

Admiral Wilson: No, we hadn't. It wasn't a matter of reluctance; it was a matter of timing. We really were just getting our act together to know what we wanted, to look ahead, to get a chance to look at tomorrow rather than today and yesterday, as it were. We were enormously busy, and, of course, the availability of materials was such that you really couldn't hope for much for a while.

We did one interesting thing. I had a very aggressive young Medical Service Corps officer named Bob Skelly, who was a jaygee and while he was there made lieutenant.† We found that the ships that were in the harbor unloading had dunnage aboard that they wanted to get rid of, so Bob took a detail of Marines and corpsmen in a couple of trucks and went

---

* General Walt's book was Strange War, Strange Strategy: A General's Report on Vietnam (New York: Funk & Wagnalls, 1970).
† Lieutenant Robert S. Skelly, MSC, USN.

down to the Tien Sha area.* They proceeded to get dunnage out of one of these freighters and load it into the trucks and started hauling it back to the camp headquarters. Well, we got about 90% of what we could get out of the ship when I got a telephone call from some Marine lieutenant colonel who said to me: "Do you realize that I have control over all of the dunnage that comes out of those ships?"

I said, "Colonel, I had no idea that you had such control over those ships."

He said, "Well, I want you to cease and desist from picking up that material."

I said, "All right, Colonel, we'll do that. We'll not bring home any more."

By that time the last truck had been loaded and was on the way, so we did exactly as I told him, but got the lumber to boot. [Laughter]

Paul Stillwell: What did you use the dunnage for?

Admiral Wilson: We made walkways between the buildings, and this was very important because of the monsoons. By the time the monsoons arrived, we had been able to construct boardwalks to connect all of our clinical buildings together, so the fellows carrying patients on stretchers didn't have to step down into the mud and risk losing their footing and all the rest of the hazards.

That was enormously important. I think there are a couple of things that people need to know about living in tents. The difference between living and existing in a tent is a deck. Once you put a deck in the tent, however you do it, whether you frame out the rest of it or not, your life improves. Your living conditions improve enormously. The same thing is true with walkways from the hospital. Once you start building sidewalks, however they are constructed, why, you're much better off. That was a great step in the right direction.

Paul Stillwell: What adjustments did you as a career naval officer have to make now that you were serving with the Marine Corps?

---

* Dunnage, often made of wood, consists of materials used in a ship's hold to support and protect cargo during a voyage.

Admiral Wilson: Well [chuckle], the Marine Corps is very different from any other military force on the face of the earth. They have their own way of doing things, and you have to learn to adjust. You have to learn to understand their gung-ho nature and do what you can to go with it. Interestingly enough, most of the Marines don't give the medical support people a hard time. They are more likely to be grateful than suspicious or prejudiced.

Paul Stillwell: It's a helpful psychology that you are wearing their uniform too.

Admiral Wilson: That's true, but they're much more likely to be helpful than critical, really. Now, as for personal adjustment, this was my first command, and I had an awful lot to learn. I had been around the Navy a lot, and I had seen a lot of things happen. But once you're on the spot, you're the guy with the responsibility, particularly in a very unstable situation like this, it gives you lots of time to think about things very critically.

For example, ordinary things. Do you let people go around armed? These are medical people. Should they be armed, or should they not be armed? If they are armed, are they well enough trained so that they are not going to shoot themselves in the foot or shoot each other? If they are not armed, what do you do about the sniper problem? We had snipers around the camp all the time. The first few weeks we were there, we had to shut the lights out a lot of evenings, because snipers out in the rice paddy would shoot us in the glow of our own lights.

Paul Stillwell: Did the Geneva Convention address that issue of armed medical personnel?

Admiral Wilson: Not really. It's quite clear in that it says they should not be armed, but it also says the enemy shouldn't shoot you. [Laughter] The Geneva Convention—there it is. So it's one of those realities.

The upshot of the whole thing was that we did not require people to be armed in the camp, except under special circumstances. We did require that they be armed when they left the compound. I personally had a .38 revolver, and I lived with it. I kept it under my pillow at night, and I wore it in my hip pocket all day, because I was in and out of the camp all the time.

Paul Stillwell: Did you ever have occasion to use it?

Admiral Wilson: No, I didn't, fortunately. I had a lot of traveling to do because of the far-flung nature of our operation. I used to travel with my bodyguard, who was my sergeant major. Ed Catallo was his name. He was a man of long experience, and he understood the Marine Corps. He was the senior enlisted Marine in the medical battalion.

We had about 125 Marines in the medical battalion eventually, and we had four Marine officers. The senior one was a captain, and he was our security officer. We had a supply officer, a motor transport officer, and one other, plus a variety of enlisted people of various kinds. A lot of them were utilities men, the electricians and plumbers and people who run the generators and mechanics who fixed the trucks and such. So we had quite a number of them, but Catallo was my senior Marine enlisted adviser, and he was a splendid gentleman. There was a price on my head of $35,000, I was told.

Paul Stillwell: How did you hear that?

Admiral Wilson: Well, just by word of mouth. I don't even know who told me. I'm not sure it's important that it was or wasn't, but this is what I was told. You know, I wasn't so foolish that I was going to go out run some risks anyway, because a dead commanding officer is no good to any command. That's no reason to shrink from doing what you need to do, because you are going to get shot at, because that's part of the game. On the other hand, there is not much point in going out where you know the risk is greater if there is no particular point in making it happen.

Anyway, Sergeant Major Catallo and I traveled together all the time, and when we traveled, depending on the situation, we would go with side arms. When the situation was a little more tense, we would take rifles and wear flak vests and helmets.

Paul Stillwell: Did you take off your rank insignia?

Admiral Wilson: No, we did not. Like everybody else who flew in helicopters and had a flak jacket with you, you sat on it for fear of getting shot by somebody on the ground and getting your backsides perforated.

I used to do a lot of flying early on in the game, because for a time there Chu Lai had all the business. For some reason or other, the Chu Lai sector had more casualties in the first four months of my presence in Vietnam than anybody else. So they would call in and say they had X number of casualties. We had only one anesthesia person in that camp, and they always called for blood. The telephone connections were so bad that I could sometimes not get any more information than just that they had casualties and needed help. So sometimes in the middle of the night, I would get an anesthesiologist, pick up a load of blood, and get in the helicopter and fly down to Chu Lai to see what their situation was.

The standard doctrine at the time was for two helicopters to go. One was a gunship, and the other one was the cargo bird, carrying the supplies and the people. The doctrine was that if your helicopter was shot down, the gunship would land right next to you, and you just got out of one chopper and into the other and don't bother with anything. Fortunately, we did not have any trouble, but it wasn't all that much fun flying night over VC territory in a helicopter. It was never my idea of a Sunday afternoon excursion. [Laughter]

There's one other thing I would like to mention to you in connection with Operation Harvest Moon. We sent a shock and resuscitation team down there under the command of Lieutenant Commander Steve James, who is an orthopedic surgeon.[*] One night during that campaign, when it was foggy and the ceiling was zero, he called me to say that he had 100 casualties, most of which had immersion foot from traveling or lying in the rice paddy during their combat period. He told me that there was an onshore wind and that he needed blankets and brandy for these casualties to keep them warm through the night. With the ceiling zero, in the darkness, it sounded like it would be very difficult at best. I called division air and asked what their thoughts were on the subject, that I was pessimistic about it. They called back and said they had two volunteer crews that would

---

[*] Lieutenant Commander Stephen H. James, MC, USN.

go out if I told them that I thought it was necessary. So I told them I'd call them back shortly.

At that point, it was decision time. Are those men who are down there who are cold and suffering from immersion foot likely to die? Unlikely. The worst thing that could probably happen to them is that some of them might get pneumonia, but that's treatable. If we hazard and lose two helicopter crews and two helicopters, that's not treatable. They are dead and gone if anything happens en route. So the decision was not to send the supplies, and we called division air and said, "The risk to your fellows is too great compared to the risk of the patients having some bad effect."

We were able to get a helicopter in there by midday the next day and evacuated those patients without significant difficulty, and nobody had any bad effects from the exposure overnight.

A couple of days after Christmas, the chaplain from the Third Battalion, Third Marine Regiment, came into the compound about 2200 saying that they had 100 men down with food poisoning. Included were both of their medical officers and all but three of their corpsmen. Believe me, when people are sick with gastroenteritis or food poisoning, they are just as ineffective as though they had been shot. There is no way in the world they can do anything functionally positive. So we put together an emergency crew of a couple of medical officers and half a dozen corpsmen with supplies of intravenous fluids and sent them over to see what they could do to get things under control.

One of the features of C-rations, or K-rations, whichever ones they were using at the time, is the fact that they are constipating. Food poisoning patients usually have nausea, vomiting, and diarrhea until their systems are cleared, and then you can ordinarily start them on an ordinary diet again. However, it's easy to say it's food poisoning, and you might be dealing with acute gastroenteritis. Acute gastroenteritis was quite common in Vietnam because of the difficulty with sanitation, getting enough screen wire to screen off the heads and to screen off the food preparation areas, the galley and the eating areas.

So one of the things that you do immediately in a case of food poisoning is to close the galley and get it cleaned up from top to bottom and stem to stern. Then you put all the patients who can tolerate any food by mouth on C rations or K rations, whatever you have. Those rations are sterile, canned, and they're constipating, so the net effect is very good for the patients who are suffering from gastroenteritis. Ordinarily, it'll stop diarrhea in its tracks overnight, and then you can arrange to have the necessary sanitation efforts completed, screening and washing down and whatever else is necessary. That's the way it worked out here. It just took a matter of a few hours for these fellows to snap back after we started treating them in this fashion.

In mid-January we had a little bit of excitement. An Air Force B-57 Canberra jet bomber crashed on the Danang airstrip while it was carrying a load of bombs and some other ammo. I think probably the plane had some of the controls or landing gear shot away and came back in with a full bomb load and ammo aboard. It did crash and burn, and there were a number of horrendous explosions and lots of pillars of bright fire and lots of smoke. We never did get any word about whether the crew got out or not. It certainly was a spectacular event, one that we didn't want to see very often.

In mid-January the NSA hospital opened up with 120 beds operational.* This was a great boon to us, because it was the first time we had any backup or any alternative medical support capability in the area.

Paul Stillwell: Did that decrease your dependence on Clark Air Force Base?

Admiral Wilson: Not really. What it did do was to spread the load of acute casualties to two hospitals instead of one. It also improved our specialty coverage, because the NSA hospital had some specialist physicians there which we did not have. They had a neurosurgeon who had worked with us for a number of months before the NSA hospital opened up. There were other specialties that they had that were very helpful to us and prevented us from having to ship patients out for that reason. Mainly, it was an alternative facility for taking care of some of the acute wounded whom we used to get in such profusion.

The difficulties in guerrilla warfare, which is really what Vietnam was all about, are legion, but in this particular case, the Viet Cong were experts at booby traps and particularly at land mines, and we had all kinds of problems with woundings from them. The VC were great at stringing fine wire or fine string across a trail and fitting it to trigger

---

* NSA—Naval Support Activity Danang.

a grenade. They had developed a great expertise in land mines. They developed a great expertise at using what we referred to as used-up batteries to detonate mines by hand.

Our LVTs, landing vehicles tracked, the amphibious tractors, each carried 450 gallons of diesel fuel in the belly tanks. We had several occasions when the VC would wait for the amphibious tractor to go over a certain spot and then from a hidden vantage point would detonate a mine underneath it. Everybody riding in the vehicle, of course, would be sprayed with burning fuel. It was a mess, and we got terrible burn patients. The VC also used punji sticks, which were sharpened bamboo sticks set into the earth or otherwise scattered around so that people stepped on them, fell into them, or however. They were usually just sharpened pieces of bamboo and sometimes had dung smeared on them for the obvious purpose of creating an infection.

I think it might be of interest at this point to stop and talk a little bit about people and how they react to combat. First of all, the corpsmen were an absolutely superb lot of people. They were of all varieties, obviously, all the way from HAs, hospitalman apprentices, up to master chief hospital corpsmen. The one thing that bound them together was their commitment to taking care of the patients. I think I mentioned earlier on that never once did I have to call a corpsman or an officer to duty. They were always ready and available and responded quickly. The corpsmen worked long hard hours, on their feet, sometimes doing tedious things, sometimes doing just plain ordinary hard work. For example, the scrub corpsmen who were on their feet 12 to 16 to 20 hours at a time. There were very few problems with the corpsmen. They were a superb group, and they worked above their heads most of the time.

The same thing is in general true with the medical officers. The care and feeding of medical officers is a difficult business, because a good physician is a confident physician, and a confident physician is one who wants to make his own decisions. When you try to fit that into a military setting, sometimes it develops conflict, but most of the fellows who came out very quickly adapted to the field medical situation. I made note earlier of the differences between peacetime practice and the necessities of wartime practice in terms of the work done, the problems that face the surgeon, and the kinds of treatments that are rendered. The difference between the two types of practice calls for understanding the principles of wartime surgery, which have to be learned in the field, because they are not well learned between wars.

When a new physician arrived at our installation, it usually took about three experiences with large numbers of casualties to accustom the individual to the system. On the occasion of the first group of casualties, the new medical officer would stand around and be minimally effective, because he was really almost overwhelmed, or at least amazed, by the numbers of casualties coming in simultaneously. He was probably asking the question, "How in the world can we make any sense out of this mess?"

The second time around, the new doctors usually were able to contribute by helping to evaluate patients, insert endo-tracheal and chest tubes, start intravenous infusions, etc. By the third time around, they were old hands, and they were almost fully capable of taking care of patients by themselves. On only one occasion did we have someone who was unable to stand the stress. This was an individual who came to us and broke down psychologically the first time he saw a large group of casualties. We sent him back to the United States immediately, for he was never going to be able to deal with battlefield problems.

Paul Stillwell: As the commanding officer, you also had the job of evaluating these doctors. I know how the skipper of a fighter squadron, for example, goes about evaluating his hot pilots. What qualities did you look for in your doctors?

Admiral Wilson: Well, we looked for several things. First of all, we looked for their clinical professional qualifications, because we needed good men to do their clinical professional thing. That was foremost in my mind. Secondly, we needed people with stable personalities, who could work long hours, retain their equanimity, not get mad, not throw instruments, not do any of the things that manifest the stress under which they were working. Thirdly, I looked upon their maturity as one of the elements of their personalities and performance. They were all young men, to be sure, in their 30s, and at the same time they were in a situation where they had to make mature judgments on a continuing basis. Their personal behavior had to be mature as well, because they were role models for the younger officers and for the corpsmen as well.

Paul Stillwell: Their personalities would also affect the patients, wouldn't they?

Admiral Wilson: Well, not so much their personality as their professional ability and their personal stability. That was what I was really counting on, and some of them became very excellent leaders. Some of them immediately understood and appreciated the field operations and responded to the needs. They made very significant contributions to the improvement of what we were doing, how we were doing it, when we were doing it, in anticipation of what might be needed later.

These thoughts bring me around to a follow-on in regard to the shock and resuscitation teams. In the fall of 1965, when we mounted out the first of those teams, the crew that went out was called the Delta Company. I told you that the Charlie Company was at Danang, the Alfa Company at Phu Bai. The Delta Company was also at Danang, and the Bravo Company was at Chu Lai. So it was logical that the outfit going out as the shock and resuscitation Team be called the Delta Team, using the Delta Team's equipments. The Delta Team was reconstituted each time an operation was mounted up.

They started out going to the field in trucks over the road. When they arrived on site and gained some experience, they found that their equipment and supply listings were about 85% correct. They had done an 85% job of anticipating what they needed. The other 15% we were able to provide immediately because of the immediacy of the available helicopter airlift. When the teams came back in off the road, they had already taken an inventory of their supplies and what they needed to replenish their supplies. They had lists of things that they wished to delete and things they wished to add. They separated out their broken and worn-out equipments for replacement as well. I recall quite clearly the day the Delta Company platoon that had been in the field for 35 days returned over the road at 1500. I reported them ready to re-deploy at 1800. They had resupplied and re-equipped themselves, and at 2000 they went out again by air. Their operation had become very finely honed.

The interesting part is that the transport mode by which the unit mounts out dictates the size, weight, and bulk of the equipment to be taken. Going out over the road made it possible to take virtually everything that the company had. Going out by fixed-wing aircraft dictated that you be careful and take as few of the big items as you could get along without. If going out by helicopter, then a completely different set of problems pertained because of the need to keep the outfit light.

Paul Stillwell: What kinds of vehicles were used for transporting over the road?

Admiral Wilson: Two-and-a-half-ton trucks and cracker-box ambulances and a few Mighty Mites, which were Jeeps. It was always the same group of people who wanted to go out. They were all volunteers. Their leader was Lieutenant Commander Roger Hauser, a regular Navy medical officer, who unfortunately is now deceased.[*] He was a superb field commander, and it was under his tutelage and guidance that this team became so well trained. The Delta Team had their equipment and supplies so carefully organized that they could start at the front of a long storage tent, and if they were going out by helicopter they could pick out the lightweight, helicopter-transportable gear from the gear near the entry. If going out by fixed wing, they could go back a little farther in the tent and include some heavier items. If they were to go out in some sort of heavy-lift mode, like trucks or even big fixed-wing aircraft, they could go back still farther and get the still heavier gear. So it was sort of a graduated arrangement that they had worked out, and it became one of the most effective field units and organizations that we had. It has survived and is a part of the Marine Corps field medical doctrine now.

Paul Stillwell: How much innovation were you able to bring to that kind of job?

Admiral Wilson: We were really able to pretty much write our own book, as they say, but it's folly to do that unless there is some real reason. We did several things that had not been done in the past. First of all, we built a fixed hospital in position and considered mobility a secondary factor of importance, because of the way the war was fought.

Secondly, we did things organizationally a little bit differently. The shock and resuscitation team is a good example. We did that because of the operational necessities at the time: the need to have some support but not necessarily the need for a whole clearing

---

[*] Lieutenant Commander Roger G. Hauser, MC, USN.

company level of support. We did it also because we needed to preserve the integrity of surgical teams at our base hospitals. We needed to have a hospital where we could function as a relatively sophisticated care center when we brought casualties in from the battle zones.

These ways of doing business in the field were not in the standard doctrine manuals of the time. We did not have any trouble in the field with our shock and resuscitation teams until the field commanders began to get involved with the patient evacuee assignments. I have mentioned that there is a golden period for getting patients onto the operating table. Lieutenant Commander Hauser was an excellent field commander. He knew what patients he had sent where and how long the various operating rooms were committed. If you have two operating rooms and you have six patients, you are tied up for 12 hours, each patient taking three to four hours. You want to get all the patients treated by at least the end of 12 hours.

As soon as you receive the seventh patient who needs an operating room, you're in overload. So that next patient suffers because he can't get in the OR in time. Lieutenant Commander Hauser was able to distribute those patients from wherever he was to hospitals up and down the coast. If he had problems in the field he sent the extra patients to Danang, and I redistributed them up and down the coast to utilize our idle surgical teams, our idle operating rooms, and our idle people or facilities.

Paul Stillwell: Could you call on the other services in that kind of situation?

Admiral Wilson: Oh, yes. We could send patients anywhere that we wanted to by simply calling and asking. We had one occasion where the hospital ship was offshore.* The hospital ships were fine in the sense that they had lots of beds, and they had some fancy equipment. But they had only three operating rooms, so they would go into overload very quickly. When the field commander in one of our operations ordered patients flown out to the hospital ship, he overloaded that ship in just a few minutes, and our whole plan for

---

* USS Repose (AH-16), which had been in mothballs, was recommissioned on 16 October 1965 and arrived on station off Chu Lai, South Vietnam, on 16 February 1966.

medical evaluation collapsed until authority was given back to Commander Hauser to make it right.

It's not that their hearts weren't in the right place. They wanted to save their helicopter time, but they just didn't understand the principle that relates to dealing with war casualties, which has to do with time and distance and/or commitment.

That brings us around to another element of wartime thinking. I spent a great deal of time in the Pacific. I spent seven years west of Pearl Harbor altogether, and I like to think that I have an appreciation for the Orient and for the Pacific basin. The thing that always comes to mind when you think of the Pacific is vast areas and distance. You are trapped in the time-distance equation. Whatever you do out there, you have to figure on how long it takes because of the distances. The time-distance factors in the Pacific are enormous because of the simple size of the geographic area. Even with fast airplanes, it's a long trip from Bangkok to San Francisco, or Bangkok to Tokyo, or wherever.

You need to know these things as you are planning for medical support, because if a patient has to withstand a very long journey, you have to have that patient that much better prepared to withstand it. You can fly patients fine for an hour or an hour and a half, but when you have to fly them for 18 hours or 16 hours, it's different, and it's tougher on the patients.

A few years after Vietnam, I had a tour of duty in London, where I had some responsibilities for planning for medical operations in the Mediterranean and Mideast as well as around the U.K. When you consider that you can fly from London to Athens in a matter of two to three hours, that the Mediterranean Sea is only 2,000 miles long, and it's only 400 miles from the top of France to the bottom of France, it's easy to see that those time-distance factors are in your favor, because you have short hauls compared to the Pacific.

Again, planning factors hinge on these time-distance factors. Later on in this discussion we will get into the matter of the bombing of the Marine Corps barracks in Beirut in October of 1983, where time-distance factors played a great part in managing the patients who were evacuated.

Paul Stillwell: You have been talking almost exclusively in dealing with the wounded. What happened to the dead?

Admiral Wilson: The medical battalion did not have responsibilities for the dead. That was a function of the graves registration portion of the Marine Corps. They had a sergeant attached to our battalion. He had his own facility for preparing the dead for shipment to Saigon, where they were embalmed and repatriated. Our role in the management of the dead was to participate in the positive identification of the remains. We did so through a combination of fingerprinting, dog tags, identification by persons in their organizational units, officers and others who knew them well from prior association in their units.

Everyone is aware of the great pain and agony that's caused when a body is misidentified and sent to the wrong family. You can only imagine the stress and grief it brings on them. So we were inordinately careful about doing a good job of positive identification. The ultimate casualties went into body bags, and then the Marine Corps provided the airplanes to fly the bodies to Saigon, where they were embalmed and then sent home.

Paul Stillwell: How did you deal with fatigue as a factor, both for the medical personnel and yourself?

Admiral Wilson: Well, it was a problem. When we had protracted periods of heavy activity, it seemed like it was concentrated in one place, so one of the best techniques was to spread the load. During one of the operations at Chu Lai we suffered 330 wounded and a very large number dead in a 30-hour period. When that action started, I went to Chu Lai and immediately selected a group of patients to be transferred, a whole C-130 load, to Danang.

Then we started working. As soon as we got enough patients treated, we evacuated them, got them out of the way so we didn't have to expend people and time and resources taking care of them. We sent them over to Clark Air Base. I deliberately did not use the surgical team at Phu Bai. I worked the teams about 18 hours, and then began to rotate them. I brought the team in from Phu Bai, and I sent a tired team up there to rest, and I kept doing that. We rotated the teams in and out of Phu Bai and in and out of Chu Lai to give them a rest.

Medical officers can work somewhere between 18 and 24 hours before they start losing their ability to do good work. And they can do that only a few days in succession. You can't work them 18 out of every 24 hours. They have to have rest, of course. By and large, we were able to keep their longest operating periods to 20 hours or under, and then, of course, when the heat's off, why, everybody collapses and gets some sleep. Then somebody gets up to do the post-op rounds to make sure that everything is going well.

As far as my personal fatigue is concerned, I did what everybody else did. I slept when I had the opportunity. My role in the scheme of things was somewhat different, of course. I wasn't doing clinical surgery. Instead, I worked at how to make sure we had enough supplies and getting the patients out so we had clear beds to offer the division.

That raises another interesting point. The objective in the field hospital is empty beds. That may sound funny, but when you are in a unit such as a medical battalion, your objective is to be ready to take the next group of casualties. If you're chockablock with casualties you have just treated, you don't have any empty beds.

We had an occasion on one Sunday when we were given a series of classified messages that pointed out where there were possible VC mortar positions. These had been identified by the intelligence people from the patrols that had been sent out. We kept getting these reports all day long, and we plotted them on a chart. We found that there were a number of them that put us within range of their mortars.

Then a message came along that said, "Make sure that everyone has a fighting hole and a place to take up a defensive position." We thought about that for a little while and decided that we could provide that for everybody but the patients. We didn't have any fighting holes for patients. Patients weren't in very good shape to take up defensive positions anyway. So we called in the helicopters and evacuated all the patients out to the hospital ship offshore. It cleaned out our beds and made us ready to take the next load of casualties. It protected the patients from any adverse effects that might have accrued to them had we undergone an attack. We called together all the officers and reviewed the security system, how they were to participate, and how we were to defend ourselves should we come under attack.

As part of our precautions, I instructed the security officer, a Marine captain in our staff, to call all the officers together and to go over the security instructions with them again, to make sure they were all fully aware of what they were to do and what other people were to do so they could fully participate in a seemly fashion.

He did this about 8:00 o'clock in the morning. Afterward there was a constant undercurrent of complaints and griping and fears and concerns about our security to the point where I called the group together again late in the afternoon, to try to restore confidence and quiet the rumors.

We again went over the security instructions. Then one of the lesser experienced medical officers spoke up and said, "Dr. Wilson, don't you think if you were to go the general and ask him, that he would send in some Marines to help protect us, because we, as a group, feel that we need protection?" That rankled my soul to a degree, because if there is one thing there is not in the chain of command, it is a group. There is only a command and a command structure. I was the commanding officer, and this was a time when I was going to be darn sure I made sure that everybody knew it.

So I told him that we weren't going to have any nonsense about this. Everybody was going to do as he was told and stand on his own two feet, and I wasn't going to brook any foolishness from anybody, not at any time. They were to stay in their foxholes as they were told and not stick their heads out until they were told or they might get shot, and I might be shooting at them. I also reminded these men that this was time to pay the piper for all the training they had received at Navy expense. This questioner was only one medical officer out of a group of maybe 15 or so, who by that time were well stressed out by recent heavy workloads, so it was logical that this should happen.

We did not get mortared, had no problems. A few weeks later, the medical officer who had asked that question became ill. When I saw him in the hospital, he broke down in tears and asked if I could forgive him, and I said, "There's nothing to forgive. People react to stress in different fashions. We're all together. We didn't have any trouble and the fact that we didn't gives us heart for the next time we hear such news. So let's forget it."

These were periodic little crises that were sort of blips on the scope as time passed. As a group, those of us who served out there in the 1965 and 1966 period were fortunate in a way because we had air superiority. The VC did not at that time have rockets, and they were not assaulting us with major weapon systems used later on in the war to such devastating effect. Our misfortunes were in terms of supplies, equipments, and facilities early on in the war.

Paul Stillwell: Did your camp ever come attack?

Admiral Wilson: The only difficulties we ever had were with snipers. They used to lie out in the rice fields and shoot at us at night. We had a ring of fighting holes around the medical battalion that were manned at night. We had a security guard during the day. We would keep the snipers at bay with rifle fire when they got too frisky, but we really never had any serious problems. We never had anybody hit.

We were being harassed by them one evening, so I called the tank battalion commander and asked him to send over one of his tanks with a searchlight on it so we could get this sniper. The young captain who came over with it sort of pooh-poohed our problem. He said, "There's nobody out there." About the time we turned the searchlight on the rice paddy, the sniper fired a round that landed between the captain's feet. [Laughter] He became an instant believer, but we never had any really serious problems with them.

Paul Stillwell: You talked about what happened after the wounded men got back to your field hospital. What kind of assistance was given to them out in the field by the corpsmen accompanying the soldiers?

Admiral Wilson: The corpsmen, of course, did the best they could. By and large, the corpsmen put on dressings. Occasionally they could get an IV started. It all depended on the tactical situation and their own personal experience. A lot of the patients came in with IVs going. All of them came in with dressings in place. Some of them came in under heart massage and some were saved by it.

I must say this for the fellows: by and large, theirs was a job of dressing and splinting, and they did very well at it. You have to realize that it's virtually impossible to do much out in the field other than that, because you're most likely pinned down. At least, you don't dare stand up straight. It may be dark or it may not be. At best, it's a grim situation, and the most you can safely do for anybody, including yourself, is to put on a splint and dress the wounds and hope to get them out soon.

Paul Stillwell: You talked about providing physical rest for the doctors and corpsmen after a long stint. Was there any provision for psychic rest? It seems to me that a steady stream of wounded bodies would get to somebody after a while.

Admiral Wilson: Well, it did after a while. They started a rest and recreation program, and we had our place in that program. We did indeed send our people off to wherever for four or five days at a time. Some went to Bangkok, and some went to Australia, and some of them even went to Honolulu. There were R&R facilities available and we did use them.

The medical officers used to get tired of certain things. There was one stretch of time in the spring of 1966 when we had a rash of land mine injuries. Every day for about two or three weeks we had two to five Marines brought in with their feet blown off or their lower legs so badly fractured that they had to be amputated. Our surgeons and orthopods got so depressed at having to do all the amputations on these young men that it was really tough on them. It was the only time I think I really saw them depressed as a group.

They were all mature enough to understand something that we don't talk about very much: a physician who gets too close to a patient is not worth much as a physician. If you get emotionally tangled up with a patient, you can't be as objective as you really need to be. You can have all kinds of sympathy in your heart and should as a personal matter, but you can't let it interfere with your work. You can't stand around wringing your hands saying, "Oh dear" when you ought to be operating. To the extent that that's true, it's an emotional struggle for physicians to face the constant influx of wounded patients and not be emotionally stricken on their behalf.

But this is part of the strength and maturity and stability that I talked about when you were asking me about fitness reports. This is the kind of maturity that's an absolute requisite, and it's one of the things that the more experienced and the more mature surgeons have to help get across to the younger ones. They can't take the loss of a patient as a personal defeat.

Paul Stillwell: Did you have any remedy for this mass depression that set in?

Admiral Wilson: I had no personal remedy. The remedy came in the fact that we didn't get as many wounded. I'm not aware of any way that you can remedy a situation like that, unless you completely change the crew, which doesn't solve the problem; it only puts it on someone else.

Paul Stillwell: You were talking about the quality of the doctors, and you moved right past clinical skills. Was that so uniformly high that it wasn't a factor?

Admiral Wilson: All the people that we got were very well trained. And when I say "all," I'm talking about the orthopedic surgeons, the general surgeons, and the anesthesiologists. We also had an internist and we had a psychiatrist. We also had a good group of general medical officers. The general medical officers weren't expected to be able to operate. We did expect them to learn to do the minor surgery debridements. They learned how to help in the operating room, to assist the surgeons and the orthopedic surgeons, which they did admirably. For the first eight months we were out there, we had all Navy-trained surgeons. We knew them, we knew the quality of their work, and we knew that some of them weren't so good, so we knew where to put our efforts at surveillance and quality control.

We then began to get some reservists, and we didn't know their qualities and capabilities, so we teamed them up with some of our experienced people till we learned about them. That's the way we maintained our surveillance over the quality of the work that was done.

Paul Stillwell: Well, just as there are some athletes that are better than others, I would think there are some doctors who have better hands. Do you put them on the toughest cases?

Admiral Wilson: Now, when you say "better hands," you have to qualify that. Some people are naturally more manually dexterous and faster in their reactions and movements than other people. That doesn't mean that they are any better; it just means that they're faster. The speed with which you work is not of importance except when you dawdle. You can't afford to let people dawdle in an operating room. They have to be doing meaningful things with their hands all the time to accomplish the work in an appropriate and timely fashion. So you can't let people dawdle, but you shouldn't be in there spurring them on to greater speed for the simple sake of it.

There were always learning curves for new surgeons and for anybody who came out there. The more of a given kind of work that someone did, the better he became at it. There was an experience function represented by this learning curve. For example, we had 24 young dental officers attached to us, basically because they didn't have any other place to go. We were sort of playing mother hen to them. These young fellows didn't have that many teeth to fix, so when the casualties came in, we assigned them to doing debridements of minor wounds. When you look at who is better at local anesthesia than a dentist, I don't know of anybody. Certainly they had manual dexterity from their own profession. All they needed to learn were the few principles involved with the proper debridement of minor wounds, which we promptly taught them. They were not only eager, but they were very good.

History has shown us that about 25% of any given casualty load requires a major operating room. The other 75% can be handled under local anesthesia or somewhere other than in an operating room, so there was a lot of minor surgery to be done. This group of young dentists was very valuable to us for this reason.

When our teams were settled in and everybody had had some experience, it was not at all unusual for us to get 45 or 50 patients in a matter of an hour. Within one hour, all 45 or 50 of those patients would have been examined and resuscitated. The major operating rooms would be up and running, the patients to follow on in the ORs would have been prioritized, were undergoing continuing resuscitation, and their cross-matched blood would be running. Some of the minor wounded would already have been treated and placed in a bunk, because our people were experienced enough so they could sort things out very quickly, find out who needed what, and get about doing it. So within an hour we could handle 50 patients and do it with aplomb and do it well. The only holdup would be OR time, and we had those OR-bound patients prioritized and under resuscitative measures, so it worked very nicely.

Paul Stillwell: What kind of reactions did you get from the wounded men—frustration at being taken out of the fight, or relief for being taken out of the fight, some of both?

Admiral Wilson: I don't recall those reactions quite as much as I do the gratitude that they were in the hands of people to take care of them when they were hurt. One of the things that we were constantly told by the troop commanders was the fact that the guys had good morale, because they knew that if they were wounded, we could help them. There was help available quickly. That's a strong motivating force for troops committed to the field.

Of the Marines who were hurt really badly, a good many of them were unconscious or semiconscious. The ones who had minor wounds were sort of glad to be in out of the field with their wounds but didn't say anything about the fights. I don't think I ever heard a Marine say, "Well, I'm glad this is a ticket home," or anything of that sort.

Paul Stillwell: Did you have any local recreation facilities for the medical personnel?

Admiral Wilson: Yes, we did. We had an officers' club where we served beer and occasionally whiskey when we could get it. We had an enlisted club which served beer and soft drinks and which we kept control of so it didn't get out of hand. We had music for the enlisted club, and there was a place for them to go and jolly one another up and have a few beers and rest and relax. We had very little trouble with it. Basically I turned supervision of the club over to the chiefs and said to them they could have the club as long as they behaved themselves. I told them I wanted no drunkenness, and I didn't want anybody disabled for duty. That's the way it worked. Same principles applied to the officers. I don't mind anybody having a drink, but they can't be disabled, not in that climate. It had its ups and downs like everything, but it worked out admirably.

Paul Stillwell: What role did your psychiatrists play?

Admiral Wilson: A very important one. There were some psychiatric casualties, and the game plan for the psychiatric casualties was to treat them as far forward as we could and get them back into their outfits as quickly as we could. The psychiatrist was always busy. It wasn't the raving maniac type of thing at all. It was the Marine who was depressed, stressed out, who was coming a little bit unglued.

You have to remember that most of those Marines, or a great proportion of them, were very young people. I don't know what the proportion is, but I would guess that probably 75% of them were under 20 years old. These were really basically kids who had really not had time to get themselves gathered together psychologically to lean on anything other than their Marine training. So there were some psychiatric casualties that our psychiatrist, Charles Smith, dealt with and very successfully. He was a superb individual in his own right, and his success rate, I thought, was remarkable under the circumstances.

Paul Stillwell: What sorts of techniques did he use?

Admiral Wilson: Basically, interview, chatting with the patients. The poor man had no equipment, really, and I felt so badly for him because he came to me and said, "I need a place to work."

I said, "What do you need?"

He said, "I need a tent, two chairs, and a table."

I said, "Well, that's little enough. We'll see if we can find that for you."
[Laughter]

Paul Stillwell: Was confidence-building his main role?

Admiral Wilson: Yes, it was. Confidence building was probably his biggest contribution. You're-doing-the-right-thing kind of talk: "There's nothing wrong with being afraid once in a while. There is nothing wrong with saying this is a dirty filthy rotten place, that you'd rather be home," those kinds of things. "It's perfectly normal to feel as you feel, and if your buddies don't feel like you, they're just not telling you." He gave them that kind of reinforcement to any particular psychic behavior.

Paul Stillwell: A sympathetic ear can often be helpful.

Admiral Wilson: That's right. Just to legitimize what you're thinking is helpful: "I'm not crazy. I'm not out of the ordinary. Everybody thinks this way; I just didn't know that before. Even the boss is afraid."

Paul Stillwell: How much did you get cut in on the operational side? How much feel did you have for how the war was going?

Admiral Wilson: I was cut in on our operational plans as a matter of being one of the planners for support. I was aware of what was going on. The general had a weekly meeting, and all battalion commanders used to go and we'd talk about it. He would talk about how things were going in various sectors.

To be honest with you, I could not get a good feel for the totality of the Vietnam proposition, and I say proposition because that's kind of the way I feel about it. It was a group of circumstances, history, ongoing actions, and activities that had no counterpart in history. When in the world did the White House ever call the bombing raids? What kind of a world is it when the field commanders don't have the authority to go ahead and win the fight? As far as I'm concerned it was like grasping a handful of Jello; it was virtually impossible to do.

The other thing was the fact that we didn't have good communications with anybody who was putting information together. We got the Stars and Stripes, for what that was worth.[*] We had radio reception, which was sometimes jammed. That also was mostly entertainment, music, and not really any great source of hard information about the international political scenery. So I really didn't have what I consider in retrospect an opportunity to be very well informed.

---

[*] Stars and Stripes was a daily tabloid newspaper published by the armed forces for the armed forces. It contained mostly news and features and was unlikely to contain the sort of critical commentary that appeared in newspapers in the United States.

Paul Stillwell: Well, and it wasn't a war like World War II where there were specific battles and campaigns and progress.

Admiral Wilson: That's right. It was more like the French and Indian War, I think, a guerrilla war. Everybody was learning. The war fighters were learning. They were learning guerrilla warfare. They had some excellent teachers out there. The VC were masters at it, and so everyone was learning, but everybody learned on a piecemeal basis. This fellow had this sector to patrol, and he went out there and patrolled that one, and somebody else had something else. There wasn't anybody who could bring it all together, particularly between the various corps areas. We never knew what was going on in the delta.

Paul Stillwell: That was a different war.

Admiral Wilson: It was a different world. That's the best answer I can give you, which really isn't very much, but it's true.

Paul Stillwell: If you took two milestones, the summer of '65 when you got there, and the spring of '66 when you left, how would you measure the change and progress between those two?

Admiral Wilson: Enormous. I like to draw the parallel between being broke and having a dime, and then between having a dime and having a lot more money. When you're broke, you're broke and that's a fact. That's not measurable; that's infinite. When you have a dime, you're not broke and you can measure your wealth. When we went out there, we were broke. By the springtime, we probably had a quarter. We were not broke. We weren't all that well off, but we were one hell of a lot better than we were when we started. Things got continually better.

I was relieved in early June of 1966. The First Medical Battalion, with the First Division, had moved into Chu Lai. The First Division eventually moved to Danang and took over our cantonment. Then the Third Medical Battalion moved on up north to Dong

Ha, but that was after my period of command of the battalion. From what I saw in terms of pictures and what I heard from my successors, it would appear that everything got better: more supplies, more equipment, more building materials, better facilities, better transportation. The entire support picture changed for the better.

I think it's fair to say that probably in the Vietnam War, ultimately, there was an excess of medical resources applied to the problem. That may sound odd, but I think it's true.

Paul Stillwell: You mentioned that this was your first command. What are the successes, the satisfactions, and the frustrations that went with that?

Admiral Wilson: Well, of course, the successes were not so many, but the ones that we did enjoy, I think, were related to the fact that we were able to take a bad situation and make something of it. We were able to organize our people and devise ways of doing business so that we could be effective in taking care of the patients and doing it in a timely and professional manner. We were getting them in and treated and out. They were handled as well as we could under the circumstances and still have time for the next group coming in. I look upon that as probably being one of the best things that we did.

I think certainly the shock and resuscitation team concept was another good one that offered us the opportunity to better utilize the people and the equipment that we had without destroying our hospital base. I think some of the physical things that we did, like redesigning the hospital for efficient patient flow, were successes.

The frustrations were always there in terms of improving facilities, getting more and better equipment, maintaining a well-trained staff because of rotations and obtaining a supply of building materials for facility development was all very frustrating. I spent more time fighting for tin roofing, I think, than I did most anything else. It was probably not true, but it just seems that way in retrospect.

Disappointments were part of it. You couldn't avoid being disappointed that you couldn't do more and do better. On the other hand, given the constraints under which we functioned, I came away with a very positive feeling, and I didn't feel as though I had to apologize to my successor. I left my successor with a well-oiled machine that knew what to do and when to do it—and did it.

Paul Stillwell: To what extent did the job call for leadership qualities?

Admiral Wilson: Well, I felt that that's what it was all about, given the fact that everyone out there—with very few exceptions—was brand new to field medicine. Somebody had to take the lead and show them the way and set the standards, set the example, be the role model, give directions, be positive and optimistic, utilize the talents of the people there to the best of our combined abilities. We had some Medical Service Corps officers who had served with the Marines a very great deal and one of those chaps, Bill Dewey, was my right arm.* He and the sergeant major were my interface with the Marine Corps in the matter of conducting operations in the field. I had had a limited experience with the Marines in the field on an exercise. I wasn't exactly green, but I certainly wasn't any vet either.

I felt that my role was to provide the environment, the milieu, in which these fellows could use their clinical talents to take care of the patients. My job was to refine the organization, structure, and function of the battalion.

Paul Stillwell: To an extent, it's like a coach for a football team.

Admiral Wilson: Absolutely, but you also were responsible for the playing field, for the gymnasium, the field house, all the supplies, and the food. [Laughter]

Paul Stillwell: Sort of a combination of coach and athletic director.

Admiral Wilson: That's right. And I'll give you an example of being in charge of facilities. As you know, in the field all the electricity is generated by portable generators which operate around the clock to keep the electrical supply going. In our case we had, I believe, six, and of those six we needed four during the day to operate the various electrical

---

* Lieutenant William A. Dewey, MSC, USN.

things such as the X-ray machine and certain laboratory equipments, as well as lights, air-conditioning, etc.

One Sunday morning I was sitting in my hooch reading, and there was a knock on the door. I answered it, and there was Major Pope, a very clean, starched Marine in his cammis. And I invited him in and asked him what I could do to help him. And he said that he was there as a representative of Lieutenant Colonel Lee, whom I recall as being the division engineer, and that Colonel Lee had been designated as the officer to be in charge of and control all of the generators in the division. Major Pope also indicated that he had information to the effect that we had an extra generator. I explained to him that we had extra generators that might not be operating during the daytime, but at night, when we had casualties—which was the most common time for them to arrive, by the way—we needed those generators to provide the exterior lighting for the receiving areas and to power the additional equipments that had to run and to power those that had to run more frequently and virtually continuously, such as suction pumps in the operating rooms and the X-ray machinery.

He allowed that it didn't make any difference that we needed those, that there were other outfits that needed them too, and that he was going to take one or two of our generators. I said to him that I would be a little bit upset if that were to be the case, and that I really didn't think that the division authority would like to have any of the quality of care degraded by the lack of power. That didn't seem to register, and he said, "I'm sorry, but that's the way it is." And he got up to leave. And he said, "I will be back to get the generator."

And I said, "Well, Major, when you do come back, if you and the colonel decide that that's what you want to do, I strongly suggest that you come with at least a squad of armed men, because you're going to have to fight your way through the gate to get the generator."

He looked at me as if I'd hit him with a ball bat, but he said, "Yes, sir," and left—never to return. That was the last I ever saw of him.

Paul Stillwell: Did you feel a sense of relief when you left Vietnam?

Admiral Wilson: Oh, yes. I don't think anybody could have had that job when I had it and not feel stressed during the time spent there. It was the kind of a climate where there was somebody around the corner ready to shoot at you all the time. You never knew what the next helicopter was going to bring. It was a life of total uncertainty, and that's bound to be stressful.

Sure, I was relieved to get out of there. I was very glad, but I didn't feel as though I had to rush out of there. I didn't force myself out of there; let's put it that way. I could have stayed longer if it had been necessary. There was nothing magic about the day I was relieved. It was a convenient date, and that's what we used. But I didn't feel stressed out to the point of having to leave under pressure.

Paul Stillwell: Anything else on that tour of duty that you would like to mention?

Admiral Wilson: Well, I can't think of it right at the moment. I'll probably think of a dozen things after we're finished. [Laughter]

Interview Number 3 with Rear Admiral Almon C. Wilson, Medical Corps, U.S. Navy (Retired)

Place: U.S. Naval Institute, Annapolis, Maryland

Date: Thursday, 16 February 1989

Interviewer: Paul Stillwell

Paul Stillwell: Admiral, I know it's going to be hard to top yesterday's session, when we talked in such detail about Vietnam. Today we move on to your next tour of duty, which you had arranged with your detailer before you went to Vietnam. That was in Yokosuka, Japan.

Admiral Wilson: Well, almost anything after Vietnam would be a letdown, after the high level of activity and tension we endured there. However, it was a relief to get to Yokosuka. As you mentioned, we had a prior knowledge that we were going to go to Yokosuka. Because of this, it was a lot easier to make the transition from Vietnam.

Almost as soon as I arrived in Japan, I had word from the Navy Surgeon General that he wanted me to come back to the United States to brief him and his staff on medical operations in Vietnam.[*] I did go back and do exactly that and subsequently returned to Japan, stopping to brief hospital staffs en route. I recall briefing at the Bureau of Medicine and Surgery and at Great Lakes and Oakland hospitals on the way back to Japan.

Paul Stillwell: Did anything come out of this briefing to the Surgeon General? Was it designed to lead to anything—increases in supply or what have you?

Admiral Wilson: I hope so, but I couldn't give you specific evidence for it. It was an information briefing, because it was the early part of the war. I was the first person out there who had significant experience with the casualty-management problems and the logistics problems. In addition to the information, it was also a briefing to pass along one major theme. That was that in spite of the shortages of supplies and specific equipment

---

[*] Vice Admiral Robert B. Brown, MC, USN, served as the Navy's Surgeon General from 1965 to 1969.

items, the patients all did as well as they possibly could because of the ingenuity of the surgeons. No patient ever suffered because of the lack of a specific item of supply or equipment. That was part of the message that I wanted to get across, particularly to the families who would have any knowledge of this briefing. It was well received, and I guess over time I probably gave that briefing maybe a dozen times to various groups, both in the United States and in Japan.

Paul Stillwell: Did you make any recommendations as part of it?

Admiral Wilson: No, it was purely an information brief.

At the time, Rear Admiral John Cowan was the surgeon for CinCPacFlt and for CinCPac.[*] Dr. Cowan was an internist, a man with previous experience with the Marines, and one of the finest gentlemen I ever met—in the Navy or anywhere else. He had a complete understanding of the problems of Vietnam, because he was out there very frequently.

He established an annual meeting, which was later termed the CinCPac surgical conference. It was held at Baguio in the Philippines, and the attendees were surgeons from all of the services in Vietnam—the Army, the Navy, the Air Force—and some of the people from the hospitals supporting Vietnam in the theater: Guam and Yokosuka and Camp Kuwae in Okinawa, as well as Clark in the Philippines. The idea was to sit all these surgeons down and get from them their thoughts and ideas about how to manage and improve the management of wartime casualties.

It's fair to say that we don't have Navy doctors with a lot of wartime experience on the staffs of the hospitals all the time. The intervals between wars are such that the attrition of experienced surgeons is very high, so we have to start over with each war with a new group. We can do our level best to provide them with training, based on experience that's recorded, but there's nothing like the experience in the field to make the surgeons aware of the problems in detail. At any rate, these Pacific surgical conferences were held

---

[*] Rear Admiral John S. Cowan, MC, USN. CinCPacFlt—Commander in Chief Pacific Fleet; CinCPac—Commander in Chief Pacific Command.

annually, and records of the proceedings were made and distributed. It was a forum for people entering the theater to know about and to learn from, and we shared experiences.

Paul Stillwell: What do you recall specifically about your new duty station in Yokosuka?

Admiral Wilson: The first thing I recall is how busy it was compared to what I knew of it years earlier when I had been stationed in the Philippines, in the late '50s and early '60s. The Yokosuka hospital at that time was operating at about a 100-bed level, and they typically had 50 or 60 patients.

When I went there to become the chief of surgery, the hospital had expanded wildly, and they had a census of about 500 and sometimes more, based on the casualties from Vietnam. The hospital was being used at the time as a kind of way station for Navy corpsmen. The procedure was that young male corpsmen, coming out of corps school and perhaps a short tour of duty at a hospital in the continental United States, would be sent out to Yokosuka in groups. Later they would be sent to Vietnam as replacements, particularly with the Marine Corps, but I suppose also with the NSA Hospital in Danang.

Paul Stillwell: What was the purpose of having a way station?

Admiral Wilson: To give the corpsmen more experience and to have some personnel in the area who were readily available if the need arose in Vietnam for perhaps larger numbers on short notice.

The hospital had become a hotbed of activity. The first year's experience in Vietnam had led to the establishment of a doctrine of managing casualties which said, "No one leaving Vietnam will go directly back to the States without having passed through one of the theater hospitals." This was because of the great time-distance factor that involved. It was a long flight from Clark Air Base, or any of the other Asian bases, to the United States. Unless the patients were very thoroughly stabilized and re-examined frequently, it was possible to ship a patient by air and have the patient do less than well en route. Admiral Cowan, the CinCPac surgeon, made the decision, and it was a wise one.

To the Air Force's great credit, they screened the evacuation patients very carefully. To the best of my knowledge, there were very few patients who passed away in the air while in the evacuation chain. The Air Force was very strict about its rules for selecting patients for evacuation, so they had a good batting average as far as not losing patients in the air.

When the war broke out in 1965, the staff at the hospital in Yokosuka was a peacetime staff. They were then augmented with corpsmen, nurses, medical officers, and medical service corps officers. By the time I arrived there in July of 1966, the hospital was really a humming operation.

As I settled into the job as chief of surgery, there were some ongoing activities that merely increased. We received casualties from Vietnam about twice a week, perhaps 30 or 40 patients each time. As that year or two wore on, those numbers increased to 70 and 80 twice a week.

The Marine Corps had a policy that if a Marine could not return to duty in 120 days, he had to be sent back to CONUS because the commander of the Fleet Marine Force was allowed only so many Marines in the theater.* Any of the ineffectives were counted against his totals, so those who were unable to return to duty quickly were returned to CONUS.

Paul Stillwell: Who made the judgment on how long it would take a man to recover?

Admiral Wilson: The clinicians did that.

There were a number of difficulties in the Yokosuka complex in managing wartime casualties. In the first place, the airhead for the MAC aircraft was at Yokota, which wasn't very far as the crow flies, but it was several hours by road because of traffic congestion in Japan.† We set up a helicopter airlift from the airhead to the hospital. This worked out very well, but it was expensive in helicopter time and resources. It was an awkward method of moving patients around, particularly in the volume we were moving. We were handling somewhere between 100 and 150 patients in and out each week—quite a

---

* CONUS—Continental United States.
† MAC—Military Airlift Command; Yokota is the site of a U.S. Air Force base west of Tokyo.

workload for the helos. We never had any problems with it, except for occasional weather problems, but it was unhandy. Yokosuka as a base had been designed to serve the surface fleet from the end of World War II. The naval air facility at Atsugi was in place, but at the time of the Vietnam War it was not a particularly strong in helicopters.

We had some terrible problems, of course. Some of the very severely wounded were with us for numbers of weeks, because they couldn't be moved. Double and triple amputees, patients with massive soft-tissue loss from mines, patients with severe fractures and with penetrating wounds of the abdomen, complicated by infection—all were part of our daily lot in life. The operating rooms were working all day every day, doing a combination of war-wound management, which was our principal occupation, as well as taking care of the local population in Yokosuka, a sort of bread-and-butter hospital trade. We treated patients with hernias, hemorrhoids, gall bladders, and thyroid problems, and the other ordinary surgical problems that are part of the surgeon's usual practice.

Paul Stillwell: What kind of working schedule did you have with all those casualties coming into the hospital?

Admiral Wilson: Well, most of the time we were in the hospital by 7:00 o'clock in the morning to make rounds on the in-patients we had. Then we ran four operating rooms every day. The orthopedic surgeons had one, the plastic people had one, the general surgeons had one or two, depending on the schedules the other specialty people needed. We had a neurosurgeon, eye, OB/GYN, ENT people, and all those folks had to have time in the operating room.* But the general surgeons and the orthopods had at least one room each all day every day. We ran them from 7:00 or 8:00 o'clock in the morning until 4:00 or 5:00 in the afternoon, and longer if we needed to.

Then there were always the emergency cases. No matter where, you always have to deal with the acute appendices, injuries from automobile accidents, broken and sprained ankles, the knifings, the shootings, and all the things that happen in society whether you are at war or not. It was a pretty busy schedule.

---

* OB/GYN—obstetrics/gynecology; ENT—ear, nose, and throat.

Paul Stillwell: How long a day did you put in, would you guess?

Admiral Wilson: Oh, I guess probably a 10- or 12-hour day was pretty standard for me. For some of my junior people, it was a lot longer. Some of them who had specific ward requirements with large heavy casualty loads with their general medical officer assistants might put in 12 or 14 or 16 hours on occasion.

You have to understand that while we were busy, it wasn't emergency busy. It was busy on a continuing basis. As people approached clinical states where they needed to have work done, we could schedule it, and so it was scheduled follow-on surgery. It was more time-oriented scheduling than it was emergency work.

Paul Stillwell: Well, let's say a planeload of patients came in from Vietnam. Would you right away sit down and schedule them all for treatment?

Admiral Wilson: No. They all had to be admitted and re-evaluated. Each patient would undergo an immediate clinical status examination and his records carefully reviewed. Continuing treatment regimes had to be established and any indicated laboratory or X-ray studies ordered. We then had to have some time to observe the patients to see how they were doing. Obviously, if someone came in bleeding or with something obviously wrong, we'd take care of it immediately. By and large, though, we needed a day or two for evaluation before we could determine what clinical course they were on and when and if they would need additional treatment.

Paul Stillwell: Did doctors accompany them on the flight from Vietnam to Japan?

Admiral Wilson: Air Force physicians, if any. I guess most of the time there was somebody aboard. But the patients were reasonably well stabilized before they were shipped, and the flights were relatively short. From hospitals on Okinawa or from Clark to Yokosuka took about seven or eight hours. So they were not too bad.

In talking about these men coming from Vietnam, we had a few very seriously wounded who came in each of these groups. One memorable case involved a young

Marine who was a triple amputee—both legs and one arm as well as multiple abdominal wounds. His condition was a particular challenge, and one of our staff surgeons, Lieutenant Commander Roger Hauser, who had been with us in Vietnam, had charge of his case. That patient received care from Dr. Hauser night and day for months. He arrested two or three times and was resuscitated and eventually recovered to the point where he could be returned to CONUS to be rehabilitated. He received two lower limb prostheses. Subsequently, however, he had a massive pulmonary infarct and died crossing the street, after all that work. But his care was the sort of thing that was supposed to be done for him, and we did it to the best of our ability. Dr. Hauser cared for him diligently, to the best of his ability.

Paul Stillwell: How much treatment or care did they get while in Vietnam, before they were shipped to you?

Admiral Wilson: All of the patients had their major lifesaving procedures performed, one place or another, either with the Marine medical units, with NSA Danang, or one of the Army hospitals. The major surgical intervention was done there. Some of these patients had been wounded only a few days before we received them. Our job was to shepherd them through their post-operative period and deal with the complications of their woundings and surgery. The complications were reasonably numerous, because almost 100% of them were struck with pieces of metal of whatever kind, bullets or shrapnel that were contaminated, so infection was the most common problem. Deep-seated infections were the real bugaboo for us, as they had been in every war.

Paul Stillwell: From an emotional standpoint, had your time in Vietnam hardened you to seeing these wounded people day after day, and just doing your job?

Admiral Wilson: Oh, yes. It's pretty hard to describe this to people who don't practice medicine or surgery, particularly wartime surgery. It's hard to make them understand that you care more than you like for people to know, and you worry more than you like people to know. At the same time, you have to discipline yourself to not let your emotions run away with your judgment, because if you get too tangled up with a patient emotionally, you lose your objectivity as a clinician and the patient suffers. So to a degree you have to isolate yourself emotionally from the patient and be very objective on his behalf to really be effective.

Paul Stillwell: I wonder if you could give an example of how that might work. How might your emotions cloud your objectivity?

Admiral Wilson: Oh, for example, you could see a young man lying in the bed who might be the same age and might resemble your son. You have to do something that you know would be painful to him, a kind of treatment perhaps, or something that would cause him distress. If you weren't convinced that it was in his best interest, you might find yourself not doing it at the proper time or in the same degree or what have you. It's no fun. Some people in medicine just can't hack wartime duty. Fortunately, they are not very numerous. It's not easy, but it's something you have to learn right from the first day you go on a clinical ward as a medical student.

Paul Stillwell: Well, there is undoubtedly kind of a screening process so that people who can't hack it get weeded out.

Admiral Wilson: Yes. You have to be able to isolate yourself intellectually from the patient sufficiently to protect your objectivity without appearing aloof or distant, and it's—

Paul Stillwell: It's an art.

Admiral Wilson: Well, that's the art of medicine.

Paul Stillwell: What do you do in the case where you know that something is in the patient's best interests and the patient doesn't want to consent to that?

Admiral Wilson: It usually doesn't come down to that kind of confrontation. In the military, of course, the individual really doesn't have much choice. For his best interest and the interest of the service, you more or less tell him what has to be done and he won't object. I have never had anybody really object. But there's another thing. You have to gain the confidence of the patient. The patient has to know that you are on his side, that you're worrying about him all the time, and that you are willing to do anything within your power to make him better.

Once you establish a rapport with patients, you don't really have much trouble getting them to agree to what you think needs to be done for them. So that never really became an issue at any time.

Paul Stillwell: Did the fact that you were an officer and many of the patients were enlisted ever become a barrier?

Admiral Wilson: No. One of the things that you do as a medical officer is never allow the officer-enlisted relationship to surface as an issue. You create a doctor-patient relationship. You don't allow breaches of military discipline or anything like that, but by the same token you don't insist on military things that are not conducive to prompt recovery. That's one of the difficulties of being a military physician. You have to be able to handle that interface smoothly to prevent difficulties, both clinical and military. But I can say this: it's rarely a problem.

In addition to the war wounds, we also received a fair amount of work from non-battle casualties. The Marines had embarked on a program of commissioning gunnery sergeants, E-7s, as second lieutenants and making them platoon officers.* Unfortunately, some of these men didn't really want to be officers and did not do well as officers. Not that their professional performance was less than good, but they didn't tolerate it psychologically, and many of them developed ulcers that led to complications, principally bleeding. We had significant numbers of officers of this category who were admitted for bleeding ulcers, and a number of them required surgical treatment.

---

* E-7 is an enlisted pay grade; the Marine gunnery sergeant is equivalent to a chief petty officer in the Navy.

Paul Stillwell: That's surprising, really, because you would expect the experienced enlisted man to be better at the job than a newly commissioned officer out of college.

Admiral Wilson: Well, it's different when you are used to taking orders and suddenly find yourself giving them.

Paul Stillwell: Well, obviously it was a condition that you found repeatedly.

Admiral Wilson: It was a pure stress-related condition, and so they had gastrectomies and pyeloroplasties and whatever else was necessary for their management. The medical service, of course, had their own sets of devils with malarias, various kinds of parasitic diseases, and dermatologic problems, and psychiatric problems that I was not involved with, being a surgeon.

The workload stayed pretty steady. It was steady because we were virtually saturated all the time. The orthopedic service was a very busy service. We had several excellent young orthopods, and they were busy 24 hours a day. Their cases obviously were those that were not going to return to duty, and so their jobs were to clean them up and get them stabilized to the point where they could go back safely just as the others.

One of the big problems from the Vietnam War was burn patients. Burn patients are a particular type of problem, because they were so demanding of meticulous technique and specific knowledge. They require a very closely coordinated team effort to manage therapy continually and correctly. The Army, to its great good credit, established a burn center in Yokohama, Japan, and all of our burn patients went there. Twice a week a special plane came out to pick up burn patients and take them to the Brooke Army Hospital burn center in San Antonio. In the plane there were special equipment and burn teams to manage the patients en route to San Antonio's burn center.

At one point in history, the commanding officer of the Yokosuka Naval Hospital, Captain Felix Ballenger, who was a thoracic surgeon and general surgeon in his own right, decided that we should do our own burn patient therapy.[*] In spite of my misgivings and protestations, he asked us to do that. In order to set this up, we had to install some extra

---

[*] Captain Felix P. Ballenger, MC, USN.

plumbing in the operating rooms to provide a wash-down capability for burn patients. We needed burn packs, which are basically dressings of specific types. He wanted to do this immediately, so we ordered all these things accomplished.

As I recall, we ordered $5,000 worth of burn supplies, and it cost $5,000 to ship them out there by air. The public works department installed the plumbing requirements virtually overnight. Within a week or ten days, we had the first of six or seven severely burned patients. We had a plastic surgeon who was a talented man, and we had assigned to him a medical officer as his assistant, as well as a group of staff nurses to manage these patients.

Paul Stillwell: The advantage I can see from setting up that facility is one that you cited earlier—you didn't have to move people so far to get them the treatment they needed.

Admiral Wilson: Correct. It's a different thing moving someone from Vietnam to Japan than to move him to the United States. Unfortunately, our experience with managing the burn patients was far less than we had desired.

Paul Stillwell: Was that because of lack of expertise.

Admiral Wilson: It was a result of probably a combination of a lack of expertise and a lack of experienced teamwork. We lost one or two of those patients. We put several of them into the air-evac system, but they had to be removed from the system at Yokota before they were even sent back to the United States. So we got out of the burn business right away after this experiment in burn management.

Paul Stillwell: What can you say about your regular clinical practice?

Admiral Wilson: The hospital was reasonably well staffed from the surgery department point of view. We had two general surgeons and a plastic surgeon, plus a good-sized group of orthopedic surgeons, obstetricians, and, of course, internists and psychiatrists and such.

The nursing staff was large and was well trained. Interestingly enough, there was no intensive care unit at the time. ICUs were just coming into widespread use at that point in history.

Paul Stillwell: Do you mean in hospitals worldwide, or just Navy hospitals.

Admiral Wilson: [Laughter] Well, my experience is pretty well limited to naval hospitals. There was no ICU at Yokosuka. One had been planned and was about to be constructed when I arrived. In the meantime, we took over one of the smaller wards and converted it to intensive care use. We had considerable need for the space.

At that time, I had assigned myself to take the officers' ward surgical problems. As you can imagine, the officer population was considerably less than the enlisted population in terms of surgical workload. And that was all well and good, because I had a great deal of administrative work to do.

Paul Stillwell: Please tell me about your administrative responsibility as chief of surgery?

Admiral Wilson: I was responsible for the quality of the records. I determined the watch schedule and supervised the OR and ICU. I sat on a lot of committees, boards, and advisory panels and occasionally on a court-martial board. As time passed I got to be more and more involved in the administration of the hospital through the executive officer's office. I came to be the hospital's representative at various international meetings with the Japanese—none of them very big and flashy, but it just took somebody wearing the uniform to provide a presence and somebody reasonably senior. So I did a lot of front work for the command at times.

Paul Stillwell: Did you review the work of your juniors from a medical standpoint, or were they capable enough that they could do a lot on their own?

Admiral Wilson: My juniors were all fully trained surgeons, and some of them had their specialty boards in general surgery and plastic surgery. I made rounds on the wards every day. I looked at every problem patient every day, and I kept close surveillance on all the patients, not from the point of view of looking over the shoulder of my juniors but from the point of view of being there if they wanted something they needed and couldn't get or wanted some consultation or some confirmation of their judgment, which is sometimes very helpful to a surgeon who is making a tough decision. So in that sense I supervised, hopefully without interfering.

Paul Stillwell: Do you recall any of those cases or examples of offering judgments or consultations?

Admiral Wilson: Well, yes, in the case of this young man I described to you who was a triple amputee. He had such complicated problems that there was always a problem in timing as to when things were done, and what was to be done to solve this particularly difficult problem. Why was the man's oxygen saturation so low? Should we put a tracheotomy tube in him and put him on continuous oxygen, or did he need that particular a treatment or that kind of procedure for his problem? And those are judgmental things. Sometimes they were big, sometimes they're small, but sometimes to share the decision through discussion was helpful for all of us.

I had some clinical problems on my own service that I shared with Dr. Ballenger, who, as I mentioned, was an experienced surgeon. It's not a point of embarrassment to do that, to consult with another person when you have a problem, because anyone can miss an obscure sign or indication. Sometimes it's just nice to have your judgment validated or verified.

Paul Stillwell: Gives you more confidence.

Admiral Wilson: Yes, it gives you moral support and kind of boosts up your confidence a bit. That's standard procedure in the surgical world and medical work in general.

For the rest of our time there, things marched on about the same way, because we were there in the early few years of the war, and it certainly continued long after we left.

Paul Stillwell: Did the patient load stay relatively steady?

Admiral Wilson: Relatively so. As I recall the numbers, the maximum capacity of the hospital was something to the order of 565 or 570, and the census usually ran from somewhere around 500, under a little bit, over a little bit. Five hundred was probably a better number than more, but it was busy, plenty busy.

Paul Stillwell: I recall there was a big rush in early '68 at the time of the Tet Offensive.*

Admiral Wilson: We certainly did feel the effects of that and had an abnormally large load. But what we did with those patients was to clear them through more rapidly. We just had to empty our beds, cancel elective surgery, use the hospital as more of an emergency place than as a standard bread-and-butter community hospital, which we did part of all the time. You absorb those loads in that fashion. Certainly the noncombatant community never raised any fuss over it. Nobody objected to having their hernia done next month rather than this month, and that sort of thing. But we were equal to those surges by managing in that fashion.

Paul Stillwell: Did you have Japanese working in the hospital?

Admiral Wilson: Yes, the support staff in the hospital was virtually all Japanese, all the secretaries, the food service people, the sanitation people, the custodians, the drivers.

Paul Stillwell: I remember the dental technicians were.

Admiral Wilson: Some of the dental technicians were, and we had some kind of arrangement with the Japanese where we could employ Americans only if there was some kind of classified information involved. I did have an American secretary for a while and

---

* On 31 January 1968 the North Vietnamese and Viet Cong launched a massive coordinated attack that came to be known as the Tet offensive because it occurred in conjunction with the lunar new year, a traditional Vietnamese holiday. Attacks were launched simultaneously against cities, towns, and military bases throughout Vietnam and resulted in many casualties.

so did the commanding officer, but there were very few Americans. Most of them were Japanese. Many of the Japanese had been in the hospital for years and years, and I mean, 20 years or more, some since right after the war. They were not only linguistically capable, they were technically capable in what they were doing and they were very loyal employees. They were as good as you could ask for.

Paul Stillwell: They had a good deal of job security, so that was helpful to them.

Admiral Wilson: Yes, of course, it was. But I came to feel they were genuinely sincere people, and I enjoyed working with them. I corresponded with some of them for years.

Paul Stillwell: How much interaction did you have with other Japanese people?

Admiral Wilson: It was quite modest, as far as we were concerned. We had interface with the Japanese military medical community in medical conferences. We had a regular meeting with the University of Tokyo surgical people, in the course of which we went to Tokyo and had meetings every month. We had a housemaid and we had a gardener who were Japanese. But as far as meeting with the Japanese public, we did not. It was difficult to do so.

Paul Stillwell: Did you manage to get any breaks from your routine at the hospital?

Admiral Wilson: Shortly before we left, the family took a trip down to Southeast Asia. We took a sort of package tour that took us initially to Bangkok for a few days, and then we boarded the MAC flight. The Military Airlift Command had a flight that left the United States each day. In fact they had two, one started east and one started west, and each flew around the world, stopping at various places. We were able to get on the flight from Bangkok to India on the westbound flight, stayed in India a week and caught the eastbound flight back to Bangkok and had a nice time looking at India, particularly the Taj Mahal at Agra. Then we came back through Hong Kong and Taiwan and Singapore before heading on to our next duty station.

Paul Stillwell: Did you get a chance to get out and tour Japan also?

Admiral Wilson: No, I didn't get to tour Japan very much. My wife and I did get to go to Nikko for a weekend. We did get to go down to Nara and Kyoto for a couple of days. We took a one day trip with a friend of ours around Mount Fuji. This Southeast Asia trip I talked about was a two-week trip. That was the only long trip we were able to get in.

I had a couple of other interesting experiences there that are worth mentioning. When I was educated in the undergraduate curriculum at Union College prior to going to medical school, it was not required that the entrants into medical school have a bachelor's degree. I found that I was terribly wanting in some of the non-scientific and more cultural and humanities types of study, so I proceeded to go back to college at night. As I mentioned earlier, my wife and son were full-time students at Sophia University in Tokyo.

I enrolled for a group of courses sufficient to get an undergraduate degree, and I did so by attending classes in the evening when I could. The professors were very lenient with me, and they said I would be considered present if my wife had a tape recorder that I could listen to when she brought it back. I was able to get to about one-half of the classes that were scheduled, due to the workload at the hospital. Under those somewhat unusual circumstances, I was able to get through the curriculum with good marks and to get an undergraduate degree during the two-year period at Yokosuka.

Paul Stillwell: Did you take a train to Tokyo for these classes?

Admiral Wilson: Yes, we went up in the early evening from Yokosuka to Tokyo, which took an hour. We'd return at the end of the evening and get home by 11:30. On the good weeks, when the workload permitted, I went three times a week. Alternatively, it was once or twice, but I got there often enough so that I could pass the courses.

Paul Stillwell: What did you major in?

Admiral Wilson: I took courses in Chinese history, Southeast Asian history, general economics and the economics of China—fascinating courses.

Another interesting event took place during the first winter we were there. In 1966 Christmas happened to fall on a Sunday. On the Friday before Christmas, at about 3:00 in the afternoon, a commander was admitted to the sick officers' quarters. He was commanding officer of USS Broome, a destroyer in port in Sasebo. He came in with a problem that required immediate attention—a lump in his breast. It was a question of whether or not the man had a tumor, so the necessity for biopsy was apparent. I said to him, "What in the world brings you to the hospital at this particular date and time?"

He said, "My ship is in. We've got five or six days in port. It's the only time I could foresee being able to get away. The doctor in Sasebo sent me up."

Here was a single man, 700 miles away from his ship during a war, and he had an unknown problem as he faced a holiday weekend. So I said, "Well, I'll tell you what we'll do. I'll do your history and physical right now, and we'll get your laboratory X-ray studies done. Then you climb into your clothes and come over to my house for dinner, because we're having some people in for Christmas holiday. But don't eat anything after 9:00 o'clock, because we're going to operate on you in the morning. We'll open up the operating room, and I'll get a special crew in, and we'll do your surgery in the morning and do a frozen section on it. Then we'll know whether or not you have a tumor. If you do have, why, then it's a different matter. But if you don't have, we should be able to get you out of the hospital by Monday and back to your ship."

When he arrived at our place, my wife met him outside. We had had a recent snowstorm, and Kit was sweeping the walk with a broom. He said, "What are you doing?"

She answered, "Just cleaning the path for you." Later on, that had some significance, and we'll get to that.

We did operate on him. Fortunately, it turned out that he had a benign lesion. He had no problems with his surgery. We were able to discharge him the first of the following week, and he went back to his ship. This was the kind of service to the fleet that I thought was extremely important—get the CO back to his ship in timely fashion.

As a follow-on to this, he brought his ship into Yokosuka some weeks later. Again, it was snowy and cold. We were invited to the ship to have dinner, and as we approached the gangway, there was an enlisted man sweeping the snow from the gangway. The commanding officer stood at the rail and said, "Mrs. Wilson, I am cleaning the walk for you." We proceeded to have a lovely dinner.

During that visit, he came over to the house for dinner at our request. During the course of conversations on both of these occasions, the subject of the Naval War College came up. I had had no exposure to it nor any significant information about it at the time, but the more we talked about it, the more interesting it sounded to me.

I thought about it for several weeks and finally wrote to BuMed. I sent a letter to Rear Admiral Frank Norris, who was head of the professional division and the detailer in BuMed. He was a fine gentleman in his own right. I asked him if I could be considered for assignment to the Naval War College. He wrote back and said that he had received my letter and talked to the Surgeon General, but it was impossible at the time to send anybody to the war college. He told me the reason was that they had sent people to the war college previously, but they didn't stay in the Navy very long afterward because they were all captains. Many of them didn't take jobs of the sort that would use the information that they received at the war college. He said he was sorry, but they wouldn't consider sending me.

Well, I thought about that for a while, and I wrote again. I said, "That reasoning isn't too good in my view. The matter of assignment is a bureau problem. They could send somebody to the right job if they wanted to. Secondly, I think that if a person is going to go to the war college, there ought to be some sort of a commitment about the length of service afterward." As part of the letter, I wrote words to the effect, "The line community runs the Navy, and if the medical department is going to support the line Navy, we need to have some people who speak the line officers' language, so that we can at least participate in a seemly fashion, using the proper approach and the proper logic to develop and deliver that support. I strongly ask for reconsideration."

Within a month, I had orders to the war college. The Surgeon General had relented. That was a great boon.

Paul Stillwell: Before we get there, I'd be interested in some of your recollections of living on the Japanese economy.

Admiral Wilson: Well, Mrs. Wilson and our son lived on the Japanese economy. I didn't, although I was able to get to Yokosuka and Yokohama a time or two during the Vietnam War, because I went to Yokosuka to deal with some logistics matters.

Mrs. Wilson had found a little Japanese house; it was near the railroad station in a suburb of Yokohama called Yamate. The access to the house was up a hill of some 200 steps or more. It was a very small house and a very compact house but an interesting house. It had a small kitchen, and with two people in it, it was very crowded. It had tatami, the rice straw mats on the decks. The woodwork, other than that, was highly polished from all the sock-covered feet that had walked over it. The bathhouse was in the garden, and a very good atsui bath it was. That's a "hotsy bath," in American slang.

It was a very comfortable place, and my wife and son enjoyed it immensely. Our son stayed in that house for some time after I arrived in Yokosuka. At that time Mrs. Wilson moved on the base, into quarters with me. She had done very well living on the Japanese economy, because through some friends and some opportunities that we were able to develop, she had access to certain portions of the exchange and commissary, which made things a lot easier for her. However, she existed in the main on the economy and was very successful at it.

Housing was very difficult out there at the time for Navy people arriving in Yokosuka. Many families had to live in hotels for several months—sometimes many months—before housing was available. We were not particularly popular because we moved right into housing, and that was based on the fact that I had been in Vietnam for a year and had not returned to the United States. The so-called points accumulated in sufficient numbers to permit me to get quarters right away. I don't think that any one of those people would have cared to live the year in a tent that I did in order to buy those early quarters.

We thoroughly enjoyed Japan. Mrs. Wilson in particular developed a great interest in Japanese art and history and became very conversant with it. Our son became proficient in the Japanese language, as well as in Japanese and other Asian studies. Matter of fact, he taught for a while in Hosei University. He taught English to some young students. At the time, he had a full beard and looked terrible. He was teaching a class of about 40 students when Hosei University finally found out that he was not possessed of a degree. So they were ready to cancel his work contract. But his students objected, so they allowed him to finish the semester. He tells some interesting stories. He used to use "Dear Abby" as an example of how to deal with English language. He and his students had a wonderful time.

He also taught English to business executives of the Kawasaki Steel Company in Kawasaki, which is a suburb just to the south of Tokyo. Interestingly enough, he used to take the train from Tokyo, where he then lived, to Kawasaki and be met by a company limousine. He thought that was great. Being 20 or 21 years old, it was big stuff.

Paul Stillwell: He must have been good at what he did.

Admiral Wilson: Oh, yes, he was, very good indeed.

He had a very interesting life. After he moved away from the house that he and his mother had rented in Yamate, he moved into an apartment in Shinjiku. It was an area in which many of the geisha entertainers lived. His landlord—or his land mistress, as it turned out—was an ex-geisha who owned a series of six or eight apartments. He and an Italian tenor were the only males in the complex, and they were very well taken care of by all the ladies of the area. He had a marvelous time there as he finished his college.

We were able to get back to Tokyo the following year, 1969, while we were at the war college, to attend his graduation. As a graduation present, we sent him home through Russia and through Europe.

He sailed from Yokohama on the <u>Bikol</u>, a Russian passenger ship. He sailed to Nachodka, the commercial port for Vladivostok. From there he took the Trans-Siberian Railroad to Chabarovsk, which is about 250 miles north of Vladivostok in Siberia. From there he flew Aeroflot to Moscow. On the same flight with him was a group of Japanese Communists going to Russia to celebrate one of the holidays. The Japanese have a propensity to eat all the time, and they are very careless about what they do with the food wrappers. This group of Japanese was living up to its reputation for littering public conveyances. These Japanese spoke neither Russian nor English. The stewardess spoke English but no Japanese. So our son Geoffrey wound being the translator between the Russian stewardess and the Japanese student passengers. Interesting experience for him.

He went not only to Moscow, but he went to Leningrad to see the Hermitage. He then took a train from Moscow to Prague through Minsk, Poland, and he had a small American flag which he set in the window of his train compartment. He said particularly in Poland, as they went through stations, the Polish people would salute the flag. It was very touching and stirring to him. He stayed a few days in Prague, went on to Paris for a few days, crossed the channel to London, and from London to Dublin, where he rented a car and drove around the southern half of Ireland to Shannon, and flew home from Shannon. He was about four months shy of being 23 years old and had just finished coming around the world. He was destined to go on in eight or nine months to go to OCS and be commissioned in the Navy.* He's still in at this reading.†

Paul Stillwell: Well, after all your experiences in Japan, you were detached and moved on to Newport.

Admiral Wilson: Yes. The three-year tour that I had anticipated at Yokosuka was cut short by one year, due to the orders I had asked for and received. It worked out quite well, however, because Mrs. Wilson also graduated from Sophia University that year, 1968. We went on to Newport, Rhode Island, that summer to attend the war college. Fortunately, we had friends in Newport, and they rented a house on our behalf. So that when we arrived in Newport from Yokosuka, we had a place to live. It was a lovely old farmhouse that looked out over the Atlantic Ocean in the distance.

At the time I entered the war college, I had been selected for captain, and the first activity of the president of the war college in relation to me was to promote me to captain, which was a nice thing to have happen to you when you go to a new duty station.

The war college has a marvelous reputation for several major reasons. First of all, it's a really splendid academic institution, with a fine reputation for dealing with significant issues in a very mature and far-sighted manner. It is a place where you develop contacts and friendships that last throughout your career. I think that the meeters and greeters who met us there said, "Of all the things that you do here at the war college, the

---

* OCS—Officer Candidate School, Newport Rhode Island.
† Geoffrey Wilson subsequently retired on 30 June 1990.

thing that you will do best and that which will mean most to you will be to meet people who will be your confreres forever." That has been true in my case.

I can't remember how many people there were in our student body in the naval warfare course, the senior course, but it was several hundred. Of course, the command and staff course for the junior officers and the naval command course for the foreign officers went on simultaneously. In particular that gave us the opportunity to meet the foreign officers, which was very interesting.

I don't remember exactly, but it seems to me there were some 30 countries represented, and they sent their very best. I don't know the percentage but I think it is well over 50 or 60% of the officers who attended that course became the Chiefs of Naval Operations in their home countries thereafter. So it was a very positive assignment for them, and they only sent the cream of their crop. Perhaps those men would have made it anyway, but going to the command course at Newport didn't hurt them.

Paul Stillwell: It gave them a leg up.

Admiral Wilson: Yes, indeed.

Since we had just arrived from Japan, we offered and were given the job of being an unofficial host for the Japanese member of the command course. He was a splendid gentleman named Masao Matsui. He was a captain and an aviator. Subsequent to his attendance at the war college, he went on up through the Japanese naval rank system to become a vice admiral in charge of their P-3 antisubmarine operations.* Then I lost track of him.

He was quite an interesting man. He had a family in Japan, but, being alone, he was very lonely. So we used to invite him to the house frequently. The house was built in such a fashion that it was sometimes difficult to hear people knocking on the door. It was not unusual for us to be sitting in the living room and have a face appear at the window to notify us that he was there. [Laughter] It was a little startling at first, but we became accustomed to it.

---

* The P-3 Orion is a Lockheed-built patrol plane.

He had purchased a second-hand car, and it looked like a nice automobile. One day he came over when I happened to be washing our car, and he asked if he could do the same. I said, "Certainly." So I went in the house for something, and when I returned he had taken the hose and was washing his car. But he had also taken off his shoes and socks and rolled up his trousers and was squatting on the hood of his automobile to wash it. That was quite a fun session. We enjoyed the foreign officers immensely.

The curriculum at the war college was a directed curriculum, in the sense that we all took similar courses and went through the same teaching, the same learning experiences. It was not a rigorous program in the sense that we had examinations and had to write essays and papers. It was very largely a sort of gentlemanly existence, where the subjects of conversation were at such a level of quality that you really didn't want to miss even an idle conversation. In that sense, it was a very mind-expanding experience.

The student body, of course, was made up of all the various kinds of people in the Navy, and we also had representatives from the Marine Corps, the Army, the Air Force, State Department, the intelligence community, including CIA. We all got to be very good friends, and some of the friendships made there were lifelong friendships. There were very valuable military contacts, including people with whom you dealt later on in life on serious matters that related to your jobs respectively.

Paul Stillwell: So that was a great benefit of the sort you were proposing to the detailer.

Admiral Wilson: Absolutely. It was an absolute 100% good product, I thought. It gave me a perspective that I never had before, and I certainly appreciated it.

Paul Stillwell: Do you have any specifics on the way your knowledge expanded?

Admiral Wilson: I think probably the biggest impact had to do with macro-economics, how the world's economy functions, how our economy fits or doesn't fit with the rest of the world. Such things as the discussion of whether we should continue to give foreign aid—what if we stopped it? What if we continued it? Why did we start it? They talked about strategy, including global strategy. And you can talk about local area strategy. What are you going to do in Central America? What's the nuclear strategy supposed to be? Remembering that this experience happened in 1968 and 1969, the Soviet threat was very strong and the question was: what kind of nuclear response should we be fostering at that time? Were our nuclear policies realistic? Those kinds of things came in.

Not that I talked every day with somebody about nuclear strategy, but as I read the newspapers, I understood more and more about what was being said in political arenas and in international meetings and what the President was saying about the current bout with the Russians, etc. While it didn't give you all that much specific information, it gave you a tremendous insight into the way the country functions. In the strategic studies, you also focused on what is the power base of the opposition, whether the opposition be large or small, or even friendly forces. What's their power base? How do you assess what they can do militarily, and how do you assess what they can do politically? To the extent that that's true, you should in theory be able to do better planning when you know the threat. When you know that the threat can attain only a given magnitude, your opportunity to plan appropriately is enhanced.

Paul Stillwell: I have a feeling that your line-officer background must have been helpful in that course.

Admiral Wilson: Oh, it was indeed. I had a chest full of ribbons, so I didn't go in there empty-handed. I at least had a modicum of knowledge of how the fleet worked, even though my experience was old. I at least had been at sea. I knew what the line officer's problems were, even though the equipments were different and the doctrine had changed. But I was still hard pressed to keep up with some of the technicalities of modern warfare, and I had to study quite hard to master those.

Paul Stillwell: In your conversations with the line officers, were you able to teach them more about the medical side of the Navy?

Admiral Wilson: Yes, yes. I had one or two of them as patients, as a matter of fact. [Laughter] I was able to bring to bear a little bit of medical perspective simply by anecdotal experience. There was no curricular opportunity for me to make an input to the course.

At the time there was a lecture afternoon made available to the Bureau of Medicine and Surgery. Unfortunately, the team they sent up there did very badly. The flag officer who went turned it over to his "master planner." His master planner happened to be a fine old gentleman of the old school of the Medical Service Corps with about 40-plus years of service who was still using a stubby pencil to do the casualty estimates. It was a disaster. To the best of my knowledge, the medical people have never been invited back, and to this day I do not believe that there is any medical planning in the curriculum. I'm not sure, but I don't think so.

Paul Stillwell: That's a pretty long-lasting effect.

Admiral Wilson: Yes, indeed.

Paul Stillwell: Many line officers tend to look down on staff corps officers in the Navy. Did you encounter that syndrome?

Admiral Wilson: I didn't tolerate it if I identified it. I tried to do my duty in the military as a medical officer in line with the requirements the line had for our services. If I did that and was convinced in my own mind that I had done well, I didn't take any nonsense from anybody. I didn't feel that I had to. I wasn't in a position to criticize their function and performance and their role, because I was not qualified in their professional realm, nor were they in mine. As long as I was satisfied that the services we were providing were up to par, I didn't think they had any complaints, and I didn't tolerate any nonsense.

Paul Stillwell: Did you do anything specifically to help build confidence on their part in the Medical Corps?

Admiral Wilson: I tried to make them understand that medical officers have a different piece of the world to deal with than the warriors, that the life they live and the problems they face have solutions that are very different. They're not cut and dried, they're not black and white, they're not mechanical, they're not something that tolerates mistakes well, and that every problem is different, and that you cannot approach every problem in the same fashion and expect the same result. Sometimes the best you can do isn't enough. I tried to get that idea across to them. It's pretty hard to do that with anybody, but with line officers who are gung-ho "let's hit 'em, Jack," forthright, A to B to C kinds of people, cause-and-effect relationship thinkers, and aggressive, it's difficult for them to throttle back and understand this more kind and gentle approach to life.

Paul Stillwell: Well, to put it in little different terms, they are used to giving orders and having them obeyed, and you can't order the patient to get well, you can't order a surgeon to do a successful operation.

Admiral Wilson: That's absolutely right. [Laughter] Amen.

Paul Stillwell: Did you get a master's degree as part of your studies?

Admiral Wilson: Yes. This was through a combination of a comprehensive exam on the war college studies and some extracurricular studies in off hours, which I did do. I received a master's degree in international affairs from George Washington University. That has served me in good stead, not because of the fact that it's a master's degree but because of the content of the studies, particularly the comparative government diplomatic histories and such studies that give us insight into how government systems work around the world.

The war college year was perhaps the best year I ever spent in the Navy, and I think a lot of people say that about the war college. It stems from the fact that we had no responsibilities in terms of a command. You're not responsible to any senior, nor are you responsible for any juniors. The year was marvelous because there was no telephone ringing. There was no medicine to be practiced, no patients to be worried about. School didn't start until 9:00 o'clock and it was frequently over by 3:00. It was a leisurely time, but a very stimulating time.

In addition to that, you are encouraged to participate in academic freedom, to sit and think. To sit and think is not a sin in the war college. To sit and think is part of what you're supposed to do. When you're beset with responsibilities that relate to a position in the command, you most often don't have time just to sit and think and ponder. This perhaps is one of the most important things that you do.

One of the principal benefits of the extension program at the time was the fact that the George Washington University extension people were very wise and very careful in the selection of their professors. We had teachers who came from the Ivy League colleges, mostly from Yale. They came to teach such courses as diplomatic history and comparative government. Those men, in their own right, were enormously stimulating intellectually. I recall very clearly how impressed I was with the personalities, background, wisdom, and talent that these men portrayed to us. In a real way they were stimulating to us intellectually.

Some years after my attendance at the war college, Stansfield Turner became the president, and he had a very different attitude about the curriculum.[*] He thought it was a country club, that it was catering to a bunch of people who didn't do anything but sit around and drink. He thought the George Washington University extension program was a ridiculous waste of time, effort, talent, and money. He therefore canceled the master's degree program. He changed the entire curriculum around, made the war college into think tanks and tried to force the students into doing things that I believe are probably improper for a war college, but I'm not a war college educator. In retrospect, I'm very pleased I went through the war college when I did, rather than now.

Paul Stillwell: How much reading was associated with your study at Newport?

Admiral Wilson: Tremendous amounts, tremendous amounts. I probably read an average of three to four hours a day. We had tremendous bibliographies to deal with. The war college, by the way, has a marvelous library. They have one of the best military libraries in the world, I'm sure. Those who involved themselves with the master's degree had to

---

[*] Vice Admiral Stansfield Turner, USN, served as president of the Naval War College from 30 June 1972 to 9 August 1974.

write a thesis, and if you haven't had to write a thesis in the past, it's quite a challenge. So we did a thesis, and that was interesting.

My wife had done a thesis for her undergraduate degree in Japan on the history of the Sino-Soviet border incursions, which started in the 17th century or before. Those incursions continued, and we sat and discussed it and decided that it might be a worthy subject to tackle from the politico-military point of view.

So I used her thesis as the basis for the history part of my own thesis, which dealt with the Sino-Soviet border as a continuing source of international tensions. It was a fascinating subject. The interesting thing is that the news about the border incursions and border difficulties was so frequently recurrent that I actually had to call a halt to putting new material in the thesis in order to be able to meet the submission deadline.

Paul Stillwell: Did you have any contact with Admiral Hayward, the president?

Admiral Wilson: Admiral Chick Hayward was the president of the war college when I went there, and he was soon relieved by Vice Admiral Colbert.* As students we didn't have much contact with them. You know, they met us and they greeted us, and they lectured to us on occasion and that sort of thing. We saw them at social functions, but we very rarely, if ever, had a one-on-one conversation.

Paul Stillwell: One of Hayward's projects was to bring in visiting speakers. Did you find that beneficial?

Admiral Wilson: Absolutely. We had some of the most marvelous speakers you can imagine. The caliber and the number of the lecturers were absolutely astounding.

Paul Stillwell: Any you recall in particular?

---

* Vice Admiral John T. Hayward, USN, served as president of the Naval War College from 15 February 1966 to 30 August 1968. Vice Admiral Richard G. Colbert, USN, held the position from 30 August 1968 to 17 August 1971.

Admiral Wilson: Henry Kissinger came.* We had the Secretary of the Navy. We had all of the major OpNav codes, all the single digits: OP-02, OP-03, OP-04, OP-05 and people from the more esoteric things, the C^3I community, for example.† We had people from the Defense Department, from State Department, professors of various types and varieties from the universities who taught courses of significance related to our studies there. I think the visiting lecturer series was probably the strongest part of the war college curriculum. We were exposed to some of the best minds in the country on the subjects at hand. The subjects were basically macro-economics, international macro-economics, national economics, international relations, national strategy, discussions of power bases—the stuff on which warfare is based.

Paul Stillwell: Did you get also specifically into naval strategy and tactics?

Admiral Wilson: Not so much into tactics. The naval warfare course has much more to do with how things get done, not what gets done. If you can relate to that statement, the naval warfare course is much more general in the nature of an overview and a senior staff approach, rather than to the operator's approach, to tactical problems. The junior course, the command and staff course, taught the younger officers how to become staff members on the major operational staffs. They had more to do with tactics than we did. We were concerned more with strategy than with tactics.

Paul Stillwell: And probably a good deal of planning too.

Admiral Wilson: Yes, indeed. I've always been interested in logistics. The only logistics we had was an optional course given by a retired admiral named Henry Eccles.‡

Paul Stillwell: He was an institution there.

---

* Henry A. Kissinger was executive director of Harvard University's international seminar from 1951 to 1969. He later served as the President's national security adviser and as Secretary of State.
† C^3I—command, control, communications, and intelligence.
‡ Rear Admiral Henry E. Eccles, USN (Ret.).

Admiral Wilson: Yes, he was. I just recently learned that he was a tombstone admiral. But he was involved with the war college for at least 20 years, perhaps more.*

Paul Stillwell: More than that, I believe.

Admiral Wilson: As the builder of the advanced bases in World War II, he had a wealth of experience in logistics.

Paul Stillwell: I interviewed him a few years ago, and he was quite a curmudgeon. I don't know if he was that way with you or not.

Admiral Wilson: Oh, he was. He was quite a sticky old wicket. He and I had some great discussions. In fact, he was my mentor as I wrote my thesis on the Sino-Soviet border conflicts. As such, he was my greatest supporter and critic. In addition, I had written an outline for an article on the subject of medical mobilization and logistics, which he urged me to publish. But, unfortunately, time was on the wrong side and I didn't get to do it, but I can tell you that later on I used the principles. He was a splendid gentleman to deal with. I really enjoyed him a great deal. He was certainly well respected by the staff and faculty at the war college.

Paul Stillwell: My problem in trying to relate with Admiral Eccles is that he thought on a higher plane than most mortals, and it was a little difficult communicating.

Admiral Wilson: He at least liked to think so.

Paul Stillwell: Well, that's true.

---

* Upon retirement from active duty in 1952, Admiral Eccles began a 25-year second career as head of the logistics department of the Naval War College. He was a prolific author; his most notable book was Logistics in the National Defense (Harrisburg, Pennsylvania: Stackpole Company, 1959). In 1985 the war college named its library in honor of Admiral Eccles.

Admiral Wilson: I think his ordinary verbal approach was almost a literary one in some respects. He talked like a book. I think he tried also to maintain that aura and aspect about himself as a part of his personal image.

Paul Stillwell: Yes. He knew his stuff.

Admiral Wilson: Yes, he did.

Paul Stillwell: Did you get involved in war games at all?

Admiral Wilson: Yes, we did. They have a superb war-gaming facility there, and we did have a war-gaming day or two. The line-officer types in the class were fascinated with it, of course, because that was their daily lot in life when they were deployed. They were all full of the tactical jargon and the decision-making jargon, and I was relegated to some minor role over in the back corner. But I enjoyed it. It was fascinating.

Since the time I attended the war college, I am told that the computer programs which are used for war gaming are enormously improved, immensely complex, inordinately flexible, and are really so much more efficacious in what they are trying to teach than when I was there that it is just beyond comparison.

Paul Stillwell: Made yours seem primitive.

Admiral Wilson: Yes, it really did. I am sure that what we saw was a lot better than what people 20 years before had seen. So it's all a matter of evolution and technology.

Paul Stillwell: How did this experience at the war college help you as a naval officer in general and as a medical officer in particular?

Admiral Wilson: It's hard to deal with the specifics of that question, because the war college studies were so general. Well, let me tell you the story of what happened in the following tour and perhaps explain a part of that question.

As the war college year drew toward an end, I went down to the Bureau of Medicine and Surgery to talk to the detailer about a next assignment. I felt that because of the correspondence and the attitude of the bureau, it certainly should be an operational assignment of some sort. So I again went to Admiral Norris and said to him, "You know that I'm about to graduate from the war college, and I really would like to talk to you about an assignment. I understand that the Sixth Fleet medical officer job is coming open in the Mediterranean. I know the Pacific pretty well; I've spent a lot of time out there. But I want to come into the bureau in the planning shop eventually, and I really need to know something about Europe to round out my experience and perception of the world."

He said, "Well, you know, the Sixth Fleet medical officer job is a commander's billet. Why don't you go to London and take the job as the medical officer for CinCUSNavEur?"*

I said, "I didn't know it was coming open."

He said, "Well, that's a captain's billet, and you're a captain."

I said, "Well, that's always been a very senior captain's billet, and I've been a captain for about 20 minutes." [Laughter]

He said, "It doesn't bother me if it doesn't bother you."

I said, "It doesn't bother me. If you'll send me, I'll go." So that's the way we went.

We went to England on the next-to-last voyage of the SS <u>United States</u>, that lovely old liner.† We rented a flat very close to Hyde Park, had wonderful living accommodations at a time when the British economy was such that it was quite inexpensive to live there. Prices were low compared to the United States. It was a thoroughly happy time.

When I reported for duty, I became the senior medical officer in the Commander Naval Activities United Kingdom clinics, which were several, as well as to be the medical officer on the staff of Admiral Wendt, who at the time was CinCUSNavEur.‡

---

* CinCUSNavEur—Commander in Chief U.S. Naval Forces Europe.
† SS <u>United States</u> was a 990-foot-long passenger liner that went into service 1952. At 53,329 gross tons, she was the third largest liner in the world. Her top speed of more than 38 knots was considered a potential military asset. She was removed from service by the United States Lines in late 1969.
‡ Admiral Waldemar F. A. Wendt, USN, served as Commander in Chief U.S. Naval Forces Europe and Commander in Chief U.S. Naval Forces Eastern Atlantic from July 1968 to June 1971.

During the two years that we spent in London, I had a great deal of interface with the CinC and his staff, doing their support job and their planning job for CinCUSNavEur operations. In the course of dealing with those people on those matters, I found that I could dredge up from the war college certain principles of operations, certain understandings of what they were talking about in terms of international and particularly NATO issues that were being discussed and managed at the time. It's difficult to place a specific experience as hinging on a specific thing that you learned in the war college, but one's perception and understanding of how the United States developed, created, and executed its strategy in concert with the other nations—particularly in a CinC setting—really were enhanced by attendance at the war college.

Paul Stillwell: Well, I think your value to them was considerably greater than if you just knew about bones and blood vessels and so forth.

Admiral Wilson: Well, I like to think that. Whether or not it was true, I like to think that.

At any rate, we finished the war college year. An interesting thing about Newport—of course, being in the Northeast—is that it has some bad weather in wintertime. It also has a reputation as being one of the first institutions to close, along with the kindergartens and elementary schools when there's bad weather. The year that we lived there, we had a completely open winter until February. In February we were snowed in twice in one week. Each of the snowfalls was in excess of two feet. It was just a freak of nature.

We broke a precedent at the war college by getting leave before graduation. One of the things they told us when we went there was that we were not going to get leave except at Christmastime, but we did indeed ask for and get leave to go to Japan to see our son graduate from college. We were able to get out there on schedule, using space-available air transportation, with the MAC system from San Francisco to Yokota and back. We enjoyed a nice interlude while we saw our son receive his college diploma.

We then packed up and went to London in the summer of 1969 and lived in a lovely Victorian flat in the west end of London, around the corner from the Royal

Lancaster Hotel on Hyde Park. It was a beautiful place that we rented for practically nothing in terms of other rents in town at the time.

I joined the staff of CinCUSNavEur and the Commander Naval Activities U.K. The Commander Naval Activities U.K. is a captain, and his responsibilities are logistic support for the operational commands and support activities in the area. The operational command is basically the submarine squadron at Holy Loch, Scotland. The support activity up there is largely a supply point for handling in-bound cargo and handling the shoreside activities of commissary and dispensary and such. NavActs U.K. also had responsibilities for supporting the communication station in Londonderry, Northern Ireland. Another station was at Thurso, on the northern tip of Scotland, a couple of smaller ones out in the hinterlands, and, of course, the U.S. military population, including the embassy in London.

CinCUSNavEur had a theater responsibility which ran from the Persian Gulf to Norway in the free western world and included stations in such places as Asmara, Ethiopia. Another was in Morocco, the old Port Lyautey, later called the naval training activity at Kenitra. And there was a communication station at Sidi Yahia.

We ran the dispensary as a three-man operation. I had a captain and lieutenant, medical officers, who really did most of the clinical work, although I did some too. I spent a good deal of time on the road. We visited each of the installations in the U.K. at least once a year and some of them every three months. In addition to that, I was on the road a great deal on CinCUSNavEur's behalf, because we had hospitals at Rota and at Naples and dispensaries in a lot of places like Kenitra, Morocco, and in Greece at Neamakri, a communication station, and Sigonella, Sicily. We had a small presence in Bahrain at the time, supporting the ComMidEast Force. We had two stations in northern Germany. Most of these on the continent, in Africa, and in the eastern Med I visited at least once a year.

We also had the naval research unit in Cairo. At the time the commanding officer was a Captain Henry Sparks, who was an internist and a very fine gentleman.[*] He invited me to visit him in Cairo and have a look at his unit, NAMRU Three.[†] Interestingly enough, it was supposed to be under the logistic support wing of the Commander in Chief

---

[*] Captain Henry A. Sparks, MC, USN, now a retired rear admiral.
[†] NAMRU—Navy Medical Research Unit.

U.S. Naval Forces Europe, although we never were asked to or did give them a dime, a person, a billet, a civil servant, space, a box of candy, or anything else.

Captain Sparks provided the funding for my trip out of what are known as counterpart funds. We sent the Egyptians wheat, which was sold in the open market, and the U.S. received Egyptian money. The money generated had to stay in Egypt. Part of it was given by our government to the NAMRU for their operating expenses, and with it they could buy tickets on airplanes. So the commanding officer sent me an airplane ticket. It saved NavEur money, and it was actually value recovered on behalf of the United States.

Anyway, I flew down there and visited the laboratory. They had been there continually since 1946, except for the time they left the country for six weeks during one of the Israeli wars. Everything they had going continued under the aegis of their Egyptian employees, and they never missed a beat in terms of their basic functions.

Paul Stillwell: Why did the U.S. Navy sponsor a medical research unit there?

Admiral Wilson: Because it was one of the best places to observe tropical diseases at the focal point. They allowed us to put the laboratory immediately adjacent to a hospital, so we had clinical material. We run a hospital of our own there now. We have one of the best laboratories in the entire world there to deal with diseases that are viciously lethal. It's a very productive unit.

Harry Hoogstrall had been there since the place had opened in 1946, and he was the world's foremost expert on ticks. Many ticks carry disease, and he was a world expert. He had ticks in his collection from all over the world.

They had a substation down in Addis Abbaba, and they said, "You might want to go down to Addis and look at the substation and see how they are doing." I said I'd be delighted. So I flew down there.

On the way back to Cairo, which I had planned, I stopped off in Asmara, Ethiopia, which was the site of a communication station now closed. It's in Eritrea, where the separatists had their stronghold. I stopped off to visit the station and then reboarded an airplane to go to Cairo. We were up in the air about an hour when the plane captain came up on the public address system, and he said, "Ladies and gentlemen, we don't have enough people who want to get on or off this airplane in Cairo, so we're going to Athens instead." [Laughter]

So, instead of going back to Cairo, I wound up in Athens. But I was en route to Bahrain to visit our Commander Middle East Force medical people. To get to Bahrain at that time, you had to go through Beirut, Lebanon. So I thought to myself, "I've been to Cairo. I've never been to Beirut. If I go to Beirut now, I have to wait a couple of days to get the scheduled airplane, and that's as good a place to wait as any. So I'll go to Beirut," which I did. I spent a couple of days in the Hotel Phoenicia, obviously named after the Phoenicians. I got to walk around Beirut and enjoy it, and it was certainly a jewel of a city at the time. This was 1970.

One day I had occasion to go to a bank to change some money or cash a traveler's check or something. The troubles were sort of on the edges and the fringes of the political scene. The Palestinians had been in Amman, Jordan, recently, and the tensions in the Mideast were beginning to build. The gentleman who waited on me in the bank said, "You're an American?"

I said, "Yes."

He said, "Please get your government to do something so that we don't have any troubles here. All we want to do is do business in peace."

I said, "I'll do my level best. I can't guarantee you anything, but I'll sure try." I thought that statement quite indicative of the attitude of the average Lebanese whom I met and have since come to know.

A little interesting sidelight. Outside Beirut there was supper club called Casino du Liban. I went out there for dinner and to watch a show. I must say that the show was equal to anything I had ever, ever seen in Las Vegas. The staging, the costumes, the productions were absolutely superb.

I went on to Bahrain, met the people there and evaluated their situation, looked at some potential assets for supporting our forces, and went on.

Paul Stillwell: What did you encounter in Bahrain?

Admiral Wilson: Nothing in particular. Bahrain, of course, was the headquarters of the Mideast Force, which was a very small force at the time. The LaSalle was there, and I think they had something that was the equivalent of a modern-day frigate, a small patrol vessel or two.* It was largely a presence to be maintained for symbolic purposes.

They had a medical officer there at the shoreside facility. He had a very modest little dispensary for what few people were there. The best medical facility was operated by the British Petroleum oil company, and they had, I think, a 20- or 25-bed hospital with two or three British physicians. It looked to be very clean, and it had a good reputation.

That was essentially a routine visit.

Paul Stillwell: What kinds of things would you look for or do in these visits?

Admiral Wilson: That's a very important question, because actually I made a staff visit and not just a medical visit. Many of these installations had not been visited by a CinCUSNavEur rep in several years. For instance, nobody had been to Asmara in two and a half years. People rarely went to Morocco.

My standard pattern, when I went to one of these stations, was to report to the commanding officer immediately to meet and greet him. The CinC told me that he couldn't solve the problems if he didn't know what they were. So I would ask the commanding officer what his mission was, what he was doing, what his problems were, the size and dimension of the problem, where his shortfalls lay, and included the medical department in that analysis of the command function and problems.

Paul Stillwell: Again, I can see some value in the war college training there, being able to communicate with these commanders.

Admiral Wilson: Yes, indeed. I developed credibility with them, and through them I was able to weld the CinCUSNavEur structure together, at least in a medical sense, because the

---

* USS La Salle (LPD-3) was originally commissioned 22 February 1964 as an amphibious transport dock. She served as an amphibious warfare ship until 1 July 1972, when her designation was changed to AGF-3, a miscellaneous flagship. She was flagship of the Middle East Force from 1972-80 and 1983-94. She subsequently became flagship for Commander Sixth Fleet.

senior medical officers knew who I was. They would call me on the telephone. We could solve problems. If they had problems, I could go to bat for them wherever it was necessary.

Paul Stillwell: Do any of those problems stand out in your mind as examples?

Admiral Wilson: Yes. I was once way up on the northern tip of Scotland, in Thurso, where we had a communication station. While I was there, Admiral Norris called from BuMed in Washington. My office in London contacted me up there and said, "Admiral Norris wants to talk with you."

So I called him, and he said, "We've got problems down in Morocco. We're having to cut back some billets. I think they're trying to take too many billets away from us in Morocco, and we can't hold out there."

I said, "Do you want me to go down there and sort it out?"

He said, "I wish you would."

So when I got back to London, I turned my hat around and did my laundry and went to Morocco. We sorted out the minimum number of billets that we had to retain in order to keep a branch dispensary in Morocco to maintain some kind of medical support for the people there. Morocco, incidentally, was supported by the hospital at Rota, Spain, but we still had to maintain some sort of in-patient capability in Morocco, at least for an interim period.

Paul Stillwell: It sounds as if you had a fairly sympathetic chief of staff who would allow you to go off and do Bureau of Medicine business like that.

Admiral Wilson: When I went there, it was made clear to CinCUSNavEur that I was the Surgeon General's representative in Europe. I dealt basically with two people in the staff. I dealt with the N-4, the logistics boss, but I actually had two codes in CinCUSNavEur. One was a code in the logistics shop, and the other one was as a special medical adviser to the CinC. The CinCUSNavEur staff was a strange group. In those days it was the kind of a place where a lot of people went who liked to be in Europe. These were individuals whose careers had not become as stellar as they had originally hoped.

Because I traveled a lot, there was a lot of ill feeling, because they thought I was out on a jaunt for pleasure, which was not the case. As a matter of fact, the trip reports, which I wrote in great detail when I returned from these trips, were farmed out among all the codes for consideration and action as appropriate. After that tour in London, when I went back to the bureau, I often referred to those trip reports, because they were the only pieces of information available in the bureau on what we had and what the conditions were in many of those places.

Admiral Wendt was very gracious, understanding, and supportive. When I wanted to go somewhere and the N-4 didn't want me to go, I'd go to the admiral and say, "Look, I've talked this over with the N-4. He doesn't think it's important. I think it's important. In my role as your adviser I would like to have your authority and go." He never said no. I didn't have to do that very often, because once I did it, the N-4 got the message.

Paul Stillwell: You weren't very popular with him, probably.

Admiral Wilson: No, I wasn't. But nobody else was doing a hell of a lot. It was a big planning operation but not much of an action operation. So I felt it important that we at least know what we were dealing with.

Admiral Wendt personally was a splendid gentleman. He had a very even disposition and temperament. He treated his staff as gentlemen. He was very perceptive, and he had a good insight into the way things operated. He's a very, very big man—about six feet, five, probably weighed 220 pounds. He had a sort of wry, sardonic manner about him at times. I recall once when we were there at a weekly staff meeting, the operations officer had been away from his desk for a week or two. He came back and he said, "Admiral Wendt, I'm back from leave now. I expect to be back up to speed by tomorrow afternoon."

Admiral Wendt, looked down, flicked the ashes from his cigarette into the ashtray, and said, "Captain, I give you permission to work nights." [Laughter]

I used to have a lot of fun in those staff meetings, because we wore civilian clothes to keep the profile of the foreign military as low as possible. The officers all came in dark gray suits, with or without pinstripes, and they all wore black neckties and looked like they were undertakers. I always felt that one of the few places that a man can show any character at all and any color in his costume is in his necktie, so I always wore brightly colored neckties in good taste.

So I'd always show up with a new and bright necktie for these Wednesday morning undertaker meetings. It was always the subject of comment. I did that for a couple of reasons: it kept my presence as the medical officer up front in the staff minds so that I wasn't relegated to a dark gray back corner. Then I always tried to have something to say, whether it was time for their flu shots or what went on somewhere else or something. I always tried to have something to say that was of interest to the group so they wouldn't ignore me totally.

The admiral had an apartment in the headquarters building in Grosvenor Square in London. He also had a lovely large country estate out some miles from the center of London. As you'd expect, he had a lot of people passing through—VIPs of various sorts, both American and other nationalities. My wife and I were frequently called upon to be fill-ins for lunches he gave in his apartment as these people were passing through London.

Paul Stillwell: That doesn't sound too unpleasant.

Admiral Wilson: No, it was a very pleasant experience.

Mrs. Wendt, Sonny Wendt, was a lovely lady in her own right and a most gracious hostess. These luncheon engagements got to be very interesting, and we enjoyed attending them. When we were in town we were usually available, so they could call on us at short notice, and we could respond. In that way we got to know the Wendts reasonably well and came to enjoy them and respect them immensely. In fact, I still keep in touch with Admiral Wendt some 15 years later.

Paul Stillwell: Your original intent had been to go to the Sixth Fleet. Did you have much chance to visit it while you were in that command?

Admiral Wilson: Yes, I did, and I had some very interesting actions that had to be taken. If you recall the history of the '70s, in 1970 the Palestinians were assaulting Amman, Jordan.* There was a large flail over there, and the United States was sorely beset as to how it should respond. Strange things were happening. The Air Force was painting some of its C-130s white and putting crews in civilian clothes so they could go into Amman as a humanitarian group and deliver some transportable hospitals to help with the casualty loads.† The Turks were denying the Air Force permission to move its air-transportable hospitals from their base in Turkey, and there was great consternation.

The Sixth Fleet was moved off the coast—something like 25 miles off the coast of the Gaza Strip—in readiness to go ashore.‡ Well, for many years the fleet medical officer, the adviser to the commander of the Sixth Fleet, was double-hatted as the medical officer in the cruiser that served as the fleet's flagship.§ In the course of the last change of flagships for the Sixth Fleet, the medical officer assigned was a lieutenant right out of his internship. So by derivation he was the Sixth Fleet medical officer. We had the whole Sixth Fleet poised to support virtually an invasion in the Mideast in some fashion or form. It didn't seem right to me that the fleet commander should have a lieutenant for his medical adviser.

The commander of the Sixth Fleet at that time was Ike Kidd, Jr.** So I went to the CinC and said, "Admiral Wendt, I don't know if you're aware of this or not, but the Sixth Fleet medical officer is a two-striper. I understand he's a good one. There's nothing wrong with him as a two-striper, but that's hardly the kind of officer to advise Admiral Kidd on his medical requirements and support functions. I think he ought to have a captain as fleet medical officer."

It turned out that, at the time, to support the Sixth Fleet, the MAC system had established what was called a "green-stripe system." It was really a method of identifying

---

* This was a group of Palestinian commandos known as PFLP—the Popular Front for the Liberation of Palestine.
† On 9 September 1970 six U.S. Air Force transports carrying medical teams arrived at Incirlik, Turkey.
‡ The Sixth Fleet deployed a number of ships to the eastern Mediterranean in mid-September 1970 for possible evacuation of airline passengers held as hostages in Jordan by Palestinian commandos. On 12 September the PFLP commandos blew up three airliners—U.S., British, and Swiss.
§ In September 1970 the Sixth Fleet flagship was the USS Springfield (CLG-7).
** Vice Admiral Isaac C. Kidd, Jr., USN, commanded the Sixth Fleet from August 1970 to October 1971.

and delivering high-priority fleet cargo to the fleet in the eastern Med. The Navy had made an arrangement with the Air Force to funnel that material through a small Air Force installation on the Athens airport. The U.S. Air Force had a small piece of property right on the edge of the Athens airstrip. So the C-141s began to just overload the hell out of that little Air Force place.* So Ike Kidd came to the CinC and wanted a captain, Supply Corps, as a freight expediter. For whatever reason, Admiral Wendt saw fit not to give it to him, but he did go to Ike Kidd and said, "I want to give you a medical officer."

Ike Kidd came back and said, "No damn way do I want a medical officer. I asked for a supply officer, and you wouldn't give me one. I don't want any medical officer."

So Admiral Wendt called me in and said, "I've got this specat from Ike Kidd. Here's what he says."†

I said, "I understand what he says, but he still needs a medical officer."

He said, "Okay, give him one."

I said, "All right, I'll get one for you."

So I called Admiral Frank Norris again and said, "I need a four-stripe medical officer for the Sixth Fleet."

He said, "I'll get back to you."

He called me back, and he identified a captain named Louis Eske.‡ He became the Sixth Fleet medical officer overnight. He is now dead. I gave the eulogy at his funeral in 1986. Among the things I included in the eulogy was a little anecdote he had told me about reporting to Ike Kidd's flagship. Dr. Eske, who had been stationed at the naval hospital in Naples, was plucked out of his hospital billet and sent to sea. He chased the flagship around the Med for about two weeks. When he finally caught up with it, he was dirty and disheveled and in need of a shave and a shower, as only you can be when you're chasing a ship at sea. He was stepping out of the shower, and in walked Admiral Kidd. Lou Eske was standing there naked as a jaybird, just out of the shower, towel wrapped around him. Ike Kidd had a piece of paper in his hand, and he said, "What in the goddamn hell are you doing here? I don't want any goddamn medical officer."

---

* C-141s are large Air Force cargo planes.
† "Specat" is the abbreviation for a special category message.
‡ Captain Louis H. Eske, MC, USNR.

Lou Eske said, "Admiral, it's taken me two weeks to get aboard this ship. If you don't want me here, you just tell me how to get off." [Laughter]

So Ike Kidd sort of harrumphed and grumbled a little bit, and he said, "All right. Get your clothes on and come have dinner with me." So he did. Dr. Eske turned Admiral Kidd's head around in about six weeks. They became firm and fast friends, and Lou Eske did a great job getting the planning for the Sixth Fleet together. When he left that job a year later, he went to the war college. He went on to be the ComCruDesPac medical officer.[*] Later he came to the bureau and put medical planning on its feet. But that's another story that we'll get into later on.

Paul Stillwell: What specifically was he able to do for Admiral Kidd?

Admiral Wilson: He was able to put in place a medical support plan for contingency purposes. You'll recall the Beirut episode in 1983.[†] At that time, we had adequate resources offshore. We had surgical teams there. We had all the necessary medical support type things in place, ready to go because of prior planning and prior actions. At the time Lou Eske reported to the Sixth Fleet, none of that capability existed in the area. He put some medical planning factors together and did some things that would have made it at least tolerable for our forces to have been committed and have reasonable medical support available had they been so committed. That was his principal function, to devise those plans and advise the CinC as to how they could work and should work, should he need them.

Paul Stillwell: Did you have civilian evacuation plans in effect when you were there?

Admiral Wilson: Yes, they were in effect. We had an evac plan. I don't recall much of the detail about it, but it was there, and there were some medical requirements for

---

[*] ComCruDesPac—Commander Cruiser-Destroyer Force Pacific Fleet.
[†] On 23 October 1983, a suicide terrorist drove a truck filled with the equivalent of 12,000 pounds of explosives into the Marine Corps barracks in Beirut, Lebanon. The resulting explosion killed 241 Americans and wounded 70.

corpsmen and nurses to attend the women and children in particular involved in this evacuation plan.

A lot of interesting things happened to us during that tour. For example, we were invited to a so-called "Save the Children Ball" up at Thurso, Scotland. The commanding officer of the communication station and his wife invited Mrs. Wilson and me to attend a ball up there. So I rearranged the schedule so that my official clinical visit to that station coincided with this social function, and Mrs. Wilson went along.

The drinking and driving laws in the U.K. are very strict, and the party was to be at a country inn, about 15 or 20 miles out of town, at a place called John o'Groat's House. John o'Groat's is significant, because it is the northernmost tip of the U.K., and it compares with Land's End, which is the southernmost tip. When they measure the length of the U.K., they always say from Land's End to John o'Groat's, so it becomes a geographic point of reference.

At any rate, we dressed for this dinner-dance and went downtown to a local hotel by taxi and had a stirrup cup. The ladies had sherry, and the gentlemen had Scotch whiskey. We then boarded a bus and went out to this dance in the country. It was a marvelous time. Everybody danced up a storm till 2:00 o'clock in the morning. We had a lovely meal, had lots of whiskey to drink, and everybody had an uproariously good time. At about 3:00 o'clock in the morning, everything stopped. Everybody sat down and had a cup of hot soup. In the meantime, it had started to snow. When we finished the soup, we all got back in the bus. The bus drove us back to town, and he dropped each and every party off at his or her own home. We thus avoided all the complications of drinking and driving. A very nice evening, very pleasant indeed.

One of the other memorable times was an occasion when Mrs. Wilson and I went on leave. We took a safari in east Africa. We flew to Nairobi and had two one-week packages lined up. We spent the first week in Kenya and in northern Tanzania, doing the usual things: riding in a Volkswagen bus. We were the only two Americans in a group of 20 people, the rest of whom were British. We went and looked at all the wild animals and went through Lake Ambaseli and the Ngorogoro Crater, and Lake Muweya and came back around by Kilimanjaro and then came up close to Nairobi and spent a day or two in the game park there, before returning to Nairobi.

We then went to Uganda. Uganda is famous for its birds. If you're a nature lover, the birds in Uganda are some of the most impressive anywhere in the world. There is an enormous variety of birds, and their plumage is unique. They're really a joy to see. They also had some crocodiles; it's the best crocodile watching in the world.

At any rate, about the middle of the week, we wound up at Murchison Falls, in northwestern Uganda, near the Sudanese border, in a lovely safari lodge close to the headwaters of the Nile River. We were there watching the crocodiles. While we were there, Idi Amin overthrew Mr. Obote in Kampala.* Immediately all the roads were closed, the airport was closed, and communications were shut down. Our only communications at all were by radiotelephone, once a day at 7:00 o'clock in the morning.

Well, my wife and I thought this not to be a serious problem. It didn't worry us, since we were out in the country. The safari lodge was wonderful. The food was good, and the Waragee gin, which was the local gin, was fine. We were prepared to wait a few days until things cooled down. Interestingly enough, the British members of this tour group became very antsy about 48 hours after this started. They said such things as, "Let's get out of here. We don't want to be murdered by a bunch of savages." As events turned out later on, they were much more correct than we were, in view of what happened to the civilian population later on.†

So we had a meeting and decided that we should get out of there. So the next morning, in darkness at 5:00 o'clock, we boarded the vans and drove onto a pontoon to be ferried across the Nile River. The power source for this pontoon ferry was an old, old Evinrude outboard motor attached to a dugout canoe lashed to the side of the pontoon. It did anything but give us a strong sense of confidence as we crossed this Nile, which was infested with crocodiles. After that, we drove about 70 miles over washboard roads to the nearest telephone. Someone called the British high commissioner, and I called the American Embassy to see if it was safe to go into Kampala. As it turned out, it was, so we drove on in.

We found that we could get out of Uganda but had to do so by sundown. It meant

---

* Apollo Milton Obote was President of Uganda until overthrown in a coup d'etat on 25 January 1971. The coup was led by Major General Idi Amin Dada, who remained in power until he fled the country in 1979.
† Idi Amin ordered the deaths of thousands of Ugandans who disagreed with his policies.

we had to get back in the buses and go another 140 miles to the border. We got to the border in time to get through, but then we had to travel 200 miles before reaching a hotel with the capacity to take all of us.

Paul Stillwell: What was the importance of sundown?

Admiral Wilson: They closed the Uganda-Kenya border at sundown. By the time we arrived at this hotel in Kenya, we had driven some 600 miles that day—from 5:00 o'clock in the morning until 1:00 o'clock the next morning, a 20-hour day. Obviously, we were fatigued to the socks. To the great good credit of the hotelkeeper, they had a whole meal waiting for this tour group. We checked in and had some cool drinks and food and went to bed, having escaped Uganda with a whole skin.

While we were in Kampala, we saw Idi Amin driving around in his victory tour. He was a huge man, riding around in a Jeep, standing up and waving to the crowd. There were machine guns in the back of the Jeep. The front of the Jeep was decorated with evergreen boughs, which is their sign of victory. I must say, it was quite an experience.

Paul Stillwell: Certainly a lot of variety in that tour of duty for you.

Admiral Wilson: I should say there was. When I returned to London, all my confreres and colleagues said, "We were wondering if we were ever going to see you again."

I said, "The thought crossed my own mind." [Laughter]

Paul Stillwell: You talked about the planning aspects of the job. What were the day-to-day type things that confronted the U.S. Navy command in Europe and the Sixth Fleet especially?

Admiral Wilson: The Sixth Fleet, of course, had its own operational schedule. In those days there was a great deal of fluctuation in the political tensions in the eastern Mediterranean. It was the time that immediately followed the Turkish-Cypriot confrontation on Cyprus, where there was still enormous tension.* We visited there once, and you could almost feel the tension in the air. The Cypriots were very uptight over the whole relationship. The Palestinians were very active at the time. There were more or less constant rumblings, with an occasional flare-up of activity, as in Amman in 1970. Plus the Soviet fleet was in the Mediterranean. Those were the Sixth Fleet's concerns and whatnot.

The CinC, of course, had logistics responsibility and actually operational responsibility for the Sixth Fleet, even though it was kind of a strange arrangement. The CinC problems weren't very severe problems. We had problems with medical planning for the CinC, simply because nobody could tell us what the proposed casualty rate should be. This was a problem that was to plague us for another five or eight years. But the CinC's problems were never very significant problems.

We had problems with the NavActs U.K. support operations in certain of the clinics because of the inadequate people in some cases. We had to relieve some people and get some new staff. Some of the people they were supporting were overly demanding. The submarine community was extremely demanding in Holy Loch. They wanted everything, and they wanted it yesterday, regardless of anyone else's problems—typical of the boomer community.† So they were somewhat of a pain in the neck and hard to live with. But, by and large, it was a day-to-day maintenance problem, where we visited the various outlying stations, where we did dependent exams, Pap smears, and general physical exams. For the military people themselves we did things like reenlistment examinations and annual physical exams.

We also did things like contract with local medical authorities. For example, we had contract physicians in some of these places where we had a very few people. When we had no physician of our own there, we contracted with a local physician. In Londonderry, for example, we had good relations with the Altnegelvin Hospital. It's the national health service hospital in Londonderry. When we first went to Londonderry, the

---

* The constitution of Cyprus, adopted in 1960, created a republic and provided for government officials of both Turkish and Greek nationality. In December 1963 the island experienced a constitutional breakdown, resulting in the separation of Greek and Turkish Cypriots.
† At the time U.S. ballistic missile submarines ("boomers") made patrols out of Holy Loch, Scotland. In 1992 the SSBNs ceased operations there because the vastly increased range of Trident ballistic missile permitted the bases to be in the United States.

"troubles" had just started. We used to fly into Aldergrove Airport, the airport for Belfast, about an hour from London by air.

It's about 60 miles from Aldergrove Airport to Londonderry. As we drove through the surrounding area, we passed buildings which were still smoldering from having been fire-bombed by the participants in the troubles between the Catholics and the Protestants. We never had any difficulties personally with the troubles, but when we went to Londonderry, it was a little bit awe-inspiring to see the second-story windows of buildings with machine guns sticking out of them and barbed-wire barriers ready to be placed across bridge entrances and armored cars patrolling the streets. This was 20 years ago, and now it's a common sight and certainly much worse. That was the beginning of it.

Paul Stillwell: And I guess the VD problem was always with you.

Admiral Wilson: We didn't really have much of a problem with that. We had a small group of people. The U.S. Navy population in the U.K. is not all that huge.

Paul Stillwell: Well, I was thinking more in terms of the whole theater.

Admiral Wilson: It really wasn't a problem for me, as I can recall. The Sixth Fleet had its own problems, but they were never as bad as in the Orient. They had problems with hepatitis. Hepatitis is quite common in Italy, in the shellfish, so we had some hepatitis problems, but we also had a preventive medicine unit in Naples, and they were on top of those problems immediately. They were a superb outfit. Captain Walt Miner got command of that at the time—superb fellow.*

Paul Stillwell: Admiral Zumwalt became CNO in 1970, and that had reverberations throughout the Navy.† Were there any in London?

---

* Captain Walter F. Miner, MC, USN.
† Admiral Elmo R. Zumwalt, Jr., USN, served as Chief of Naval Operations from 1 July 1970 to 29 June 1974.

Admiral Wilson: Not initially. He came through London like a whirlwind and made his presence known, gave us his big, toothy grin but really didn't leave any great mark on the system at that point, other than his flashy presence. At least he made no mark that I was aware of. I was not really in a position to talk at CNO level about any policy or personnel matters. I don't know what he told Admiral Wendt, but Admiral Wendt retired from London.* Admiral Wendt had an airplane and a chauffeur and car and all the usual perks he was used to having. He said, "When I retired, I flew back to Norfolk and drove my own Volkswagen home." [Laughter]

Paul Stillwell: Did you have to gear up for medical support for dependents going into Greece when the overseas home-porting program went there?

Admiral Wilson: Yes and no. Admiral Zumwalt had a bee in his bonnet that he wanted to home-port some ships in Athens but didn't want to build anything on the beach to support them. The Athens homeport idea came after a rather lengthy evolution during which a homeport selection group was formed and sent all around Europe trying to find a suitable port.

The final selection was Athens, but in the process of doing that, a team of about six officers and one chief yeoman were put together to evaluate various ports. I was on that team for a couple of trips, and we went to Athens, Leghorn, Italy, and Naples to do a comparative analysis and evaluation of these ports as possibilities for home-porting a portion of the Sixth Fleet. We were under the heaviest of cautions about letting out the secret of our mission. We were not able to deal with anybody but the embassy people wherever we went. We had only one yeoman, and he was really busy typing the reports.

I went and dug up all the medical information. It was not too difficult because the embassies publish a book that has a description of all the local areas. That includes everything: the geography, topography, local products, local economy, size of the population, and demographics. It also talks about the water supply and the medical facilities and food supply and the diseases endemic in the area. I was able to obtain these books and really use them to write up summary reports to indicate whether or not this was

---

* Wendt retired 1 July 1971.

a place that could be used for a homeport and, if so, what were the health hazards and what were the day-to-day dos and don'ts to stay healthy.

I duly went to my hotel room with a rented typewriter and wrote all these reports in my poor typing and handed it to the yeoman who smoothed it up. We did this day after day, week after week, for several weeks in a number of home ports, including La Maddalena in Sardinia, as well as the others I mentioned.

Eventually CNO decided Athens was the place to go. Then we went to Athens to find out where to put a dispensary or a hospital to support whoever was sent there. We worked out a couple of very fine arrangements, one of which was to invest $100,000 to finish a floor on a private hospital that was partially completed. For an investment of $100,000 we could have had the use of a whole floor of a hospital. CNO simply would not hear of it, so they wound up making a jury-rigged clinic in a storefront in Athens.

Admiral Zumwalt didn't want to build anything on the beach. He took one of the hospital ships and converted it into a dependent-support ship by putting the commissary and exchange in it and changing the clinical facilities around. Of course, that never flew, except to spend the money on the hospital ship, which never went over there herself.[*]

A few warships went over there for a while, but then Zumwalt left and the home-porting thing dissolved. Captain Cary Landis was a line officer who was the leader of this home port search team.[†] He eventually went to Athens to set up the home port arrangements and shortly thereafter died of a heart attack.

Paul Stillwell: Do you have any comments on the Zumwalt impact on the Navy as a whole during that era?

Admiral Wilson: Yes. He became CNO during the time we were in London. We began to get his Z-grams, of course, and they were very confusing to everyone.[‡] The general laxity

---

[*] The hospital ship Sanctuary (AH-17), which had served off Vietnam, was converted in 1971-72 to a dependent-support ship, including medical and exchange facilities. She was intended for support of U.S. Navy families in Greece but wound up serving in other roles instead.
[†] Captain Cary E. Landis, USN.
[‡] Z-grams were consecutively numbered policy directives from Chief of Naval Operations Zumwalt that attempted to deal with such issues as enlisted rights and privileges, equal opportunity, and Navy families. Junior personnel viewed them much more favorably than did their seniors. See U.S. Naval Institute Proceedings, May 1971, pages 291-298.

that he supported in terms of personal appearance among the troops and his emphasis on UPWARD seminars and racial awareness and his willingness to go to a command and listen to an enlisted man put his commanding officer on report, just gave us all kinds of heartburn.* I don't think I'm saying anything here that hasn't been said dozens and dozens of times before—that the Navy took a real downturn during his term as CNO. It took us a number of years to recover our image, discipline, and respect for the chain of command, which included the respect for the authority and accountability of petty officers. Those issues and items came across our desks and into our line of thinking, just as they did across the rest of the Navy, and we were all horrified by it, to be truthful.

During our tour in London, the bureau finally determined that the medical department was 100 years old, that it was formally organized and recognized and authorized by Congress in 1871. They had been looking for many years for specific authorization in the Congressional Record or in some law that firmly identified the date of origin of the Navy Medical Department, and until that time had been unable to find such a date.

We thought that, in view of the fact that it was the 100th anniversary, that it would be appropriate that we Americans in London celebrate that occasion with a party. So I went to Admiral Wendt and told him what I had in mind, and he thought that was a good idea. So we invited the Surgeons General of the British armed services—that is, the Navy, Air Force, and Army—and the senior dentist from the Royal Navy. We also invited a senior surgeon from the Middlesex hospital, Mr. Handley, along with his chief resident—chief registrar, as they're called over there, a man named John McLeod, a thoroughgoing Scotsman.

To manage the acute problems that occurred with military people living in London, we used the Middlesex hospital as our treatment facility, and our liaison was with John McLeod and with Mr. Handley, so they were invited guests as well. We had the flag officers from the CinCUSNavEur staff, including Admiral Wendt, Admiral Trum, and Admiral Leroy V. Swanson.†

---

* UPWARD—Understanding Personal Worth and Racial Dignity.
† Rear Admiral Herman J. Trum III, USN, was deputy chief of staff for operations and plans; Rear Admiral Leroy V. Swanson, USN, was deputy commander in chief and chief of staff.

We contracted for a party room at the Dorchester Hotel and were told it was the same one used for Prince Philip's bachelor party before he was married to Queen Elizabeth.[*] We contacted the party arranger at the Dorchester Hotel, and they agreed that we could do two very important things. We could provide our own liquors, booze of all kinds, and provide the meat for the entree. As you may know, the British don't hang their beef and let it mature at all before they market it. So to an American palate—at least to ours—it tasted quite fresh. So Kit, my wife, went up to the commissary and bought 40 pounds of standing rib roast. We bought a case of champagne and several cases of assorted whiskeys, gins, cordials, beers, etc.

On the appointed night, we had a small string orchestra, provided by the local Army. Everybody was all dressed up in their best uniform, formal uniform. As the crowd gathered, they entered a small anteroom where the bar was set up. We met one another, and socialized, had a drink, listened to the music, and had quite a nice time of it.

The Surgeon General of the Army was a very tall, imposing fellow. He was probably six feet, four inches tall, very ramrod straight, and—as we learned later—quite British. The first thing he did when he arrived was to walk over and look at the seating arrangements, ostensibly to see whether he was seated appropriately in terms of his seniority. When he was satisfied with that, he joined the rest of the people and looked down from on high to see and deal with the rest of us.

The meal was beautifully cooked, served by waiters wearing white gloves. We saw one of them stick a meal behind the curtain; apparently they enjoyed that later. It was very well done. We had good wines at the table. The conversation was lively, and in general everybody enjoyed the event. We had a birthday cake, and I had a slide presentation that I gave. Admiral Wendt spoke, and some of the British armed forces officers spoke. Then we had an after-dinner drink and closed up the party. It was said by a good many that it was a fine party. In fact, one of the flag officers' wives said it was the best party she'd attended since she'd been there, and she'd been there two years. So we felt as though that was a reasonably positive response to our effort.

It's interesting now to note that 1871 was not the proper date. Since then they have found out that it was some other date, and I don't even know what that one is. Anyway, it

---

[*] The event took place on Friday, 5 March 1971, in the Park Suite, Dorchester Hotel, Park Lane, London.

was a good party for a good reason—with the information we had at the time—and we all enjoyed the hell out of it.

Paul Stillwell: Do you have any other items from that tour of duty to put on the record?

Admiral Wilson: I think that covers most of the interesting ones. We were short-toured in Europe by one year. As a matter of fact, we'd been there only ten months when Rear Admiral Norris called from the bureau and asked if I'd like to come back to the bureau to join their planning staff. I told them at the time that I really didn't want to, because we had just finished a ten-month tour, and were just getting started into the work that I felt had to be done in the office for Europe. I said I really needed at least another year to do what I thought out to be done, and I really couldn't ask Mrs. Wilson to move again on such short notice. After that, I added, "Having said that, are you under any pressure from the Surgeon General for me to come back?"

He said, "No pressure."

So I said, "Okay, let's delay it a year." Which they did. We were still short-toured by a year, leaving at the end of two years instead of three. By then I felt that we had established the communications networks. We had done what could be done reasonably in the planning sector, and we had established good relations with the other services and had good contracts for supplying medical services to the small units around. I felt at that point that I had accomplished what I came there to do, and it was time to leave.

Interview Number 4 with Rear Admiral Almon C. Wilson, Medical Corps, U.S. Navy (Retired)

Place: Bureau of Medicine and Surgery, Washington, D.C.

Date: Wednesday, 16 September 1992

Interviewer: Paul Stillwell

Paul Stillwell: Admiral, last time we had just finished up discussion of your tour of duty in London. After that you were transferred to Washington, where you did more planning.

Admiral Wilson: Yes. I came to Washington in the summer of 1971 as the deputy director of the planning division at the Bureau of Medicine and Surgery, at that time called Code 41-1. The director at the time was Captain Dermot Murray.[*] Dermot was a very interesting fellow. He was born in Dublin, Ireland, and for a while he sailed on cruise ships as the ship's doctor. Then he emigrated and somewhere along the line—I don't know whether it was in Ireland or here—he became an anesthesiologist. He was a very well thought of as an anesthesiologist. He left clinical services and came to the bureau to become the deputy director and eventually the director of the planning division.

At that time, the planning division had two components. One was contingency planning, and the other was facilities planning and management. Far and away the most important of the two was the facilities shop. The contingency planning was still being done with a stubby pencil by the same person who went to the war college and did a bad job. So the main focus of my activities became the facilities world. As the deputy director of the division, I spent my first year really learning the ins and outs of the facilities business from the bureau's point of view.

The Bureau of Medicine and Surgery has a unique relationship with the engineers. To the best of my knowledge, BuMed is the only organization in the Navy that has its own facilities division design staff. We have and have had on the staff of the bureau for years and years architects and engineers whose job it is to supervise the design and observe the

---

[*] Captain Dermot A. Murray, MC, USN.

construction of our medical facilities all over the world. These range from little clinics and dental clinics to hospitals, small and large. Being a frustrated engineer at heart, the facilities division very quickly became a very pleasant job for me, and I looked forward to going to work every morning.

On top of that, the staff in the facilities shop was absolutely superb. Commander Lloyd Nichols had been in the business for a long time.* He was well connected with the various people in the facilities divisions in the Department of Defense as well as in the Naval Facilities Engineering Command. We had a virtual genius in David Fisher, who at the time was a lieutenant.† He went on to become the Surgeon General's principal programmer as a captain and eventually went on to have a command of his own. In addition, there was a series of civil engineers, all lieutenant commanders, who came through the shop and did the engineering advisory work for us and were, of course, in part liaison people with the Naval Facilities Engineering Command. Most went on to become captains and have their own commands.

Our role in facilities was, first of all, to program the various jobs that had to be done, including the construction of various hospitals. We fought for the construction money with the Surgeon General's testimony before Congress and with the testimony of the Chief of Civil Engineers. We programmed the facilities work in a five-year plan to fit with the budget cycle.

When a program was approved, the Naval Facilities Engineering Command arranged to hire an architectural engineering firm to do the design work. In the Naval Facilities Engineering Command there was a medical design desk run by a civilian named Ron Johnson, and we had our own architects at BuMed. They put their heads together and defined the requirements for the architectural engineers who were to actually do the drawings for the construction. This involved writing a space program. A space program is simply a statement of how many square feet are needed in each space in the hospital. That is an enormous job that originally was done by hand, and a very arduous task it was.

In 1972 I became the director of the division, and we suddenly were asked by Secretary of Defense Melvin Laird how much money it would require for the Navy to

---

* Commander Lloyd B. Nichols, MSC, USN.
† Lieutenant David H. Fisher, MSC, USNR.

replace, refurbish, or modernize its medical and dental facilities in toto.* We really scurried around. For several days we were as busy as could be, trying to get these figures together. We finally came up with a figure of $694 million in 1972 dollars. We filed that report, thought nothing more about it, and went on about our business.

About that time we decided that while NavFac, the Naval Facilities Engineering Command, had a responsibility for supervising the construction of these completed designs, BuMed had a responsibility, along with NavFac and the architectural engineers, to see that those hospitals and clinics were correctly constructed from the point of view of medical and dental functions.

We trained a group of MSC officers whom we referred to as MCLOs, military construction liaison officers. They were ordered on site to where a hospital was being built. Their function was twofold. It was to review the architectural drawings and to equip the hospitals, i.e., to arrange for the development of equipment listings and to make sure that the proper equipment was purchased.

By proper equipment, we mean the equipments that have been recommended by the specialty advisers to the Surgeon General. The Surgeon General has an adviser in each of the clinical specialties, and they are the ones who determine what equipment should go in the new hospital. Nobody but the physician running the X-ray department knows better what to buy. So the MCLO was charged with getting the proper guidance from the SG's office by way of the specialty advisers and to purchase that equipment.

The system worked extremely well. On many occasions we found rooms where the doors were swung the wrong way so you couldn't get a bed in and out handily. We found rooms that had doors so narrow you couldn't get a hospital bed with an orthopedic frame through it. We found hospital rooms so arranged that you couldn't get one bed in without taking the other bed out. We found sinks with drains on the opposite sides of the room. Or we saw drains and sinks with no water supply. These were little things but important things. So the MCLO system came into being about this time and soon demonstrated its worth.

---

* Melvin R. Laird served as Secretary of Defense from 22 January 1969 to 29 January 1973.

Paul Stillwell: I'm surprised there weren't some standard specifications that they could work from. It sounds as if they were almost working from scratch.

Admiral Wilson: Well, there were specifications that were handed to the architects, but they had to do with more general things. You should not have to tell an architect to put a drain under a sink that has a water supply.

Paul Stillwell: You're right about that. [Laughter]

Admiral Wilson: Those are kind of "you-ought-to-know-its." But if you are not familiar with designing hospitals, you might not be aware of the space and width requirements for big doors for beds with orthopedic frames attached to them. So we had to make sure that they knew that sort of thing. That was one of the reasons why they were involved with the architects in the design.

It was also necessary for our people to help the architects align the services. For example, an emergency room has a large requirement for X-rays because of fractures coming in. Therefore, you put the X-ray department in reasonable proximity to the emergency room. The same thing is true of the laboratory. You don't put it way away, or, if you must, you put a satellite laboratory near the emergency room. You don't separate the operating room and the recovery room, for example. The ICUs, particularly the surgical ICU, should be near the operating room.

Well, there are all kinds of nuances like these. Where do you put the delivery rooms in relation to the obstetrics clinic, and is there a reason for putting them close and all that sort of thing? So we collectively, meaning the facilities part of the BuMed planning division, had a great deal to do with the ultimate space program and design that was used to build new facilities.

After Mr. Laird inquired about how much money was necessary, the money oddly enough began to be forthcoming. They gave us money to do many of these projects. In the next five years, beginning with fiscal '73, I believe, BuMed programmed and completed 68 different MilCon projects, all the way from hospitals to medical clinics to dental clinics to laboratories.* It was an amazing injection of money, but we were, of course, pleased to get it.

When you talk about projects in that collective size, and we've just described the difficulty of putting together a simple space program to support the design, it becomes immediately apparent that you can't do a multitude of projects without some kind of improved capability. With that in mind, I went down to see Admiral Harry Etter, who was at the time the flag officer in charge of the Code 04, which was the logistics code.† He was the Assistant Chief of the Bureau of Medicine and Surgery for Planning and Logistics. I went down to him and said, "Admiral Etter, we've got to have some computer service to start managing this big facilities construction load that's upcoming."

He looked at me kind of funny and said, "Computers? What for?"

I said, "For the space program and ultimately for the equipment program."

He said, "How much is it going to cost—$50,000?"

I said, "I don't know. I don't know whether it's going to cost $50,000, $250,000, or a million. But I can tell you this—we have to have it, and neither one of us has a choice. There's no going back. We're committed now, and to make it happen we've got to have computer assistance."

So he snarled a little bit and said, "Okay, get me a price tag."

I went and got him a price tag. I don't remember what it was and it doesn't matter. Very shortly we had a computer programmer on the scene virtually full time, writing a computer program that would enable us to generate space programs for medical facilities on demand. It was quite interesting.

All the spaces were workload-driven. For example, if you told the computer that you expected 100,000 outpatient visits to the OB clinic every year, the computer would calculate how many square feet of waiting space you needed, how many doctors' offices, how many examining rooms, how many square feet for administrative space, how large the waiting room should be, how many seats should be in it, how many bathrooms you should have, and how many fixtures in the bathrooms, and what size the bathroom ought to be. Space requirements for cleaning gear, linen storage, all the various other components of a

---

* MilCon—military construction.
† Rear Admiral Harry S. Etter, MC, USN.

functional unit were ground into this particular space. The same thing would happen under the heading of surgical clinic, operating room—whatever piece or part of the hospital you wanted to talk about. The program worked very well.

It took time to evolve, and the computer program had to be debugged and altered many times but eventually became the really strong support that was needed for a large MilCon program.

Well, it's one thing to build a facility. It's another to equip it, so the next thing was to find out how we could computerize the equipping of these hospitals. Well, many things are standard. You know, a doctor in an examining room needs what a doctor in an examining room needs across the hall, unless he's doing something special like babies or GYN clinic functions or something of that sort. By and large, all the doctors' offices were the same. Their exam rooms were the same in space. They all had to have a stool to sit on, had to have a wastebasket. They had to have a lavatory with a paper towel dispenser and a soap dish and a mirror and a medicine cabinet and all that sort of thing.

So there was much that was standard for many spaces in the hospital. We could identify from the space program how many doctors' offices there were. By simply punching the number of office spaces we needed, we could tell how many exam tables, soap dispensers, examining stools, goose-neck lamps, wastebaskets, whatever else fit in the exam room, how many we needed to order for the whole hospital. So those two computer-based programs were some of the strongest steps that we made into modern management. Those were very much welcomed by the staff and also by the people with whom we dealt in the facilities world.

Military construction is a very expensive part of the budget. The dollar figures are huge, and you find yourself making changes in millions of dollars. It doesn't seem very significant if you raise the price from $29.2 million to $31.6 million. It's only a couple of numbers, and it's hard to remember that those are millions of dollars you're working with. Anyway, the MilCon program is very fluid, and it's very much subject to attack by people who want money for other purposes--to build ships or to buy airplanes or build submarines or whatever. You have to fight for those military construction dollars, and they have to be well managed, which NavFac did and we helped. But it was a fascinating business, which made it a lot of fun to go to work.

We did a lot of traveling to go to design conferences all over the country, depending on where the architects had their offices. We met a lot of people, and we looked at a lot of land where they were going to build facilities. It was enlightening to see how facilities were planned and rose out of the ground to become functional. It wasn't usually possible for someone spending a normal tour to see very much construction come out of the ground that you had planned, because the cycle was so long from the beginning of it to the end of it—from the time you programmed it until it was beneficially occupied.

In the course of doing some of these site visits, we had some very interesting experiences. For example, we had a dispensary down in New Orleans. It was a World War II dispensary made out of wood, had 15 beds, and was designed to take care of people who had the sniffles or the flu or catarrhal fever, as it was commonly diagnosed in World War II. This was for patients who needed an overnight or maybe two nights in a hospital with light care just to recover from the very mild illness.

At the time, F. Edward Hebert was the chairman of the subcommittee on defense of the House Appropriations Committee.[*] He turned out to be a great pork barreler, just like Mendel Rivers before him.[†] Mendel Rivers had all the military that he could handle moved into the Charleston area while he was in that position. Eddie Hebert did the same thing. Incidentally, he is the same Hebert who is responsible for the establishment of the Department of Defense medical school, called Uniformed Services University of the Health Sciences, which is named after him.

Anyway, we were sent down to New Orleans to do a site visit, to look at some property that might be used for a replacement facility. We took with us a DoD consultant named Dr. Kenneth Babcock, a kind of a dour fellow who was a surgeon by medical trade and probably in his late 60s or early 70s.[‡] We went to New Orleans and met with the local politicians, the naval district engineer, and all the other interested parties. At the time there was a marine hospital in New Orleans, owned by the U.S. Public Health Service. There was a lot of talk about closing it down.

---

[*] Representative F. Edward Hebert (Democrat-Louisiana).
[†] Representative L. Mendel Rivers (Democrat-South Carolina), who had served as chairman of the House Armed Services Committee.
[‡] DoD—Department of Defense.

The property that was selected by the Navy to build its new hospital was in Algiers. Algiers is across the Mississippi River from New Orleans. There's a bridge over the river, but the bridge is frequently closed due to accidents or the other natural phenomena that close bridges. So there was a great to-do about whether the people on the Algiers side could have access to the so-called marine hospital that belonged to the Public Health Service. The other issue was, "What size should the hospital be?" It turned out that that one number was 100 beds, and the other number was 210 beds, and we were replacing a dispensary with 15 beds, with no increase in population! Well, the powers that be took all our findings, and a pronouncement was made that we were to build a hospital in New Orleans. It was a 100-bed version, but we were to put it on a foundation that would take another 100 beds.

We started construction of the hospital in three phases. We had a demolition contract, a foundation contract, and a construction contract. As we were getting pretty well along into the first 100 beds, the phone rang one day. It was Captain Beaver, a Civil Engineer Corps officer who was the district engineer for the commandant of that district at the time.[*] He said to me over the phone, "The commandant of the naval district and I have just had lunch with Mr. Eddie Hebert. Mr. Hebert says, 'Go ahead and put on that extra 100 beds on that hospital you're building.'"

I asked him to repeat the message, because I knew the first 100 was unnecessary, and certainly the second 100 would be. So he said, "Go ahead and build the second 100 beds."

So I said, "Okay."

I dropped the phone and called up Admiral Charlie Minter, who at the time was the Deputy Chief of Naval Operations for Logistics.[†] It was in his shop where the programming for money for facilities was accomplished. I said, "Admiral Minter, this is Al Wilson. I've just had a call from the New Orleans naval district engineer that Mr. Hebert says to go ahead and put on those other 100 beds."

Then he said something that shouldn't go in print and then, "Wait a minute." When he came back, he said, "Go ahead and build the SOB." So we did. We built a 200- or 210-

---

[*] Captain John F. Beaver, CEC, USN.
[†] Vice Admiral Charles S. Minter, Jr., USN, whose oral history is in the Naval Institute collection.

bed hospital in New Orleans that was not needed. Nobody, I believe to this day, knows how the second 100 beds got up there. Because there was never a document. There was never a piece of paper that crossed my desk that ever addressed the subject or the authority for it. That's what was happening at the time, how the Navy was run and how the political impacts were imparted to the services, in this particular instance in the military construction world.

A little later on during this three-year tour of duty, Bolivia came to the State Department and asked for some assistance to help some of their people in the more remote areas. They had decided that the Bolivian Navy would do some people-to-people work, and we were asked to help them find a way to do that. I was selected to go down there with two other captains, both of whom spoke Spanish, one of whom was a Medical Service Corps officer. The other was a medical officer who was a public health-type expert. Their roles were supply and public health matters; mine was in the facilities area.

CNO sent us down there, and we were met at La Paz airport. The airport is at 12,600 feet elevation. When we stepped off the airplane, the thin air immediately engulfed us, and we were gasping for breath without having taken a step. I had a briefcase, and when I had walked probably 50 yards with that briefcase, I was utterly exhausted—huffing, puffing, and panting. Our hosts had met us with oxygen tanks, and we all stopped and took a few breaths of oxygen from the tanks to get to feel better. They drove us down to our hotel in the city of La Paz, which was about 1,000 feet lower, and we put up in a nice hotel. The next morning they got us up early, and we went out on Lake Titicaca. Lake Titicaca is at 12,000 feet, and the planned evolution was quite simple and quite ingenious and turned out to be quite effective.

The Americans had had a program ongoing there for some time in the lower part of Bolivia, which we'll talk about later in more detail. It was a boat-building operation. Up on Lake Titicaca, at 12,000 feet, the Seabees had constructed a pontoon barge. It consisted merely of several large metal pontoons welded together to make a big platform. On that platform they had constructed a dispensary. Several rooms had been equipped with various and sundry medical equipments. On the stern were two enormous outboard engines. I don't know how many horsepower, but they were sufficiently large to propel this barge around the lake so it could visit the villages which had no access by road. As you may or may not know, the people who live in those areas that have no roads either walk to town or paddle in in some very unusual Lake Titicaca boats made out of reeds.

Paul Stillwell: It sounds like an ingenious way of providing medical care.

Admiral Wilson: It certainly was. At any rate, we spent an entire day, 12 hours, going around the lake shore, after having visited and inspected the medical barge. We returned to the hotel at approximately 7:00 in the evening. I walked up two flights of stairs, from the ground floor to the first floor. It took me at least five minutes to accomplish 12 or 15 steps. When I reached my room, I had chest pain, pain down my arms, and felt just limp as a rag. Fortunately, I had put a couple bottles of oxygen in my briefcase. I immediately strapped on one of those tanks, opened the valve, and stayed there very quietly until my chest pain went away and I felt better. With that warning about the rarefied air, we were very careful about our activities and our exertion levels thereafter.

We went on to visit other portions of Bolivia, a country that is so poverty stricken that it's deplorable. We went to a naval installation on the shores of Lake Titicaca, where the buildings were on the top of a rather steep bank that sloped down to the water. There was no flushing water for the toilets in that building, because the electric motor had burned out. It was a three-quarter horse motor which at the time could probably have been purchased in the United States for about $75.00. It had burned out, and they didn't have the money to replace it. They were completely without toilet-flushing water, or hand-washing water, bathing water, or any other kind of water, in that entire naval complex, which included their dental and medical clinic.

The object of our visit was to help by giving them ideas if we had any and, more importantly, to determine what their equipment requirements were and to see if we could identify equipment in our surplus inventory to help them. We then went down to the tropical portion of Bolivia. Bolivia, as you will recall, sits astride the Andes Mountains, and that part which is on the mountain is at 12,000 or 13,000 feet. As you go down the east slope of those Andes Mountains, you come out onto a tropical plain, which is separated from Brazil by a river. The foliage is jungle, and the heat and humidity are tropical.

There at a place called Trinidad was their Navy headquarters, a place where they did boat building. The other place was called Riberalta. At Riberalta they broke out the Marine guard to form an honor guard, and those with shoes were put in the front row. The barefoot Marines stood in the back row. We were so moved by this pathetic sight that we could barely contain ourselves. Eventually we were able to provide them with uniforms through some sort of program that the CNO dreamed up.

We stayed down there a day or two assessing their needs. This time we were looking at their brown-water navy. The Bolivians had two navies. They have the high-water navy at Lake Titicaca, and they have their brown-water navy down on the rivers that feed into the river dividing Bolivia from Brazil. Their riverboats are about 50 or 60 feet long, and they look like miniature steam packets from the Mississippi—not that they're stern wheelers, but they resemble them. These are the navy river patrol boats. The idea was that they were going to equip these boats with dispensaries, man them with medically trained people, supply them with medical supplies, and dispense medical services as they went up and down the rivers.

We flew back up on top of the Andes mountain range, after having been down in the jungle. We flew in an old R6D, which you will recall is a four-engine plane that was common during World War II. The Air Force liaison officer had it. They used to fly meat from the jungle ranches up to the Andes in it because they didn't need refrigeration. They flew so high that it kept cold. We flew in this airplane that had a whole bunch of beef carcasses in it swinging around while we were getting a ride up to where it was cool. The only problem was, what little bit of altitude acclimatization we had acquired in our first few days there was totally lost, so we were back to the huffing and puffing that we had experienced on arrival.

Fortunately, we only had to stay a couple of days. We had an out-brief with the Chief of Naval Operations in Bolivia, then went down to Lima, Peru, and then on home through Panama. As a requirement from this trip, we wrote a report and sent it over to CNO. A great deal of support equipment was sent down to Bolivia, particularly medical and dental equipment. We heard later that the barge had been very successful on the lake and provided a lot of good medical care to the population around the lake as it made its circuit.

Now, let me add an interesting side note about the Washington bureaucracy. The portion of Admiral Zumwalt's staff in the CNO's office having to deal with this particular project consisted of a couple of captains who had a small office over in the Pentagon. When we returned, the other officers and I sat down and filled out a fact sheet for ourselves. We wrote up a very fine, well-designed, well-crafted trip report that gave all the information, all of our recommendations and cited all of the possible solutions to the problems that had been identified.

We got the report back saying "That's nice, that's nice, lot of information in here, but we'd like you to put it in this format, a different format." So reluctantly we rewrote it in this alternate format. Lo and behold, a few days later, they came back and said, "Well, our minds have been changed now. We want your information in a different display."

I said to them, "All the information that we have is in those first reports. How you display it is no concern of mine, because I'm not going to write that damn thing another time for anybody, and that includes you particularly." [Laughter] We never heard from them again. Thus endeth the chapter.

Paul Stillwell: Were any of the recommendations implemented?

Admiral Wilson: Yes, yes. The U.S. Navy sent a lot of equipment down there, a lot of dental equipment in particular, and I think they supported the barge on Lake Titicaca rather well.

Paul Stillwell: How did it come to be a U.S. Navy project?

Admiral Wilson: Oh, it was one of those Navy-to-Navy things. One of Zumwalt's programs was a Navy-to-Navy evolution, if you'll recall that. He went down to South America and got to know all the senior naval officers. It was basically a give-away program that he wanted to use to cultivate the South Americans, as I understand it. Someone else may interpret it differently.

Paul Stillwell: Sounds like a good thing, for whatever reason.

Admiral Wilson: Yes, but it sounded like it should have been a State Department evolution, not a Navy evolution. But anyway, that's what happened. That's how we got wrapped up in it. But it was an experience; I'll say that.

Paul Stillwell: On the military construction that you were talking about earlier, you said you got this requirement from SecDef's office to tell you about what kind of money you'd need. Do you have any idea why that kind of largess was forthcoming?

Admiral Wilson: I can't remember the detail, but somebody had brought to the Secretary of Defense's attention the sad state of military medical facilities around the globe. We had some really bad places. We had lots of hospitals that were of World War II vintage, built out of clapboards and fire-consumable in under five minutes. I truly don't know the stimulus to the SecDef to make that offer.

Paul Stillwell: Presumably the other services were benefiting also.

Admiral Wilson: Oh, yes. It was a DoD offer, not just an offer to the Navy.

Paul Stillwell: Did you have any discussions with your counterparts in the other services?

Admiral Wilson: Only in general. We all ran our own programs. If they wanted to replace Walter Reed, or the Eisenhower, or whatever hospital they were interested in, that was their business. Just like we said we'd like to replace Corpus Christi or Charleston or Jacksonville or Pensacola or wherever, the services had their own priorities.

Paul Stillwell: How did you go about establishing your set of priorities?

Admiral Wilson: We established priorities rather simply. We said we wanted to first get rid of all the cantonment hospitals. Those were the World War II hospitals built very quickly out of wood. Among them was Oakland, which had been replaced by the time we received this money. Oakland had been a cantonment hospital originally. Corpus Christi, St. Albans, Orlando, and Jacksonville had been cantonment hospitals.[*]

Anyway, we decided to replace all the wooden ones first, for pure and simple safety factors. Then we started replacing the oldest ones, those that would have cost the most to modernize. We started talking about modernization programs. Some places were very solid but needed to be modernized and needed to have air-conditioning, new plumbing, water supplies, and electrical upgrades and replacements.

Then the other "index" we used was density of population versus the availability of space. After the war the population shifts were considerable, and what had been a large naval installation might now be a little place and vice versa. For example, at Mayport, Florida, which was growing, we found ourselves with a very small dispensary.[†] We replaced it with a 56,000-foot dispensary.

So basically it replacement of cantonment wooden hospitals, followed by needs for the space required to meet population increases. On top of that, we tried to accommodate the fleet, put things on the coast where the fleet could have access to them rather than inland.

---

[*] St. Albans was the naval hospital that supported personnel in the New York City area.
[†] Mayport supported both the aircraft carriers and surface ships home-ported there, as well as the naval air station at nearby Jacksonville, Florida.

Interview Number 5 with Rear Admiral Almon C. Wilson, Medical Corps, U.S. Navy (Retired)

Place: Bureau of Medicine and Surgery, Washington, D.C.

Date: Thursday, 17 September 1992

Interviewer: Paul Stillwell

Paul Stillwell: Good morning, Admiral. Let's start with something that we were discussing before the tape started—that one of your collateral duties while at BuMed was to serve as the physician for the Chairman of the Joint Chiefs of Staff.

Admiral Wilson: I inherited the job from Paul Kaufman, who had been the Chairman's physician.[*] He moved on to a job that didn't permit him to spend the time, so I assumed the duties of the Chairman's physician. I traveled with him when he left the country. Most of these flights were to multiple sites in Europe for short meetings. On one occasion we went to Pearl Harbor, and I remember that trip because it was the first one, and we took an intelligence officer along with us. His wife met him in Honolulu, and they stayed with some friends. While they were there, their friends' house burned down, and this intelligence officer and his wife lost all of the clothing they had brought with them. The Chairman, Admiral Tom Moorer, who was a very kindly fellow, invited the intelligence officer's wife to return to the United States in his airplane, which she did.[†]

When I traveled with the Chairman, I carried along a group of medical cases containing various kinds of equipment and medication. I had a square box with a handle on the top that contained all the medications I thought we might need. Another box contained resuscitation equipment, such as endo-tracheal tubes and laryngoscopes, and chest tubes. In another box I had intravenous fluids, the idea being that we could handle certain things with aplomb, but certainly not any major disastrous trauma. However, we

---

[*] Captain Paul Kaufman, MC, USN.
[†] Admiral Thomas H. Moorer, USN, served as Chairman of the Joint Chiefs of Staff from 3 July 1970 to 30 June 1974. His oral history is in the Naval Institute collection.

carried the things that were necessary to deal with the common things that happen to travelers.

In the course of this experience of two years with Admiral Moorer, we made trips to Brussels, to Ankara, Turkey, to The Hague, among other places. Sometimes the trips repeated themselves. The last trip I made was a memorable one, because we went to Teheran. This was shortly after the Yom Kippur War of 1973.* We went to Teheran and spent a week there. He went conference with the Shah and his people.† Admiral Moorer was attempting to sell F-14 airplanes, as I recall the mission. I was not a part of the negotiations.

On all of these trips, I had a lot of spare time because the Chairman was never ill, and only occasionally did I provide an aspirin for a hung-over staffer. I had a car and driver at my disposal, so I went shopping. We were very interested in oriental carpets, so I usually wound up with a load of oriental carpets to bring home. When we went to Brussels, I bought French wine.

The trip to Teheran was interesting for a variety of reasons. First off, Teheran is a very interesting city. It is very modern in some parts, and outside of Teheran is an enormous set of grounds which were used for the 2,500th anniversary of the Persian Empire celebration.‡ There are these magnificent buildings, statues, and obelisks. It was truly a sight to behold.

At any rate, the carpet shopping in Teheran was not bad. We had a good hotel, and we had some Russian caviar, which is always a treat. On one occasion I was asked to see a British general who was part of the contingent meeting with Admiral Moorer at the time on some planning issue for Southeast Asia. I think this was a SEATO meeting, Southeast Asia Treaty Organization. At any rate, I was asked to see this gentleman because he had severe diarrhea and nausea and vomiting. I went over to see him, and he was indeed ill. I

---

* The Yom Kippur War started on 6 October 1973. Egyptian and Syrian forces began major coordinated ground offensives against Israeli positions, seeking to improve territorial claims in the wake of the Six-Day War of 1967. Supported in part by weapons supplied by the United States, Israeli forces counterattacked and drove back the Arabs. A cease-fire finally took effect on 25 October.
† Mohammad Reza Pahlavi (1919-1980) became Shah of Iran (or Persia, as it was then known) in 1941 and held office until his regime was ousted in 1979 by the Ayatollah Khomeini.
‡ A week of lavish entertainment and pageantry marked the 2,500th anniversary of the Persian Empire. The Shah launched the celebration on 12 October 1971 in a specially built tent city on the site of ancient Persepolis.

gave him a couple of liters of intravenous fluid and some medication to control his diarrhea and nausea, and he responded promptly. At about 10:00 o'clock in the morning his wife asked me if I wanted a drink of Scotch whiskey, and I was very grateful but I didn't think 10:00 o'clock in the morning was quite late enough in the day for my taste, so I had to decline.

From there we went on to Isfahan, which is south of Teheran, more or less en route to their naval base city on the Persian Gulf. It's very old, and they showed us a bridge, some 600 years old, that has been in continuous use. We stayed at a brand-new hotel, and its most elegant characteristics were the beautiful mosaic tiles used to decorate the entryway foyers and all the public spaces. It was truly a magnificent place.

We actually went there to sort of get out of the way of the Shah and to lower our profile while we were waiting to go on to Bahrain and Kuwait. After a few days in Isfahan, we flew on to Bahrain, where we met with the Emir. The Chairman had a negotiating session with him, and we toured the island without any great adventures overtaking us. As you know, the island is relatively small. It's mostly oil. Bahrain had taken a lot of money from British Petroleum up front to be able to develop Bahrain early on after oil was discovered. As a result, Bahrain was quite well developed. They had a good road system, quite a modern city in Manama, and a very large, very modern up-to-date hotel.

We then flew on to Kuwait. In Teheran I had bought a couple of two-liter bottles of Scotch whiskey at a wonderfully low price and I had them in my luggage. Somewhere between Bahrain and Kuwait they got smashed, so I wound up with a suitcase full of Scotch-soaked clothing, which I had to wash in a bathtub. At any rate, we were in Kuwait, and the Kuwaiti Government people who were our hosts showed us around town and we saw some memorable things. For example, there's a golf course outside of Kuwait City, and there isn't a blade of grass anywhere. The greens are oiled down to provide a firm hard surface from which to tee off and on which to putt. So you see these black spots in an otherwise almost white desert; they identify a golf course.

There is a four-lane highway that runs from somewhere to Kuwait City, and it ends abruptly just outside the city. It goes nowhere. On this stretch of highway we saw all kinds of very expensive automobiles: Rolls-Royces, Cadillacs, Ferraris—all the world's leading automobiles were being run up and down this short strip of highway.

The Kuwaitis were very cordial. We had a reception hosted by the American ambassador to Kuwait. It was a very nice affair, as they usually are. During the course of the evening, I was asked to see a gentleman from the State Department who was prostrated with an acute gastroenteritis. We took him back to his hotel, and I treated him with some oral medications and also a couple of bottles of intravenous fluids. I remember hanging the intravenous fluids from the light fixture at the head of his bed to let them run in rapidly. He recovered quite quickly and resumed his duties.

The Chairman conducted his negotiations with the Kuwaitis, and then we left. The routing was interesting. We were not permitted to fly over the Arabian Peninsula, so to get to Teheran originally we had to fly the entire length of the Mediterranean Sea. We refueled in Naples and stayed overnight en route. Then we had to fly all the way to the end of the Mediterranean, over Turkey, and around to Iran that way. From Iran we went on to Bahrain and Kuwait. Then we had to retrace our steps, and our return flight from Kuwait, I believe, was 17 hours in air. We refueled in Rota, Spain, on the way back.

Paul Stillwell: What was the prohibition against flying over Saudi Arabia?

Admiral Wilson: It was a matter of diplomatic clearance in airspace. The relationship between the United States and the occupiers of the Arabian Peninsula was not sufficiently good so we could overfly them. There was a lot of tension, at that time between the Saudis and Israelis, so it wasn't possible. On the trip we made to Ankara, it was interesting from a technical point of view. The Chairman had a KC-135 Air Force aircraft at his disposal all the time. He was prohibited from flying commercial aircraft because of his clearances and the sensitivity of what he knew and his person as a possible hostage.

Paul Stillwell: This was during a time of a lot of airplane hijackings.

Admiral Wilson: Yes, it was. Because of these dangers, he always flew in his private airplane. This airplane was unique in several ways. First of all, it had accommodations for several aircrews. For passengers it had bunks, facing seats with tables between them, and a galley. When the Chairman went on one of these missions, he took with him a standard group of people. The group usually consisted of his wife, his public affairs officer, his area specialist, his writer, who was a chief yeoman, and his medical officer, me. The crew of the airplane varied in size according to the length of the trip. When we went to Teheran and had to fly such long distances, we had three Air Force crews aboard, and they rotated flight duties to preclude fatigue problems. The Chairman was virtually a workaholic, and he could sleep for two or three hours in one of the bunks in the airplane and arise fully refreshed and ready for a whole day's work. He was an amazing man.

Paul Stillwell: What else do you recall about him?

Admiral Wilson: Well, he was a very close-mouthed man, as far as I was concerned. He was very cordial to me, but he certainly never discussed anything of significance, particularly on the military level. My interface with him was purely social, both militarily social and on occasion I was asked to come to his residence over at Fort Myer to treat some of his family.

I remember treating his wife's mother one evening. Afterward he invited me to have a cocktail and I accepted. As I was about to leave, he said, "Wait a minute." He sent his steward to bring up something; he handed it to me, and it turned out to be a duck. At that time we had just gone through a sort of mini scandal in town where many of our senior people had been accused of availing themselves of a duck blind and duck refuge on the Eastern Shore of Maryland. I think it was Northrop.

Paul Stillwell: I don't know.

Admiral Wilson: It was one of the major aircraft companies. Admiral Moorer had taken a lot of flak in the media about this issue, and he handed me this duck which came from that place. I said, "Admiral, this is pretty good; you take the flak but I get the duck." [Laughter]

He said, "Can you imagine those people trying to think they could buy me with a damn frozen duck?" That was typical. He was a very honest, straightforward working man.

Paul Stillwell: Was he inclined to small talk at all, since he wasn't talking substantive things?

Admiral Wilson: He was not inclined to small talk at all. On the airplane he either worked or played gin rummy, and he was an expert at gin rummy. He took a lot of money from the public affairs officer. I never got involved.

Paul Stillwell: I suspect that the communication setup was superb on that plane.

Admiral Wilson: Absolutely wonderful. As a matter of fact, once while we were in the air we were flying over the southern tip of Italy. I was talking to the pilot, just chatting to pass the time, and the communicator said, "Do you want to talk to your wife?"

I said, "I'd love to."

He said, "Here. Take this telephone."

So he did something, and all of a sudden the operator on the other end said, "What number would you like to talk to?"

I gave him my home phone number, and my wife answered. She said, "Where are you?"

I said, "Well, I'm in the air at about 35,000 feet. We're just passing over Sigonella."

She said, "Good heavens." Anyway, we passed the time of day, got the latest news, but that's how good the communications were. He could speak with the Pentagon at the drop of a hat from anywhere in the world.

This airplane was also unusual because there was no luggage space in it. All the space in the belly of the aircraft that is ordinarily used for luggage by the commercial airliners was converted into fuel tanks. When we went to Ankara, we took off from Andrews Air Force Base outside Washington with a full fuel load. In fact, the fuel load was so great that the pilot needed the entire Andrews Air Force Base runway to get airborne, and even at that very slowly. We flew across the entire Atlantic Ocean, the entire length of the Mediterranean ocean, and halfway across Turkey without refueling. It was a long, long trip. The pilot claimed we came in on the fumes in the tanks.

Paul Stillwell: Where was the luggage stowed?

Admiral Wilson: On the same deck as the passenger compartments. There were luggage spaces along the sides of the fuselage, behind the crew's quarters and before the bunks. These are large airplanes, of course, so there was plenty of space.

Paul Stillwell: Did you get any impression on whether the admiral was fond of creature comforts, or did that seem important to him?

Admiral Wilson: Not really. We, of course, had mess attendants aboard, and they prepared beautiful food. We paid for it, but it was nicely served and the bar was open. We used to drink Bloody Marys before dinner. It was a very informal but working atmosphere for them. He wore sort of coverall suit while traveling. His aide was one of the members of the team he brought along. His aides complained that he was really tough on uniforms, so anytime he went they had to bring three or four or five uniforms just to last him a couple of days. But he was very much a down-to-earth fellow, not haughty in any sense of the word, very businesslike all the time, however. He had a good sense of humor, but it was not apparent on a minute-to-minute basis, because he was so engrossed in what he was doing.

I was transferred away from the Bureau of Medicine and Surgery shortly before he retired, and I consider him really one of the great naval officers in our time. He'd had most of the major jobs in the Navy.

The next part of my career involved having a hospital command. The Surgeon General at the time was Admiral Don Custis, who, by the way, was a splendid gentleman, and a very good Surgeon General.[*] He was the first to really point the way for what is now

---

[*] Vice Admiral Donald L. Custis, MC, USN, served as the Navy's Surgeon General from 1973 to 1976.

considered modern management. The bureau had been run forever on the old-boy system, out of somebody's hip pocket, and there were fiefdoms all over the place. The comptroller was almost a law unto himself. He had hidden pots of money that he dispensed if he liked the project and if the requester was a friend. Unfortunately, but truly, he raised a successor who fit the mold beautifully and continued to carry on with that kind of activity in the comptroller role for many years thereafter.

This was at a time when there was a change going on in the government, and the Bureau of Medicine and Surgery was very slow about coming around to newer management ways. Their response to change was slow as could be.

Paul Stillwell: If it's not broken, don't fix it.

Admiral Wilson: Well, that plus the fact that they didn't have any trained managers. In those days anybody who had had command of a hospital was said to be a manager. That statement leaves enormous room for debate. Commands were assumed by people because they knew somebody and had come up through the system and had done their time in the right places, etc., etc.

Paul Stillwell: So this was a very thoroughgoing old-boy network.

Admiral Wilson: Absolutely. Nepotism was rampant. I know of an officer who probably got a command because he did a hysterectomy on the wife of a Surgeon General and she had a good result. I couldn't prove that to anybody, but his talents otherwise were not all that superior, certainly as a manager, to my own knowledge.

Paul Stillwell: I interviewed a former Chief of Chaplains, and he described a parallel situation in the Chaplain Corps.[*] In the '70s the chaplains really had to change the way they did business and get on with the PPBS system—planning, programming, and budgeting—and justify their requirements.

---

[*] This is in the Naval Institute oral history of Rear Admiral Neil M. Stevenson, CHC, USN (Ret.).

Admiral Wilson: Absolutely. A lot of people are afraid of medical people, because they don't understand the language of medicine. It's all a deep mystery to them. I think the line officers felt same way, because they were prone to give the medical department what they needed—within reason. Then the medical department passed it around as they saw fit—sometimes well, sometimes not so well—depending on the priority of the leadership at the time.

Even the Surgeons General were not very talented managers sometimes. They got by through the efforts of their staff, both in uniform and out of uniform, and sort of muddled along. But after Robert McNamara became Secretary of Defense and "systems analysis" became the buzzword in Washington, then the PPBS, the Planning, Programming and Budgeting System, became the mode of management.* It was very, very difficult to change the leadership's ideas about such things and get them to understand that if they didn't participate in the system, they were simply not going to get the assets to make things happen. The resources were going to be denied them because they didn't fit in the budgeting system, and they were not sufficiently documented for their true validity. This was to go on for a number of years.

Paul Stillwell: How did men rise to become Surgeon General? What was the system that picked these leaders?

Admiral Wilson: That's a very difficult question to answer.

Paul Stillwell: I'd be interested in your perceptions, in any event.

Admiral Wilson: Those of us who were junior in the system all had our favorite flag officers because of the fact that we either knew them, we knew their reputations and liked them, or had a great deal of respect for their talents, whatever they happened to be. There were some officers who were essentially groomed to be Surgeon General. I think R. B. Brown, whom we discussed before, was probably the best example. R. B. Brown had been a professor of surgery at Penn, I believe, during the late '30s, early '40s. He came into the

---

* Robert S. McNamara served as Secretary of Defense from 21 January 1961 to 29 February 1968.

Navy in World War II, went out, returned, stayed, became the chief of surgery at Bethesda, had a tour in a hospital ship in the Korean War, and then came back and spent the rest of his time at Bethesda. He eventually became the Surgeon General in 1965.

He was a man who was very well liked by the people who knew him. He was an excellent surgeon, a wonderful teacher. He was very well respected in the military and the civilian community and professional surgical circles. He was a very impressive gentleman. He never wore an unshined shoe; you could always see your face in his shoes. His pants were always pressed. He was the epitome of a meticulously dressed individual. He was a tall, spare man with graying hair and a very steely look in his eye. He was not prone to be loquacious, and he a person who spoke to the point, to the crux of the matter at hand, without fanfare.

As Surgeon General, I didn't have terribly much personal experience with him. I did have a couple of experiences with him. He came to Vietnam to look at the operation in the Third Medical Battalion headquarters in Danang in either late 1965 or early 1966. He sat and listened and really made no specific comment except to say the usual things: "You're doing a good job, keep it up, we're behind you, etc." I really didn't realize how far behind us he was until I learned later what happened when he came back to BuMed. After having been given a list of our most serious problems—and there were some very serious ones—he came back and assured the people at the bureau who asked that all was well: "There are really no big problems out there; things are going along all right." It really marred my perception of his image to have him do that. I think it was due to the fact that he really did not have an insight into combat medicine, even though he had been in a hospital ship. So he was of the old school caliber of management.

He was succeeded by George Davis, who was a very imposing appearing man.[*] He was very tall, very well groomed, in good physical shape. He was quite articulate, but, again, not very outgoing. He tended to be quite reserved, and he didn't say very much when you had a conversation with him. He was in that sense somewhat unapproachable to many, and that included some of his flag officers at the time. He was very well thought of. He was thought to be very smart, he was considered to have a good rapport with the line,

---

[*] Vice Admiral George M. Davis, MC, USN, served as the Navy's Surgeon General from 1969 to 1973.

but I don't specifically recall any great improvement in anything while he was the Surgeon General. He was Don Custis's predecessor.

Don Custis became the SG in 1973, and he was a breath of fresh air. He was a small man in his stature, but he was a large man in his mien and manner. He had broken service. He did not have, I think, more than probably 16 years' active duty when he came to the job of Surgeon General. He had risen very rapidly from a captain commanding the hospital at Bethesda Naval Medical Center under a flag officer named Felix Ballenger, who was a loser, a very ineffectual officer.* Don Custis was not only promoted to rear admiral, but he almost immediately thereafter became the Surgeon General. So he went from four stripes to three stars in a matter of a few months—to the consternation of many in the old-boy system, I'll tell you.

Paul Stillwell: How did he manage to get elevated?

Admiral Wilson: I don't really know except that he had demonstrated to everybody that he was an outstanding figure in his attitudes, in his insights, in his manner of dealing with people. He had management instincts that showed. Other than that, I don't know.

Paul Stillwell: Let me play the devil's advocate. Is it necessary to have a physician as the commanding officer of a naval hospital or as Surgeon General of the Navy?

Admiral Wilson: Good question. I have a very parochial viewpoint on that subject, being a medical officer. I think it's important that a medical officer be the Surgeon General, by all means. Because if you're going to be the leader of a medical organization, you have to understand the profession, and you really don't understand the profession unless you're a physician. Now, I say that, knowing that there are lots and lots of people who are not physicians but who understand a lot about medicine. I stand by the fact that you really can't understand it as well if you're not a physician, and I don't mean to sound haughty about it, and that's true for the Surgeon General.

---

* As a captain, Ballenger had commanded the naval hospital at Yokosuka, Japan, when Wilson was there in the 1960s.

As far as hospital command is concerned, I feel the same way. I am one of the greatest supporters of the Medical Service Corps that was ever in the Navy medical department. I have a great deal of respect for them. I've had a marvelous experience with many of them who were very challenging people, and some of them have been good commanding officers. Command of a military hospital is different from being the administrator of a civilian hospital. The commanding officer of a naval hospital is the guy who is ultimately responsible for the clinical care of the patients who are treated. I don't think it's fair to place that burden on someone who is not a physician first.

Secondly, the commanding officer has to make certain judgments in terms of patient management and patient disposition that require a clinical background. Not to say that a non-physician couldn't get advice on the issue, but the commanding officer, being a physician, has a personal feel for it much better. It has to do in some cases with management, in particular in terms of establishing priorities: do you treat the patient here, do you send the patient elsewhere, and if it costs you money, is that the way you want to spend the money? That's the way I feel about it. I feel that clinical facilities should be run by medical officers. I have absolutely no argument with the Medical Service Corps officers who do their administrative thing admirably and are absolutely requisite to the good function of the medical department. But I don't think they ought to be responsible for clinical functions.

Paul Stillwell: Where are the doctors supposed to get this management training or ability or whatever to be the leaders, the commanders?

Admiral Wilson: In the past there was no set pattern for them. In recent years, some effort has been made to provide them with formal course work to become managers—or better managers. It's not only the techniques of medical management that are important. The longer you're in the Navy, the more you understand how important it is to understand the Naval organization and how it functions. You can't really be effective in an organization unless you make the organization work for your target enterprises. We all have priorities. There are some priorities that are established by other people that you cannot avoid. But your own priorities surface, and that's what management is all about.

Within the structure of the naval organization there are lines of responsibility that go on to the line officers, and there are lines of support that are available to you. If you fully understand the lines of support, you can garner for yourselves a lot of resources, be they money, people, attitudinal support, or opportunities to try new things. All kinds of opportunities occur if you know what the system offers and what it requires and how to gain access to the assets that are useful to you.

If you take the attitude that the system cannot be changed, then you're contributing to the archaic old-boy system. The Navy is a dynamic organization. It's today's Navy; it's not the 1880s Navy. While there are timeless fundamental rules of conduct, interpersonal relationships, chain of command, principles that deal with training your juniors and successors, there are also specific management activities that must change with the times. If you run across something of a nature that doesn't fit with the realities of your world, you owe it to the system to define that problem, to seek relief either in exception if it's a very narrow problem, or for a change in the regulation if it's a widespread problem.

Part of your responsibility is to help keep the system modern. I've told people forever and nine days that the career Navy medical officer's job is not only to treat the patients for whom we have responsibility, but to be the caretakers of a system that can be expanded in wartime to deal with the wartime problems. We have to make that system as modern as the civilian community's, so that we're not sitting around on our hands letting the medical system in the military deteriorate to an unacceptable level. That's hard to sell to some Navy physicians who are so clinically oriented they don't have an interest or insight into peripheral matters that pertain.

Paul Stillwell: In the 1980s the Navy's medical system did deteriorate to an unacceptable situation.

Admiral Wilson: Yes.
But, anyway, Admiral Custis, the Surgeon General from 1973 to 1976, tried his best to get into the PPBS system. He was criticized roundly and soundly for more or less end-running Admiral Zumwalt to gain some congressional support for some programs that he needed to have.

Paul Stillwell: Such as?

Admiral Wilson: I can't remember the specifics now, but Zumwalt was sort of standoffish. He went to see Zumwalt one time, and Zumwalt had a captain who was CNO's gatekeeper. The captain said Custis couldn't see the CNO. Custis said, "I don't work for you. I work for CNO and I want to see him. If I have to walk up the front of you and down the back of you I'll do it. Don't give me all this gatekeeper stuff."

I guess he got to see him. Anyway, Don Custis was very good to his people. He respected your abilities, he respected your talents, and he was helpful with your problems. He did not interfere with the operation of your area of responsibility as long as you did it well. If you had problems, he was very approachable and helpful.

Paul Stillwell: Sounds as if he also had some leadership qualities that his predecessors lacked.

Admiral Wilson: Oh, he certainly did. He was a good leader in the sense that he knew his people, he came around to see them, knew them by name, knew what their jobs were, knew what their problems were, and, as I say, he was very approachable. He was very much a part of the team that was trying to do a tough job at a tough time.

About this same time, of course, the draft ended, so our medical officer procurement system really went to smash in a hurry.[*] With all of this, they started closing hospitals. Closing hospitals is very difficult, because no congressman wants to have anything adverse happen in his district. I remember clearly that Admiral Etter went to a conference with Joseph Addabbo, who was the chairman of the Subcommittee on Defense Appropriations of the House Appropriations Committee.[†] He went to a meeting over at the VA headquarters here in Washington, and Congressman Addabbo called Admiral Etter every name you can imagine except gentleman, because we were proposing to close the St.

---

[*] In 1972 the Defense Department announced it would end draft calls in mid-1973. Secretary of Defense Melvin Laird announced on 27 January 1973 that the use of the military draft had ended as of then, several months prior to plan.
[†] Representative Joseph P. Addabbo (Democrat-New York).

Albans Hospital, which was in his district. As a net result of Mr. Addabbo's efforts, the Navy has been forced to run a clinic in the building that was once a naval hospital for the benefit of the Navy people in the New York area while the rest of the hospital was converted to veterans' use.

But that was the power of each congressman, and they were very ugly people, some of them, and Joseph Addabbo, who is now dead, was one of the worst. He was profane to the point of being obscene in his commentary, and Admiral Etter was a thoroughgoing gentleman in all of his dealings with everybody. So in that sense there was congressional abuse of people. Fortunately, we didn't see it very often, but it did happen.

Closing installations down is always a very difficult proposition, not only from the congressional opposition point of view but from the internal point of view. We all have a sense of history and all hate to see the closing of time-honored duty stations and hospitals where you've worked hard and taken care of patients. We hated to see them go by the board. We closed Chelsea in Boston; St. Albans, New York; and Portsmouth, New Hampshire.

Paul Stillwell: The one at the Naval Academy also.

Admiral Wilson: Yes, we closed the naval hospital at Annapolis and converted it to a clinic. All this because the Vietnam War was winding down, and the draft had ceased to exist. We didn't have enough people to staff all those hospitals. The entire medical department contracted for a while.

Paul Stillwell: And it had to think of new ways to get doctors.

Admiral Wilson: That's correct. We had always had good residency training programs as an enticement to physicians to come into and stay in the Navy. Then the services began offering bonuses for physicians, and these bonuses increased over time. They had started in the early '50s with medical officer pay at $100.00 a month. By the late '70s it had come to the point where a captain medical officer with 16 or 18 years service was drawing something to the order of $16,000 more than his line counterpart. That was a very great point of disgruntlement with our line friends. Yet the Congress understood the problem. They understood that they had to go into the marketplace to buy physicians, and the bonus method was the way they bought physicians into the service—not only in the Navy, but also in the Army and Air Force, because these were standard pay scales.

I mentioned earlier that the facilities had a shot in the arm when a lot of money was pumped in. So at a time when we had the medical staffs contracting we had all kinds of money for expansion. Then the age-old question came up. What size should a hospital be? If you can't staff it, why build it? The question then was, "If you can perceive the need for a given size hospital, build the hospital, because you can get people by the draft much more quickly than you can erect a hospital." Trying to balance those two types of opinions against one another in this time of drawdown was a very difficult thing to do.

As always, we had our critics in the Pentagon, particularly in OMB, and to a degree in the facilities side of the Department of Defense.[*] This was not in the health affairs section but in the Defense Department "public works" departments. Fortunately, we had some friends in those departments who were knowledgeable about medical operations, and we did pretty well. But one of the things they did, for example, was reduce the size of hospital rooms to save the cost in hospital construction. When you reduce the size of a hospital room, you immediately cause difficulties in terms of maneuverability of beds, the problems of adding bedside therapeutic support equipments, and certainly the aura and aspect of the room as a spacious environment in which to recover.

We went through a series of evolutions about space, and usually they were downgraded. This was a time of great change. We were trying to change into the management mode. We were trying to change into using the PPBS system. We were trying to realign the medical department assets to deal with the loss of the draft and the closure of hospitals.

We wound up discontinuing some vital services in some of our hospitals, like obstetric services that were farmed out to the local communities, causing great dismay to the Navy people and great cost to the CHAMPUS program.[†] The CHAMPUS program took a very large hit, because literally thousands of people who had been cared for by

---

[*] OMB—Office of Management and Budget.
[†] CHAMPUS—Civilian Health and Medical Program of the Uniformed Services.

uniformed physicians in the past were now cast out on to the civilian market simply because we did not have the people to take care of them. Things were in great state of flux.

Modernization, management, systems approach to problems, conformity with the budget system, lack of medical officers versus shortages of money—all of these things combined at one time to make a very difficult period. Now, having said that, I'm sure that history will show that other people at other times suffered through similar difficulties. We knew that, and we felt that it was our turn more or less. The one thing that pervaded the issue, however, was the need to be sure that even though we didn't take care of everybody, that we took proper care of the ones we did treat. To let the quality of medical support or care dwindle would have been the worst kind of sin. I'll say this—that everyone who had anything to do with patients defended the quality of care above anything and everything. On that score I am very proud of the department.

Paul Stillwell: And that helps make your point—why do you need a physician in charge?

Admiral Wilson: Correct.

Paul Stillwell: Against that background then, you went on to your new duty station.

Admiral Wilson: I went out to Great Lakes as the commanding officer of the hospital there. I had several opportunities. I could have had command of the naval hospital at Camp Pendleton or the hospital at Charleston, S.C., or at Great Lakes. I chose Great Lakes, mainly because it had big quarters and my mother-in-law was with us. She was an invalid, and we needed the large place in proximity to the hospital.

There were some things at Great Lakes that I wanted to learn. For example, I had no insight into recruits and their problems that pertained. We duly moved out to Great Lakes, and I relieved Bill Turville, who was a flag officer.[*] The commanding officer's billet had just been downgraded from a flag billet to a captain's billet. So I assumed command as the newest CO on the street at Great Lakes.

---

[*] Rear Admiral William C. Turville, MC, USN.

At that time, Great Lakes was a monster in a sense, because in my command assumption briefings I was advised that there were 47 different commands with commanding officers in the Great Lakes complex. The operation was under the command of Admiral Warren O'Neil who was a flier and a lower-half flag officer.[*] He had been told by Zumwalt that he, Zumwalt, was attempting to upgrade the quality of the naval district commands. So putting a flag officer in the naval district command was a leg up for his career, which turned out to be pure hogwash. I have never known of a district commander flag officer—with rare, rare exception—who ever went on to anything much better in terms of a career step.

Paul Stillwell: Well, it was usually a twilight tour.

Admiral Wilson: Indeed it was. Since that time, in recent years, there have been some who have gone on to bigger and better things.

Paul Stillwell: But then the Navy eliminated the naval districts.

Admiral Wilson: Yes, they did, but they still have a few equivalents left. But they were not exactly barn-burners for duty stations.

Great Lakes at the time was on backside of some very bad racial rioting incidents that had been prevalent there in the late '60s and early '70s. There was still a great deal of tension between the black and white communities, both civilian and within the Navy itself. For those who are not familiar with Great Lakes, it consists of two major commands. The Recruit Training Command had approximately 10,000 recruits on hand most of the time, with ups and downs depending on the season. There were more in the summer as the kids got out of high school. Across the highway from the Recruit Training Command was the Service Schools Command, where they had a great number of specialty schools, into which they assigned large numbers of recruits for periods up to one year of training. The Service Schools Command was one of the larger and more important commands in the complex.

---

[*] Rear Admiral Warren H. O'Neil, USN.

At the same time, Admiral Zumwalt was pushing his racial awareness programs. Training in race relations was the mode of the day, just as sexual harassment is today as the spin-off from the 1991 Tailhook Association fiasco.* We as commanding officers were directed to establish UPWARD seminars. The system that they employed at the time had some very interesting aspects. A command would survey its people to find someone who was interested in participating, being a so-called facilitator for UPWARD seminar discussions. It was best if he or the assistant—and they always had two in the program—was a minority, for obvious reasons.

We were just a bit slow getting off the mark on this program, but we finally did get one going. The man who had been chosen by my predecessor as facilitator was a young reserve lieutenant (j.g.) who had been had come up through the ranks from hospital corpsman first class. He was very racially aware and went around asking the black people on the staff, both civilian and military, if they had any complaints and showed that he was really looking for racial discrimination problems.

I had a series of complaints about the seminars after they started, principally from civil servants who claimed that they were being harassed and didn't want to attend. At that time we were directed to select people, both military and civilian, to attend these classes. The complaints from the civilians became quite severe. One woman was brought into my office almost in hysterics. So I elected to go and observe the class.

Paul Stillwell: What was the substance of the complaints?

Admiral Wilson: The substance was that the facilitator in the UPWARD seminar was focusing on this woman's private life and telling her that what she was doing was wrong. She was guilty of something or other in terms of racial discrimination, and she had not responded well.

---

* Following the Tailhook Association's 1991 convention in Las Vegas, a number of women complained of being mistreated by naval officers in attendance. There were other allegations of inappropriate behavior. A long, largely inconclusive investigation followed. The upshot was damage to the Navy's overall reputation and to that of naval aviation in particular. For a detailed analysis, see "Tailhook: What Happened, Why & What's to be Learned," U.S. Naval Institute Proceedings, September 1994, pages 89-103.

Paul Stillwell: What did you find out once you sat in on the session yourself?

Admiral Wilson: First of all, one of my senior people, a captain department head, came to me and said, "I don't know about this guy. He was talking to us in this UPWARD seminar. He volunteered the fact that if he was walking down the street with a group of blacks and they started to assault a white man that he would help the blacks."

I said, "My God, he's supposed to be the guy trying to get the racism to simmer down. That's no attitude for him." So I went to look at the seminar. I took the chief of psychiatry, Gary Almy, who was very used to group dynamics.[*] He ran group therapy programs all the time. I took him along to be an objective observer about the group dynamics and leadership. We walked in there, and, according to the people who ran the symposium, we completely disrupted their train of thought, destroyed the atmosphere and sense of trust they had built between one another, and in essence just spoiled their entire session.

Paul Stillwell: Was there some kind of centralized curriculum that had come out of Washington?

Admiral Wilson: Oh, yes, there was a very standard, almost a cookbook, curriculum. But what happened was that we had taken a very, very diverse group of people and put them all together. They had come from enormously disparate backgrounds, and when the discussions got around to value judgments, certain of these value judgments were laid on the group, and some of the people couldn't tolerate it. Somebody said, "It's wrong to live with a black man," or something of that sort. Well, if there's a white gal sitting there who's living with a black man, that doesn't make her feel too secure. So we had instances where the sensitivity of the people was severely assaulted.

In the meantime, the man who had been running the seminar had been acting in a fashion that led me to believe that when he made a mistake and was admonished about it, he never learned from it. He'd do the same thing again. This happened on several occasions. In fact, I called him in one time to talk to him about the seminars.

---

[*] Lieutenant Commander Gary L. Almy, MC, USN.

I said, "We're getting a bad reputation. Cool it, straighten it out, settle it down." It didn't happen. Finally, after having gone there, I decided to stop it. I shut the seminar down and called him into the office with his white cohort. I said to them, "I don't think that the program is running the way it should. People are being terribly disrupted by it. The manner in which you conduct it doesn't seem to be appropriate for the subject material." Then he went through a long defense of his way of doing it.

Paul Stillwell: Did you get the idea that this was kind of an ego thing with him, to be able to run it?

Admiral Wilson: Oh, yes, because he considered himself to be a sort of champion among the blacks. But what came out later on is the fact that he was not black. He was a very dark-skinned man, but he was Puerto Rican who had been raised in a series of black foster families. He identified with the black community, even though he himself was not an African by ancestry.

Paul Stillwell: Well, he was still a minority.

Admiral Wilson: Yes, still a minority, no question. At any rate, at the same time I said to him, "You know, it might be well for you to go and talk to Dr. Almy. He does a lot with these group dynamics and groups. I'd like to have you be interviewed by him." He immediately became suspicious. At the time, I was getting ready to come to Washington for a COs' conference. I said, "I'd like you to go talk to the administrative officer and get lined up with Dr. Almy." Then he went out.

Now, my administrative officer was a by-the-book guy. You know, it was either this way or that way. If it was in the book, you did it, and if it wasn't in the book you didn't do it.

So, unbeknownst to me, the facilitator said to him, "I don't want to do that."

My AO said to him, "Well if you don't want to be seen, then the captain can order you to be admitted. You have your choice."

The facilitator said, "The captain is going to have to order me admitted."

"Okay, that's the way you want it, we'll admit you." I found out about it, I think, before I came to Washington. But it sounded to me like it was the facilitator's choice. Anyway, it wasn't presented to be as a "Do it or else."

Paul Stillwell: So you didn't have all the facts?

Admiral Wilson: Well, I guess not, but I still had the responsibility. At any rate, when they admitted this man to the psychiatric service for evaluation, all hell broke. His wife telegraphed everybody in Washington, I guess including the President. The first thing I knew about it was when I was at Bethesda, and I got a telephone call saying, "What the hell is going on out there in Great Lakes? You're locking some guy up."

I said, "Hold the phone. There's more to the story than that."

They said, "Well, you better get back home, because things are busting loose."

Well, I immediately returned to Great Lakes, and on Friday night virtually the entire Navy Inspector General's team descended on me. They brought with them people like Commander Buddie Penn, who was their minority affairs guy for a long time.[*] He was in Pers forever on a minority affairs desk of some sort. This team immediately began to look down their noses at me as if I were some sort of ogre who was trying to trample the system.

Then they formulated a formal investigation. They got a rear admiral from Whidbey Island who was commander of the Patrol Wings Pacific or something. I can't remember his name offhand. But this happened in 1974. He had an attorney assigned to him by the naval district. They interviewed all kinds of people, all over the command, under oath. A real deal.

I had a chance to give my side of the story, and I, of course, told Admiral Custis, the Surgeon General, what was going on. He sent out Bob Strange, who was the psychiatric consultant to the Surgeon General.[†] Because I was sort of under the gun for admitting this guy to the psych service, the question was, "Did you have any right to put

---

[*] Commander Buddie Joe Penn, USN.
[†] Captain Robert E. Strange, MC, USN.

this man on the psych service?" It turned out that Bob Strange felt that I had just reason for doing so, and said so.

At any rate, after all of this mess settled down, the upshot of the whole thing was that the CNO was going to give me some kind of letter. A letter of caution, I think was the term that they used. Admiral Custis, who had been fully appraised of all these issues, told CNO that if he wrote out a letter for me, to write one out for him, because he approved of the way I had managed it. So that, of course, made me feel the strong support the SG always provided.

Then the lieutenant (j.g.) who had been the facilitator was released from the service. He had been picked up from the enlisted ranks, partly, I believe, on the basis that there was a big move afoot to commission minorities. They commissioned a lot of minorities in the Medical Service Corps. He was a reservist, and his performance of duty had been such that the Medical Service Corps was not going to recommend his retention on active duty as a reserve Medical Service Corps officer. So, in essence, what happened to him at Great Lakes in relation to his being released from the Navy was distinct, different, and separate from the actions that I had taken. But that was hard to realize for anybody who didn't know the details that separated the issues.

Paul Stillwell: Especially the lieutenant (j.g.).

Admiral Wilson: Yes. His immediate allegation was that I had caused him to be kicked out of the service after X number of years.

Things went along, and in December of that year, 1974, I suddenly received notification that this former facilitator was bringing suit in federal court. I was charged with 12 counts of malfeasance of office, in essence, indicating that I had hospitalized him against his will. Each of these 12 different counts was demanding $750,000. There were five defendants: the commanding officer, the administrative officer, the chief of psychiatry, the director of clinical services, and the commandant of the naval district, Admiral Warren O'Neil.

The U.S. attorney's office in Chicago was designated to defend us. This suit went on for ten years and didn't end until after I was retired. At one point we were all set to go to trial. We all gathered in Chicago and made depositions. According to our attorney, the depositions were such that they were very damning to the plaintiff, and he would have lost on the basis of the depositions. At any rate the plaintiffs eventually failed to respond to some filing deadline in the legal process. Ten years after the fact, the case was finally dropped.

Paul Stillwell: Did the U.S. Government pay all of your defense fees?

Admiral Wilson: They certainly did. On a number of occasions, I was advised that such and such an action was going to be taking place, and that if I thought if advisable this was the time to get a civilian attorney. But I never thought it advisable to do that, so I stuck with the government attorneys all along.

Paul Stillwell: This whole thing couldn't have been very helpful to your own mental well-being.

Admiral Wilson: Well, no. It was a constant worry, of course, but I didn't have any sense of guilt for having done what I did, because I felt personally justified in the judgments I had made. There was certainly nothing racial about it. As far as I was concerned, it was a management decision.

But it too was part of the times. We talk about what happens specifically, but when you try to put this in context with the rest of what was going on in the Navy, it makes an interesting pattern. At that time they had had trouble with race riots in the aircraft carriers in San Diego.* There had been race riots in various and sundry military installations around the world, not only in the Navy but in other services as well. Then along came Admiral Zumwalt, apparently with a charter to change all of this and increase our racial awareness through various mechanisms.

---

* Racial disturbances broke out in the carrier Kitty Hawk (CVA-63) on 12 October 1972; in the oiler Hassayampa (AO-145) on 16 October 1972; and in the carrier Constellation (CVA-64) on 3 November 1972. See Captain Paul B. Ryan, USN (Ret.), "USS Constellation Flare-up: Was it Mutiny?" U.S. Naval Institute Proceedings, January 1976, pages 46-53.

He chose this method of UPWARD seminars, and from the point of view of the psychologists, if not the psychiatrists, it's important to know that people in general are by and large compensators. None of us is perfectly well balanced. Each and every one of us has a methodology for existing in his environment by a series of compensatory mechanisms. Everybody has to feel that he does something better than someone else. People have feelings that they are better than somebody else, for whatever reason. It is very, very internal and may not ever, ever surface verbally, whether the person is ever asked or not.

Paul Stillwell: And we rationalize our shortcomings.

Admiral Wilson: Absolutely. So if you take a group of people who are variously close to the brink of breaking down their compensatory mechanisms and put their compensations or compensatory links under great stress, some of them are going to break. That's what happened to one or two of these civil servants. The stability in their particular psyches was disrupted sufficiently so that they had an adverse reaction to this whole experience.

Paul Stillwell: Well, the whole mechanism was designed to be confrontational, wasn't it, to force people to deal with their feelings?

Admiral Wilson: Yes it was, but that very term leads you on to the next phase, which is the sensitivity session. Confrontation and sensitivity were buzzwords at the time. Sensitivity sessions were supposed to bring all your basic fears and flaws and whatever you had deep down in your deep compartments out so you could look at them and say, "Oh well, I've gotten rid of that phobia now." It doesn't work that way. You can destroy people by assaulting their defense mechanisms. I think that the idea of taking people almost randomly from commands, running them through a short course in being a facilitator for one of these confrontational seminars was a very dangerous thing to do. I will never know if or how many unsuspecting people were psychologically disrupted by this kind of experience. I'm sure we were not the only command that had this kind of problems.

Paul Stillwell: I'm sure you were not. And it probably could have been much better done by people who had a career background in that field.

Admiral Wilson: Absolutely. Well, the upshot of the whole thing was the entire UPWARD seminar was shut down, Navy-wide.

Paul Stillwell: As a result of your specific experience?

Admiral Wilson: I think so. They shut it down Navy-wide. I didn't hear of anything like it until relatively recently. Now, that doesn't mean it didn't happen. But I don't remember anything like this having been in the wind from 1974 through '84. Do you?

Paul Stillwell: No.

Admiral Wilson: That whole UPWARD seminar effort went to naught. Or I shouldn't say "went to naught," but it was discontinued in the form and fashion in which it had been originally delivered.

Paul Stillwell: Did you in fact get a letter of any sort from the CNO of a negative nature?

Admiral Wilson: The CNO sent me a very mollifying letter that said, in essence, "We know that you're a good guy and that you made a judgment this time that you might not make another time in view of what you have learned from this one and what you now know," and all sorts of other waffle words of that nature. In essence it said, "The guys that we sent out to look at you think you're guilty, but there are some other things that make it necessary for me not to do anything to you." The CNO himself didn't know what went on out there. Even after he got the report from the investigators, he never really knew personally. He's the boss and he doesn't have time to read a lot.

Paul Stillwell: Did the IG's report draw any conclusions?

Admiral Wilson: Yes, they drew conclusions that I ought to be investigated for racial discrimination. They thought I had used poor judgment in referring the facilitator to the psychiatrist. I didn't believe that, obviously. So I did what I did, and I thought with reasonable management rationale. But, rightly or wrongly, as the recipient of all of the attention by the IG, I was pretty much put off by it. I felt somewhat abused, and as though I was being used as a target. Of course, I didn't like that.

Paul Stillwell: With the benefit of hindsight, is there another approach you might have taken that would have been more constructive?

Admiral Wilson: Oh, probably. I like to think I've learned something in the last 20 years. Maybe there's a better approach that I could gin up now than then. But if I were to face the same circumstance tomorrow, other circumstances would be different too, so there's no going back.

In the Zumwalt era the chain of command was disrupted as well. Zumwalt was very fond of going out to a command and talking to the junior people. He did this at Oakland one time. He went out there and either some patient or some staff member, a very junior type person, made some adverse comment about the commander of the hospital, Rear Admiral Paul Mahin.* Paul Mahin was a good admiral, a good medical officer, a good commanding officer. But, by whatever route and mechanism, Zumwalt told the Surgeon General that Mahin should never have another command, and he never did while Zumwalt was CNO.

Zumwalt was fond of going out and doing that sort of thing, delving down into the organization to find somebody who had some bad words to say about the chain of command somewhere and then plucking out people for their alleged mismanagement, according to these lower ranking people. That did anything but endear him to the officer corps. At the same time, he had brought around himself a kitchen cabinet of people like

---

* Rear Admiral Harry Paul Mahin, MC, USN.

the Bagley brothers.* There were some others who hung on his method of management and his style. One of them was this IG who came out to Great Lakes, who incidentally retired and went into the Episcopal ministry.†

Paul Stillwell: There were both pluses and minuses to the Zumwalt approach. One plus is that sometimes there are legitimate gripes that don't surface by other mechanisms.

Admiral Wilson: No question about it. But you don't solve the problem by destroying the system that over time has proved to be a good one.

Paul Stillwell: One could argue that every gripe was regarded as legitimate. There wasn't an adequate filtering process.

Admiral Wilson: Yes, but to take the initial low-rank-level gripe and use it as the screened fact is hardly real in military service, or any other organization for that matter. The other thing that had happened during that period of time was that petty officers, particularly chief petty officers, lost their authority. Chiefs were no longer looked up to. They put everybody in a hat, as it were—the coat and dress necktie like chiefs wore.‡ The chiefs had a great deal of their stature that came from wearing "the hat" and a coat rather than a jumper.

Paul Stillwell: The other part of it was the perception that the chain of command had been seriously weakened.

Admiral Wilson: Yes, to the point that being a chief didn't mean much anymore to a lot of them. I didn't think that was right. When I took command of this hospital, I perceived that

---

* During the course of his tenure as CNO, Admiral Zumwalt promoted both David H. Bagley and his brother, Worth H. Bagley, to the rank of four-star admiral.
† In 1974 Rear Admiral Burton H. Shepherd, USN, was Acting Naval Inspector General. As a captain, he had been Admiral Zumwalt's executive assistant. In January 2000 he delivered the homily at Zumwalt's funeral.
‡ During Zumwalt's tenure, Navy enlisted personnel in pay grades E-1 through E-6 were put into uniforms quite similar to those traditionally worn by chief petty officers. In later years, the lower-rated personnel again returned to traditional sailor uniforms with jumpers, white hats, and bell-bottom trousers.

that was the case, so we started reorganizing the enlisted group. We assigned everyone a division officer. They had a division chief, and everybody in his work place had a leading petty officer, whether he was in their division or not. At least he had somebody he could refer to. We made it clear that their route to the command was up this chain of command. Moreover, that chain of command was not to impede a legitimate complaint; it was to solve the problem at the lowest possible level, and there was to be strict accountability. If you were second class petty officer, you had things that you were responsible for and you damn well did them, and that applied all along the line.

It was the same old system that had been around forever. We rejuvenated it, and people immediately felt better about it. It sold wonderfully well among the involved people, which was very heartening to me, because it reestablished people's stature in their own eyes, which is the best place to reestablish it. Our people began to feel more like a Navy; they began to feel better organized; they felt they had a better handle on what was going on about them. They were participating.

Petty officers had responsibilities as well as privileges because of their rank. A second and first class could indeed do things that a third class and an HN could not.[*] The perks went with the responsibility. We tried to reestablish some of that, and there's a piece in one of the U.S. Navy Medicine volumes about it. It was under the authorship of Master Chief Rogers. It would be in about 1974. That program worked out from the management point of view.

About this same time I had a personal near-miss by a series of lucky happenstance events. I was discovered to have an early cancer in one my kidneys. I had a biopsy done, and they told me that it was possibly malignant. So when they got it out, they sent it away, and it said probably malignant, possibly cancer. I was in the zone for flag selection, so I said to the pathologists, "Look, we've got to have an answer. If I've got a cancer that is life threatening, I've got to tell the SG, because he doesn't want any terminal guys on his flag candidate list." It was finally resolved that it was not malignant, but a pre-malignant lesion. So I went back home, breathing a sigh of relief.

Then I went on and I was selected for flag and frocked at Great Lakes in the summer of 1976. Admiral Arentzen at the time had been selected to be the Surgeon

---

[*] HN—hospitalman, an E-3 striking for hospital corpsman.

General.* He called me on the phone and asked me if I would be willing to come back to the bureau to be his Code 4, the logistics guy. I agreed to do that. Very shortly thereafter, we received orders back to BuMed, and that was the start of a whole new era in my career.

Before leaving the Great Lakes era in my career, I should point out some lessons that I learned there, particularly in relation to managing people and evaluating and dealing with recruits. First of all, the recruits came from all over the country, but a great many of them came from the Great Plains states: kids from Iowa, Nebraska, and other farm communities. A lot of them also came from the inner city of Chicago and other cities in the Midwest, so immediately there were two groups of people: those who were streetwise and in many cases from single-parent families, some of them on welfare, some of them gang members, some had been in the drug culture, a typical inner city cross-section in any modern-day city.

You place these inner-city kids up against a group of kids who had been out on the farm, who had been going to church ever since they were three years old, and probably hadn't been more than 200 or 300 miles away from home at the most. When you take those along with an intermediate group of young people from the middle class who had never been told "no" in their lives and probably never worn a pair of leather shoes, you immediately had a group that was disparate in backgrounds and with very different attitudes and experiences. Bringing them all together, of course, is the job of the Recruit Training Command, and I must say they did it very well.

The hospital ran a recruit evaluation unit, composed of a group of psychiatrists and psychologists who functioned at the Recruit Training Command to evaluate recruits and to weed out those who couldn't make it or wouldn't make it. The job of this group of psychiatrists and psychologists was to evaluate the recruits and see whether or not they had any emotional responses or psychological problems that would make it impossible for them to be trained as recruits. They did a pretty good job weeding out most of them. Some horrible things happened, such as recruits who would go out on their first liberty and hang themselves. We had a couple of such incidents while I was there. They were simply unable to cope with their new environment and took the only way out they knew.

---

* Vice Admiral Willard P. Arentzen, MC, USN, served as the Navy's Surgeon General from 1976 to 1980.

We had some other experiences along that line that went on farther through the system. The obvious reason for weeding out the psychologically unfit at the outset is not only for the individual's well-being but also for the Navy's well-being. There's no sense in spending time and money and effort trying to train people who are incapable or unwilling or for whatever reason not trainable. However, some of them slipped through, and we had some in the corpsman group who slipped through to us. These cases surfaced at mast, mostly.*

Mast is another issue, and it fits nicely with this recruit discussion because mast is a purely judgmental thing on the part of the commanding officer holding it. In an effort to be fair, you have to develop some kind of standard pattern of approach to the problems. I asked for observers in my mast meetings all the time. I insisted that the division officer, the leading petty officer, and the division petty officer be in attendance for any of their personnel who came to mast. I listened to their words about the qualities or lack thereof of the person who was at mast.

In addition, I asked the master chief petty officer of the command, and always a couple of his invited guests—usually petty officers, sometimes officers—from some totally unrelated department. I did this for the sake of trying to get across to the people that there was some element of thought being put into what was being done to or for the people brought to mast.

For example, if you have some youngster from one of the affluent societies who goes home on a weekend and doesn't come back until Monday afternoon because he went out with all his friends and got drunk over the weekend, that's quite different from the young black man from the inner city of Chicago who doesn't get back because his mother is ill, and he can't get somebody to take care of her until Monday. Unless you probe these people and find out these things, you tend to lump them all together and give them all the same kind of punishment.

I made it a point to sit down with all the attendees after the mast, especially if I had given different punishments for similar alleged violations. I sat down and gave them the

---

* Captain's mast is a sort of court in which the commanding officer of a unit listens to requests, awards non-judicial punishment, or issues commendations. Most often captain's mast is used for punishment of lesser offenses than those that merit courts-martial.

rationale for it, so that they could go out and spread the word among their people when the mast list comes out, it says, "Joe Doakes, AOL two hours and 30 minutes" and the next guy gets the same thing for three hours.* One guy gets restricted for two weeks, and the other guy gets a warning. What the hell's the difference, you know, 30 minutes? So we had to have some way of getting the word out to the crowd that they were being treated as fairly as we could on an individual basis.

Paul Stillwell: Did you also communicate the rationale to the offenders?

Admiral Wilson: Oh, indeed. For example, when we talked to a young black kid who had trouble with his mother being ill, we said to him, "Have you been able to get social workers to help? Does welfare help you? Can we do anything for you? Are you aware of the fact that you should call us and tell us that you are going to be late for a good reason? Then you don't appear at mast." Sure.

Then we had a group of people who came back to mast time after time after time, two, three, four, five times, always for the same offense—absent over leave or some other minor offense. It became apparent that there was something quite wrong with these people vis-à-vis the service, because they were not conforming to what was ordinary standard behavior.

I sent a few of them over for an outpatient consultation with the psychologist and the psychiatrist. It turned out that a good many of these people—these kids, 18, 19, 17 years old—were constitutionally incapable of dealing with the super-organized military institution. Not their fault. Their psyches were put together in such a form, demonstrable to the psychiatrists and psychologists, that they were flatly unable to live in the kind of society which the Navy represented.

We made representation of this to BuPers, and they allowed us to separate these people.† Again, there's no point in trying to beat somebody into doing something that they cannot do, not because they don't want to but because they are unable to. So these kinds of things are all reflections of the people coming through the recruit depot, that bespeaks

---

* AOL—absent over liberty.
† BuPers—Bureau of Naval Personnel.

the variances between people's backgrounds and their psychological developments, and their psychological capabilities. That was an interesting lesson learned.

In terms of the staff, Great Lakes unfortunately had been the repository of a group of medical officers who had geographic wishes that had been fulfilled for years. Some of the staff members had been there up to ten years. We tried to get this changed, mostly because in the military service one of the benefits is the transfer system. It brings new blood to the command and brings new ideas, and it prevents the command from getting stuck in the mud clinically and ideologically in terms of clinical matter, management, and people relations. We had a bit of a problem with that.

At the same time, we were being subjected to the general drawdown in the military occurring during the period of 1974 and 1976. We went from 275 total officers down to 60% of that number, over a period of two years.

We also were invaded, if you will, by the Chicago Medical School. The Chicago Med School had been in business quite a while. It was established in Chicago especially to provide a medical school opportunity for Jewish students who had suffered some kind of discriminatory exclusion from some med schools for some years past. This school was funded by some very wealthy Jewish people and an organization that supported the school. The board of trustees was a group of very smart, very diplomatic Jewish people. They had lost their hospital affiliation in Chicago and were looking for a clinical place in which to place their students for clinical work. They were very insistent and very aggressive about trying to get them into our hospital. We did allow them in eventually for outpatient services for their junior and senior students. We were not in a position to allow them to get involved with in-patients because of a variety of military/civilian interfaces and responsibility issues.

Paul Stillwell: Well, you'd have liability for what they did.

Admiral Wilson: Absolutely. At the same time we did start some sharing with the local Veterans Administration Hospital. For example, we had a cardiac catheterization capability but no cardiologist, and they had a cardiologist but no cardiac cath capability.

So we welded those two together and came up with a service that was of benefit to both hospitals.

Within the hospital I kept track of things largely by going out on the wards and holding weekly staff meetings. I had morning staff meetings with the chief nurse and the director of clinical services, and I kept in close touch with the comptroller. He gave me good financial computer printouts so that we knew where we were and where we were supposed to be financially and what our targets were. In general, it was a very reasonable experience, except for the fact that so many of the staff people had been there for so long that they had lost their orientation to the hospital and had gone out into the community, so that to get social functions to work in the hospital as a hospital social group was inordinately difficult and virtually impossible. My wife was very active in this effort, trying to get the groups together to have fun together. It was difficult because of this dilution and dispersion of interest into their civilian communities.

Paul Stillwell: You talked about the mental health of these recruits. What can you say in general about their physical health?

Admiral Wilson: That was a matter that was taken care of at the recruiting station. A few people got by with physical defects which we caught when they were in boot camp, and they were discharged if severe enough. By and large, they were screened by the AFEES, as they were called—Armed Forces Enlistment Examination Stations—and they caught most of the gross things.

Paul Stillwell: So for 18 year olds, you should have a pretty healthy population.

Admiral Wilson: Yes. When you talk about healthy, you talk about a couple of different things. You can talk about physical health, but there were a lot of drug users in those days. It's pretty hard for a habitual drug user to be healthy, and so that was a problem.

Paul Stillwell: And the Navy was much more tolerant then than it became later.

Admiral Wilson: Yes. Later it became, I think, a bar to enlistment if you'd been a drug user of any kind. Is that not so? I haven't been around the issue for quite some time.

Paul Stillwell: I don't know, but there was, as they put it, zero tolerance for use while in the Navy.*

Admiral Wilson: Yes. But that was a time when the drug problem was a very severe one, and the Navy was getting very strong in its antagonism and in its mechanisms and regulations to deal with it.

Paul Stillwell: Did you have any specific drug-treatment programs in your hospital?

Admiral Wilson: No. We had an alcohol rehab center but no drug rehab at the time.

Paul Stillwell: What were your methods of dealing with drug use?

Admiral Wilson: At the time I think we were discharging them. I don't recall specifically what administrative management we did. The Navy ran several drug rehab services, but I would have to refer you to someone else in the medical department who knows more about that than I. I'm sorry to have that void, but it's there.

Paul Stillwell: How did your program of alcohol treatment work?

Admiral Wilson: An alcohol rehab treatment center was established shortly after I left Great Lakes. It offered the standard treatment. There was a dry-them-out ward and an acute toxicity treatment area. They started rehab treatment with counselors, Alcoholics Anonymous, church orientation, general counseling and group therapy, medications, and the standard programs that everybody uses. It was apparently reasonably effective.

---

* The zero-tolerance policy was instituted during the tenure of Admiral Thomas B. Hayward, USN, as Chief of Naval Operations from 1978 to 1982.

Paul Stillwell: I interviewed one retired chief who had been through that program, and he said they had role-playing that was extremely effective, because it revealed that the source of his alcoholism was that his girlfriend's parents, 15 or 20 years before, had not allowed her to marry him, and alcohol was his compensatory mechanism.* Finally, knowing that, he was able to deal with it.

Admiral Wilson: Good. Well, it's hard to know why people drink. He was lucky to find out. Some people drink for social purposes, and it gets out of hand. Then they become addicted or at least habituated to alcohol. It varies from person to person. But they have been quite successful over the years now in helping people who have had the problem.

Paul Stillwell: Another issue, then, would be how did you go about administering this command? What ways did you have of monitoring the health of the hospital and its ability to do its job well?

Admiral Wilson: Basically, we kept an eye on it by going out in it. I went out on the wards as frequently as I could, and that meant at least two or three or four times a week. I'd go visit the wards, look and talk to the patients, nurses, the physicians, and see what the wards looked like. Of course, I always had access to such things as infection reports and accidental incidents, like if somebody got the wrong medication, if somebody put the wrong medication in the IV or gave somebody the wrong pill, which pointed up that we needed to have better supervision or more training or whatever was involved.

I kept in close touch with the service chiefs to know what their problems were, and if they were sensing any problems, or if they had problems that were out of hand in terms of the hospital's capacity to deal with them. For example, our cardiology people frequently had to send folks down to Chicago to have cardiac-bypass surgery done. We didn't have that capacity. We had other clinical problems that we had to send out.

I made those decisions based on information provided by and in consultation with the service chiefs. The services ran very well. There were differences between them, some better than others, but by and large, they were busy. The physicians for the most part

---

* See the Naval Institute oral history of Master Chief Boatswain's Mate Carl M. Brashear, USN (Ret.).

were well motivated. We had a few reservists who were problems, but that's true in any walk of life where you have people from a multiplicity of backgrounds. You always have one or two who don't conform to the standard that the others use.

We had no more specific problems with the staff than you would expect. So I left there with the idea that at least they weren't throwing me out when I left. I looked upon that as a success. [Laughter]

Paul Stillwell: You mentioned that you had some civilian employees. How did the administration of them differ from the military personnel?

Admiral Wilson: Many of the civilian employees had been there for years and years. As you know, there are two kinds of people around that area. There are the people whose ethnic origins go back to Scandinavia and Germany, and there are the people from the black community. The black community does the usual thing. They are the custodians, do the more menial jobs because they don't have the education. The other civil servants are the secretaries and the receptionists and the supervisors of various functions.

The nice thing about it is that the Northern European work ethic pertains in that area, or did when we were there, and people came to work. There was no such thing as unwarranted absenteeism. There were not people who were chronic complainers about having to work. People weren't closing up their desks and bringing out their purses at 3:30 in anticipation of a 4:30 shutdown. Our civilian nurse staff was very well trained and capable, worked hard, were reliable and well respected for their professional skills. We had a good group of people, and some of them, like the housekeeping superintendent, had been there for well over 20 years.

Paul Stillwell: You had civilian nurses because there weren't enough Navy nurses to staff it?

Admiral Wilson: Yes. It's common practice to have civilian nurses on dependent services, OB and GYN. It's not universally true, but where they are found, that's where they usually are—there and in some of the outpatient clinics. The military wards usually do not have civilian workers on them.

Paul Stillwell: The line officers that I have talked to discuss the satisfactions of command. How would you talk about the job of being in command?

Admiral Wilson: Well, having a command is a fine thing, because it is supposed to represent the culmination of a long and perhaps tedious if not serpentine course that you've taken over the period of your career. But I really never felt about it as being the zenith of my career in any sense of the word.

Doctors are strange people, and I know because I am one. They don't march to the same drummer that other people do. They are very independent, and they guard their independence very jealously. It's part of your lot in life to have to persuade them to do things. So your armamentarium is far less authoritarian than it is persuasive in its nature. To the extent that that's true, you deal with all levels of independence between and among them, particularly the older physicians. The younger ones are still malleable to some extent, but some of the older ones who have less to lose than others in their career benefits are tough to deal with. I didn't find it a particularly or overly enjoyable evolution. In fact, it was quite boring.

After you get to a command, you get a feel for how it functions, the dynamics of it, you identify the problems, identify the solutions and set the mechanisms in motion to solve those problems, what do you do then? Then you go back and do routine ordinary things. You make rounds on the wards every day, you talk to all the service chiefs, you go and look at the grounds, make sure they are all right, check with the maintenance men and see how we're coming on fixing the water coolers for the air-conditioning units, etc., etc. It becomes a massive repetitive detail that's really not very interesting and certainly not very intellectually challenging.

So, in summary, a command sort of has become a time-honored necessity if you are going on up in the medical department system in terms of rank for a medical officer. But, as I pointed out to you earlier, the care and feeding of medical offers is a complete pain in the ass. Pardon my profanity, but it's true.

Paul Stillwell: Do you have any examples of how you had to use this persuasion rather than being able to direct various activities?

Admiral Wilson: Oh, sure. I had a chief of medicine out there who had been there for about ten years, and we wanted to do something about changing the way some of the service was managed. This fellow had all kinds of complaints: "We've never done it that way before. We've done it this way forever, and it has worked fine. Why do you have to come in here and change things? This is my service, I don't see the need for it, and my people don't agree with you, and some of them do, but most of them don't."

At that point, you say to him, "Well, doctor, we all have to make a little progress some time. I don't think this is going to hurt you. I urge you to try it for a while, and if it doesn't work, then we can talk about it some more. But for the moment, let's go ahead and make this change in the hope that it's going to be a better way to do things." That's the kind of approach that I used, and most of the time it worked. At least I didn't have any mutinies.

Paul Stillwell: What do you remember about living at Great Lakes? That's certainly different from the usual seacoast environment that the Navy is in.

Admiral Wilson: Yes. We lived in a huge set of quarters. It was 6,000-square-feet house with seven bedrooms. It had four baths on the second floor alone, and a huge living room which we always referred to as the Holiday Inn. That living room was probably 20 feet wide and a minimum of 50 feet long. We had four divans in it, and we had room to walk around all behind them, and leave a dance floor-sized space in the middle. It was huge. It was a lovely old house in a way. It was a brick house, built in 1906 at a cost of $25,000.

Paul Stillwell: Big money back then.

Admiral Wilson: Yes, indeed. It was originally heated by steam from a central steam plant quite a ways away on the main part of the base. But that system failed, so they put in an independent heating system. It was a nice house, but at the time I went there as a captain, they had discontinued stewards for commanding officers, so we had to maintain this great big house that was really a showplace for the command. We had a cleaning lady who came in every week, and she could do one floor one week, and one floor the next week. So it was a bit of a challenge on that score.

We had an open house for the staff on two Sunday afternoons. We had 250 invitations that went out for each Sunday, and we programmed people in by the hour: 2:00 to 3:00, 3:00 to 4:00, 4:00 to 5:00. Unfortunately, the guests didn't watch the clock very well, because pretty soon we had a whole house full. The house could accommodate about 125 to 150 people without bulging at the seams, but I can tell you from experience the liquor bills were tremendous. We did this two weekends in a row, to accommodate the entire staff. But it was an experience, and I like to think it brought the staff a little closer together. Whether or not that's true is anybody's guess.

Paul Stillwell: That North Shore area has some very fancy posh communities. Did you get involved with the civilian community at all?

Admiral Wilson: We got involved with the Navy League. The Navy League was very supportive of the base, and we were invited by the Navy League to a number of their functions. In fact, the Navy League gave a farewell party for Admiral O'Neil and for me when we left, which was very nice of them. The Midwesterners are great patriots. There's more patriotism in Midwesterners than most people realize. For some reason or other, they are great supporters of the Navy. I think more sailors come out of the Midwest than come out of any other area in the country. It's surprising, but true.

Other than that, we used to go to Chicago once in a while. All the commanding officers would be invited to some kind of a luncheon sponsored by somebody, and we'd sit down there with community figures. At that time, Big Jim Thompson, who shortly became Governor of Illinois, was prosecuting attorney of Chicago.[*] I sat next to him and I really didn't know who he was, so as a matter of conversation, I said, "What do you do for a living?"

---

[*] James R. Thompson, Jr., served as Governor of Illinois from 1977 to 1991.

He introduced himself to me by saying, "I put people in jail."

I said, "Oh, you're that Jim Thompson." [Laughter]

Very nice man. Very nice community. Very supportive. Chicago is a great town for the military. They very much enjoy having the military around, and so the interface between the base and community was very smooth.

Paul Stillwell: Anything else on Great Lakes?

Admiral Wilson: I don't think so. We left there, came back to Washington, had to find a house, which is always an interesting proposition but we managed. Then went on to the next thing, which was the bureau again.

Paul Stillwell: What did your duties entail for Admiral Arentzen?

Admiral Wilson: Well, the names were changing while I was away. I became the Assistant Chief of the Bureau of Medicine and Surgery for Material Resources. That really entailed a whole group of functions, including the old jobs I had had here before, logistics and planning. This job also included the budget. The people who formulated and executed the budget were under the aegis of my office. I think I have alluded in the past to the fact that certain of the areas of the bureau became little enclaves, including the office of the comptroller, and this continued while I was there.

Paul Stillwell: Did you have to take a quick course in PPBS?

Admiral Wilson: No, I didn't have to do that. I had been sent to what was laughingly referred to as the charm school up at Newport, or the knife-and-fork school. It's a two-week indoctrination course for new flag officers. Unfortunately, they don't have it anymore. It was very enlightening. It had to do with organizational management, and was really a most intensive course in management given by some of the country's best authorities on the subject. On a standard day, you went to class having read a book by the lecturer. He spent the morning going through the book, pointing out the highlights and making the book really come alive for you. In the afternoon we used the principles of the book in some sort of practical applications to demonstrate the effectiveness and the utilization of the techniques. It was described as being a "mind-bender," and the content of the material was so great in quantity, and the pace of its exposition and our supposed assimilation was so concentrated that it really was extremely fatiguing. However, it was most stimulating.

So most of us went to that as a management school. The rest of management capability came from experience and the seat of the pants. During the next four years, BuMed would develop some management opportunities for people, and that was one of the good things they did.

As indicated, I was invited back here to BuMed by Admiral Arentzen to be his material resource manager. It was quite immediately apparent that his management style was different from his predecessor's. Admiral Arentzen was a small man in stature. He had had a couple of hospital commands, had been interested in a wide variety of subjects, including military construction and design, as well as hospital operations. He was not well oriented to fleet and field operations. I felt—as I got to know him more, and never changed my mind—that he knew very little about the Navy as an organization. He had really no feel for the organization of the fighting forces of the Navy and had only a fair concept of the interface with the medical department and the line.

Paul Stillwell: Would parochial be a fair term?

Admiral Wilson: Parochial is fine. I think perhaps unenlightened might be used too—unfortunately but truly. It immediately became apparent that several things were going to pertain to his tenure as the Surgeon General. First of all, he brought with him some people from his last command in San Diego, especially Jim Quinn, who was a captain who had been with him not only in San Diego but also in Portsmouth, Virginia.* They were very close to one another. Jim Quinn made it a point to be in the Surgeon General's office at 6:00 o'clock every morning, and the Surgeon General was there. There were several more people who met every morning.

---

* Captain James J. Quinn, MC, USN.

Paul Stillwell: Was Quinn the executive assistant?

Admiral Wilson: Well, originally, he was a part of the code that I ran, but he didn't stay there long because I asked him not to see the Surgeon General unless I knew about it. That's the way the chain of command works, and I couldn't possibly think of anything that he had to discuss with him that we had discussed. Jim Quinn allowed as how he only had one loyalty at a time, and it certainly wasn't to me. I allowed as how that wasn't how I worked. Shortly thereafter he was transferred to the SG's personal staff as some sort of special assistant.

This kitchen cabinet kind of operation not only started but grew over time. He developed a very close-to-the-vest kind of management system and really used his close associates, some of whom were very junior, like one of the members was a lieutenant, Medical Service Corps, whose background is still kind of a mystery to me. I don't know where he came from or where he went, and I wasn't very impressed with what he exhibited to me as talent, but he was one of the favored few of the Surgeon General.

Paul Stillwell: Quinn was one of those who came to grief over the Billig affair.[*]

Admiral Wilson: Eventually, yes. It was very quickly apparent that Admiral Arentzen was going to be a micro-manager. He immediately took unto his bosom a whole host of small items that had been delegated forever.

For example, flag officers could not sign temporary additional duty orders. They all had to go through the Surgeon General's office. There were other little things like that that he took over completely. He fancied himself a great designer of facilities, and he involved himself in the design of new hospitals and clinics all the time. I've alluded to that in past sessions of interview.

He also fancied himself to be the world's expert on hospital beds. He fancied that he knew more about the various designs and efficiencies and desirabilities and properties

---

[*] Commander Donal M. Billig, MC, USN, was found guilty by a military court-martial in February 1986 of involuntary manslaughter in the deaths of two patients and negligent homicide in the death of another.

of hospital beds than anyone you ever knew. He proceeded to take two of us down to Atlanta one time to show us the difference between several kinds of hospital beds and help us select office furniture for the commanding officers' offices in the hospital. This kind of stuff was really irritating, because duties are delegated to people who are in the business. We had architects and people from NavFac who knew interior design work, who were used to doing that.* A medical installation executive office is no different from any other kind of executive office. It's a desk and a chair and a file cabinet and a telephone, and whatever else is the personal desire of the occupant. But he involved himself in all these decisions.

He took an overwhelming interest in the detailing of people. He personally had to approve virtually every assignment, particularly for medical officers. Some careers were somewhat bent out of shape by his antagonism. Some of them had a personal bias to them, and he so curtailed the authority and the stature of the head of the MSC that a couple of them quit. They were just roundly and soundly disgusted and said they quit. If you want to enlarge on that scene, you should talk to Captain Al Schwab who lives in San Diego now.† The other one was Captain Bill Green.‡ Both of them were heads of the Medical Service Corps, and both of them got out somewhat before they would have otherwise because of the climate.

Some of the flag officers were treated with disdain. Some flag officers were sort of roundly and soundly ignored. They came to work, sat in their offices, did their thing, whatever it was. But their work never surfaced, and it was never asked about. Any major decisions that were made in relationship to it were probably done in the front office, and so their contributions were sort of thrown aside, if you will.

All this time we were trying to our thing to get into the PPBS system, into the Planning, Programming, Budgeting System. It was very uphill work because the SG apparently didn't understand it. He didn't want to bend the BuMed system of doing things to the point where it could conform to the PPBS requirements. We had a Medical Service Corps officer over in OP-96, CNO's analysis shop at the time. They were responsible for analyzing program submissions to see if they were conforming with the PPBS system, and

---

* NavFac—Naval Facilities Engineering Command.
† Captain Albert J. Schwab, MSC, USN (Ret.).
‡ Captain William J. Green, MSC, USN (Ret.).

we were not. This Medical Service Corps officer came back and told the SG, and the SG accused him of being disloyal and trying to disrupt the way we did business. He damn near sank that officer in terms of promotion. Later on, I spent a lot of effort protecting that officer from the SG, simply because he was being so unfair to him at a place and time when the man was trying to help. It was a sad commentary that this was happening.

Paul Stillwell: Did Admiral Arentzen have any redeeming qualities to go along with all those you have enumerated.

Admiral Wilson: Oh yes, he did. He was very much interested in improving the quality of the talents of our Medical Service Corps officers in fiscal and supply matters, and established a fiscal and supply course at the School of Health Sciences to fulfill that need.

He also started a sort of mini-war college. He brought in officers who were interested and gave them a better perspective of the Navy and the medical department and how things work and how we plan to do things. It's called SMRRC, Senior Medical Readiness Review Course. It has been in existence quite a long time now, and it's very well thought of. There are two levels of the executive-type training available, one for the junior people, and one for the more senior folks. Will Arentzen instituted those. He was aware of the need to broaden the base of medical officer and MSC knowledge in support of the department.

As time has passed, fiscal and supply matters have become more complex as the computer has come into being, so fiscal responsibility and almost instant response to fiscal inquiry is necessary. We didn't have enough fiscal and supply officers, so we just made a school for them and it's worked well—to his great credit, no doubt about it. That was a good legacy that he left.

He also was supportive of an activity to set up what we came to call the C^4 course, which is the combat casualty care course in concert with the other services, and which was carried out down in Fort Sam Houston under the aegis of the Army's Health Command System. At any rate, he was very supportive of that effort and helped make it work. So he did have some very redeeming features which were effective at the time, but his unfortunate management style detracted greatly from his popularity and effectiveness.

About this time, 1976, the fleet hospital issue came up. There'd been a series of two studies, one of which was a Navy review study of its own about medical support, and the other one was conducted by a combination of people: OSD, GAO, and OMB. All the conclusions were the same. Nobody had enough medical assets to support the committed combat forces. The services were essentially told to go home and get busy and do something about it.

Having been in Vietnam—and I've told you the story about how bad things were there and how I was determined that it shouldn't happen again—we started the fleet hospital program. It was a very long and tortuous route. Fortunately, we were able to start off with the right kind of people.

Paul Stillwell: Was your war college background helpful as you approached this problem?

Admiral Wilson: Absolutely. It helped a great deal.

Paul Stillwell: Please tell me about the fleet hospital program.

Admiral Wilson: I think we mentioned that the various parts of DoD and other portions of the government had studied the requirements for medical support and found them to be inadequate among all the services. When I arrived here, I more or less assumed the responsibility for doing something about it. The question became what to do about it, so I sat down with some of my people to discuss the matter.

One of those people was Commander Ron Turco, who was my executive assistant.[*] He had had some field experience with the Marines. Also, there was a lieutenant in CEC named Tom Gibb, who was assigned to our facilities division.[†] He had done some work down at Camp Lejeune on putting van bodies on military trucks, Marine trucks, and equipping those vans as operating rooms, dental clinics, and such for field deployment and use.[‡] They had been modestly successful. The question came as to what kind of a hospital

---

[*] Lieutenant Commander Ronald F. Turco, MSC, USN.
[†] Lieutenant Thomas W. Gibb, Jr., CEC, USNR.
[‡] Camp Lejeune, in North Carolina, is the largest Marine Corps base on the East Coast. It is the home of the Second Marine Division.

did we want to design, how could we justify it, what size should it be, what form should it take?

Fortunately, a whole series of related events occurred almost simultaneously. A commander named Bob White, a Medical Service Corps officer, was the first Navy medical department person to delve into the use of computers in the medical department.[*] He had built a computer model called MedCon I, which was a computer program designed to predict casualty generation as a result of conflict. It had such inputs as the committed forces by number, the intensity of the conflict, the nature of the enemy and its size, etc. Out of this came numbers that were supposed to equate with the daily numbers of casualties and the accumulated numbers of casualties. From that, we hoped, one could determine the number of beds required to take care of the casualties.

In middle or late 1976, we began working with a man named Vance Gordon, who at the time was a lieutenant and was from the Naval School of Health Sciences, NSHS.[†] He had succeeded Bob White in his role of computer model maker. He proceeded to improve and expand the capacities of the medical contingency model, casualty predictor, into what has since become known as MedCon II as a program name. Shortly thereafter, some other people showed up on the scene, more or less out of the blue. In mid-1977 Captain Lou Eske reported for duty at BuMed and became the medical contingency planning officer. He was a very bright man.

Paul Stillwell: You previously mentioned Captain Eske's achievements on Admiral Kidd's staff.

Admiral Wilson: Right. He's the same one. He worked with a commander named Bill Hirschfeld, who was a dentist, who had had some experience teaching dental officers out at the Navy Dental School at Bethesda.[‡] He had been teaching them operational dentistry, operational in the sense of field operations, both afloat and ashore. A man named Bill Dial

---

[*] Commander Robert L. White, MSC, USN.
[†] Lieutenant Charles Vance Gordon, Jr., MSC, USN. Wilson had met his father during the course of a tour of duty in the Far East in the early 1950s. See interview #1.
[‡] Commander William E. Hirschfeld, DC, USN.

came to us with an interest in planning and there were one or two others who came on the scene later, but these men formed the crux of a planning group.*

It just so happened that I had an interest in planning as well and had assumed the responsibility for putting together this approach to solving the lack of medical facilities for the Navy. We sat down together, sometimes in ones and twos, and started to think about what the fleet hospital should look like. We didn't even call it fleet hospital in the original version. It was called Navy mobile hospital or something of that sort.

Anyway, we decided that several things pertained. First of all, we had to have a hospital that could be moved. It didn't have to be mobile in the sense of having wheels, but it needed to be relocatable. It needed to be sophisticated enough to provide the necessary services to the wounded and the ill as close to the front as could be logically assumed. Fourthly, it should incorporate equipments that were off the shelf for a couple of reasons. First, so-called "hardened" equipments for the military are very expensive, and many hardened versions of equipments that were necessary were obsolete or not in existence. In view of the technology available in the packaging industry, we felt that we could quite likely take off-the-shelf medical devices, pack them appropriately, and expect them to survive transport into the field in a functional state.

This concept had the added advantage of the fact that the people who would be using them would be familiar with them. They would have been tried and tested and known to be effective. The people would know how to interpret the results that came from them. The spare parts would be in the commercial inventory, and our biomedical technicians could repair them.

There's a very long and complex road that has to be traversed to get from an idea to a facility in being. Among the first things that had to happen is you have to demonstrate the need. Through the efforts of Vance Gordon we were able to identify the casualty numbers through the use of the computer model, MedCon II. The Navy was a little bit loath to believe it, so the program was submitted to OP-96, the Chief Naval Operations Analysis Group, for validation. They farmed it out to a contractor, and the contractor did, indeed, validate the computer program that was being used to produce the numbers.

---

* Lieutenant William S. Dial, MSC, USN.

Then we ran into the Department of Defense nay-sayers, who wanted to take the program and look at it. We handed it over to them. They massaged it, analyzed it, and came back and said they agreed with it 100%. They recommended to the powers that be that it become the standard DoD casualty-estimating program.

In the meantime, to make this project work, a paper known as the Navy Development Concept Paper, NDCP, had to be generated. It's a piece of paper that says, "Here's the problem; here's what we intend doing about it; this is the concept; this is how we plan to lay it out and prosecute the idea." We hired that done. It was done very ably by a corporation called ALM. It was a well done piece of work and it served us well.

In the meantime, we had garnered support from other people. An engineer from NavFac, Commander Ray Smith, had begun to put together some ideas about what sort of buildings we should use.[*] The question was: how can we provide a better environment in which to treat patients?

Slowly but surely, out of all these ruminations, meetings, and discussions came a little mnemonic which turned out to be TTEE, standing for Time, Talent, Equipment, and Environment. Time meaning enough hospitals to allow the doctors time enough to treat the casualties. Talent meaning the training among the physicians to do the job properly. Equipment was the equipment to be provided to the talented and trained people so they could do their jobs. The Environment meant not only a place that was reasonably safe from being blown up, but also meant a place that was either sufficiently heated or adequately cooled to be workable as an environment and one that hopefully minimized external contamination, like dust and dirt from the surrounding atmosphere.

Using these basic tenets, we started to think about structures and how to acquire and test them. In the course of working on this project, it obviously became necessary to find someone in the Navy world to promote and support the program financially. The sponsor for medical support was the Deputy Chief of Naval Operations for Logistics, OP-04. In that organization there is a code OP-41, the functions of which are designed to provide logistics in fuel, ammunition, and medical support. It was always a flag billet, but

---

[*] Commander Ray A. Smith, CEC, USN.

when we were commencing this program it was filled by a brilliant Supply Corps captain named Andy Giordano.*

When we briefed him on the subject, he was very much in favor of it. Some money had been put in the OP-41 support program as a starter package. This action was taken when we first thought of the program and simply to get the program name up in front of the programmers, knowing full well that it would probably not be funded. Somewhere in the program, Lloyd Gray, a civil servant comptroller-type working for Captain Giordano in OP-41, managed to sequester $2 million. He did this for a couple of reasons. First of all, he and I had a great rapport. I had taken great pains to brief him in detail about what this program was all about. If I recall correctly, he had been in the Marine Corps in World War II.

The upshot of the whole thing was that lurking there in the background, unexpended and available, were two millions of dollars. We needed those dollars to develop the program, so we put together a presentation for a CEB, CNO's Executive Board. We presented the program to Admiral Bob Long, who was VCNO at the time, sitting in for CNO.† We told him what it was all about, told him there were $2 million in the pot, and asked his permission to use those $2 million for further planning, procurement, and testing. He agreed to that.

About this time, in conversation with Captain Giordano, we were advised that what we were considering entailed a very large logistics support requirement. He said we needed to address the logistics problems early, so we could identify the requirements and determine how the logistics side of the problem could be solved. He offered to send us a tiger team. A tiger team had no meaning to me at the time, but it turned out to be a group of three officers who were very experienced in logistic support matters. They came to the bureau and briefed us on all of the difficulties that we would see down the road. They were unequivocally correct in every single solitary thing they said. We did encounter all of

---

* Captain Andrew A. Giordano, SC, USN. Giordano later became at rear admiral and served as Commander Naval Supply Systems Command and Chief of the Supply Corps from June 1981 until his retirement in June 1984.
† Admiral Robert L. J. Long, USN, served as Vice Chief of Naval Operations from July 1977 to September 1979. His oral history is in the Naval Institute collection.

the pitfalls that they had mentioned, but, in the meantime, we took their advice to heart and included in the program mechanisms to deal with all of those logistics requirements.

Designing an installation is one thing; getting it is another. We felt the need to have a portion of the fleet hospital program oriented to the acquisition of the actual hospitals once we had them programmed, designed, and funded. To that end we established at Port Hueneme a Fleet Hospital Support Office. This was about 1979. We had enlisted the services of the Naval Facilities Engineering Command, Civil Engineer Support Office at Port Hueneme, California. On one of our visits out there, it was recommended to me by the commanding officer at Port Hueneme that we listen to the advice of a man who had a great logistics background who might be of assistance to us in getting on with the fleet hospital project. His name was Captain Lawrence D. Hagedorn, Supply Corps, USN. He had been at Hueneme for some time, had been the logistician supporting the buildup of Diego Garcia, and was a very experienced officer.[*]

He came to our meeting, learned about the program, understood it, and shortly thereafter I asked him if he would be interested in joining the program. He said, "Yes, I would, but I am retiring."

I said, "Let me take care of that part if you want to stay."

He said, "I do, I'd be glad to work on it."

So I went to BuPers, and they were able to retire and retain him for assignment to us. I also went to the head of the Supply Corps, a man named Gene Grinstead.[†] He was a crusty old soul. When I walked into his office, he said, "What in the hell do you want?"

I said, "Not much. I just want one of your captains and his billet." This was at a time when billets and captains were in very short supply.

At any rate, I explained to him why I wanted him and what utilization we expected to make of him. When I walked out, I had his concurrence in providing both. It turned out that Captain Hagedorn was more than we anticipated. He turned into one of the principal

---

[*] Diego Garcia is an atoll about 1,000 miles south of India; it was formerly British territory. In the 1970s the U.S. Navy made a significant investment in facilities there to support ships operating in the Indian Ocean. See Kirby Harrison, "Diego Garcia: the Seabees at Work," U.S. Naval Institute Proceedings, August 1979, pages 53-61.
[†] Rear Admiral Eugene A. Grinstead, Jr., SC, USN, who was Chief of the Supply Corps prior to Rear Admiral Giordano.

supporters of the program in the early phases when it was in severe jeopardy. Without him the project would quite likely have failed.

Paul Stillwell: Did he head up this new office you established?

Admiral Wilson: He became the officer in charge of the Fleet Hospital Support Office at Port Hueneme, and he immediately started building a plan for the logistic support of the hospital. He began an acquisition plan. We had decided that we would like to take some panelized structures, quite like the structures used to build prefabricated houses, partitions complete with electrical and plumbing fittings and use those as the "building blocks" for the hospitals. We went to the panelized housing industry, purchased a large number of these panels, partitions, and took them out to Twenty-Nine Palms to test them in the desert.[*] Again, Captain Hagedorn engineered this entire operation. He purchased the pieces and parts, arranged the trucking, arranged the Seabee support to prepare the site, all the logistic support necessary to conduct a test in the field. The fleet hospital project office group wrote a protocol for evaluating the effectiveness of the installation in the field.

We did the summer testing, the hot-weather testing, in Twenty-Nine Palms in the summer of 1980. Shortly thereafter, during the winter, we took the hospital to Pickel Meadows, which is a cold-weather training site for Marines near Bridgeport, California.[†] It is way up in the Sierras, where the weather is cold and snowy. We tested our concept out there, and we learned a number of things.

Among the structures we had with us was an ISO container, an International Shipping Organization container configured as a galley. Actually, it didn't belong to us; it belonged to the Navy, but it was there. We had brought along an ISO container that we were interested in that expanded on both sides. It had nothing inside; it was simply a box, but it was expandable, and we brought it along as a prototype to examine. We learned a number of things. First of all, we learned that it was very cumbersome to install prefabricated house panels and make them suitably square and strong and leak-proof.

---

[*] Twenty-Nine Palms, California, is the site of a Marine Corps Air-Ground Combat Center.
[†] Pickel Meadows is the site of the Marine Corps Mountain Warfare Training Center. Pickel was an early settler in the region.

Leaks in the roof were a constant problem. We also learned that they did not go up and come down and go back up again without considerable mortality in their structural integrity. Therefore, we determined right then and there that those panel structures were not appropriate for the hospitals.

We went back to the drawing board, seized upon a group of ISO container models that expanded either one or both sides, which were fully capable of storing the equipments and part of the supplies for a variety of functions. For example, we could put an entire operating room in one box, and in a matter of 30 to 40 minutes, spot the box, open it up, and start unloading or unpackaging the supplies inside, and in a few hours have a completely equipped and functioning operating room. The same thing was true for a central sterile supply room, for laboratory, pharmacy, X-ray, etc.—the critical elements.

At the same time, we went into consultation with the Army laboratory at Natick, Massachusetts, where they were developing a new tent made out of improved materials, of different design that had an insulated lining and was capable of being heated or air-conditioned. In consultation with them, we were able to change the dimensions of this hospital tent slightly, so that it would accept hospital cots at right angles to the walls and leave us sufficiently wide aisles between beds to accommodate patient traffic. These became known as temper tents. They were temper because they were temporary mobile personnel.

But they were good tents in the sense that they were made out of fabric which didn't mold. We put flies over them; that's an extra canvas rigged several inches above the tent; they could reduce the temperatures inside by as much as 10 degrees. The tents used fiberglass frames that offered stability to the tent itself but caused no obstruction in the middle of the tent as tent poles had in the past. There was an insulated fabric pad that went down on the ground to be a floor, if you will. Lighting was provided by the same sort of fixtures that had been used in the Army MUST units.[*] We found some heat pumps capable of providing heat or cool air, and these were hooked up to the temper tents and provided very adequate air-conditioning, both heat and cooling, for these tents.

---

[*] MUST units were inflatable tents designed, used, and ultimately discarded by the Army after having been unsuccessfully tried in Vietnam.

With the advent of the ISO containers and the temper tents we were in pretty good shape. It wasn't until 1981 that we established a Fleet Hospital Project Office. In the meantime, all these efforts had been going on as part-time activities of the participants and largely free labor, except for the things that Captain Hagedorn did in developing logistics plans and fielding the trial units at Twenty-Nine Palms and at Bridgeport.

Paul Stillwell: You could go through $2 million pretty quickly. Did you get supplemental funding?

Admiral Wilson: Not difficult at all to spend $2 million. Somehow or other, we were able to muddle through with that amount. We had additional problems. The ABFC system is the Advanced Base Functional Component system in the Navy. It consists of a listing of facilities that are supposed to be available in storage to be deployed when there is a contingency and a need for these facilities is recognized. In the inventory there were dispensaries, galleys, commissaries, mess halls, hangars, motor pool facilities—all kinds of facilities needed in an advance base. The components were all distributed to various storage sites by their Supply Corps classification. Motor vehicles are one class, structural materials in another class, fuel in another class, barracks and the equipment for it are in another class, etc. These classes might be stored in completely separate places, so when you wanted one of these facilities and called it up out of inventory, it would have to be assembled from all these various depots.

Not only that, different commands having the requirement for the same kind of facility might compete for that facility and finally not get one, because things were double counted. Command A had a requirement for 100 trucks and so did Command B, but at the truck depot there were only 100 trucks, and both of them were counting the trucks as theirs. So there were glitches in the system. The worst problem we saw in the ABFC system for the fleet hospitals was this vast dispersion of pieces and parts all over the country. We felt that since the strategic thinking dealt with a come-as-you-are war, we needed to be able to pick up a hospital in one piece, transport it somewhere, set it down, and make it go without having to go all over the country to get the components.

Through the efforts of a Bob Soluri, a civil servant at NavFac, we were able to get an exemption from the ABFC system that permitted us to retain all the parts and pieces in one place. They were duly listed in the ADFC catalogue as being what they are, hospitals of 250, 550, and 1,000 beds.

Paul Stillwell: Did you settle on Port Hueneme as a storage site?

Admiral Wilson: We did not. As time passed, we felt the need for a space in which to receive and assimilate the materials making up the fleet hospital. Port Hueneme did not have such space. They did have the space at Alameda. We were able to acquire six huge warehouses and some other space, so we moved the Fleet Hospital Support Office from Port Hueneme to Alameda, and it's been there since about 1980 or 1981.

Paul Stillwell: Was there a point at which you went from the testing phase to the actual operation of it?

Admiral Wilson: Testing and operation were not very close together. The testing showed us that we were on the wrong track. The availability of the ISO containers led us to believe that there was more opportunity in their utilization and in the temper tents than we could ever hope to find in manufactured panels.

About this time the design efforts became bogged down. The Civil Engineer Support Office could no longer afford the people and the time to do our design work, so we had to go to an outside architectural engineering firm. We were able to get some money to hire an A&E, and we got the Ehrenkrantz Group from New York City. They provided us with two gentlemen who turned out to be absolutely sterling performers. They took the information we gave them in briefings and massaged it. They looked at what we had done, were constructively critical, and came back with an alternative that was really marvelous to see.

The final design was a hospital consisting of a combination of ISO containers, temper tents, and of ordinary run-of-the-mill general-purpose tents. The hospitals had their own power systems, their own power generators and distribution systems, a water distribution system, and a sewage collection system.

On the staff were Seabees who would clear the site and do some of the early utility and facility installations to get the hospitals up and running. The rest of the hospital staff were mostly medical people with some scattering of communicators, yeomen, storekeepers, and other rates as appropriate to the functions that were involved.

Up to this point, it had all been hard work and hard fought. We faced a great deal of adversity from a variety of sources. First of all, the Surgeon General was not very receptive to the idea. He developed a personal antagonism to me for whatever reason and took the program away from me for a year—mid-1979 to mid-1980. It was restored when Admiral Cox became Surgeon General.* By then the program had grown and progressed and was really on track. Will Arentzen forbade me to have anything to do with the fleet hospital program during this year that he gave it to Admiral Lowery.† Admiral Lowery did not believe in the program, he did not think it would work, he did not think it was possible to procure it, and he rather artfully neglected it without completely neglecting it.

To Captain Hagedorn's great good credit, he kept the program going by continuing his efforts to develop a logistics base and an acquisition plan. He and I conferred sub rosa during this entire time so that in essence I continued to have the managerial authority for the program, even though only two people knew it. [Laughter]

Eventually, in 1981, the Fleet Hospital Project Office came into being. Admiral Cox provided a billet, and I went to that job as the project officer. I stayed there for approximately 18 months, until we completed most of the hard-fought part of the program. The difficulties in getting the program off dead center were multiple, but many of them were political. We spent lots of hours on many days over in the halls of the Senate and congressional office buildings, sitting in waiting rooms, trying to convince staffers and members of Congress to support the fleet hospital program because it met a national requirement.

In the meantime, as a matter of management technique, we elected to put the program through the most rigorous paces the acquisition system demanded. There is a

---

* Vice Admiral J. William Cox, MC, USN, served as the Navy's Surgeon General from 1980 to 1983.
† Rear Admiral Clinton H. Lowery, MC, USN.

series of acquisition categories for projects that are being purchased by the federal government, and we elected to put the fleet hospital program into the category that was most rigorous in terms of the review processes required of the program. There were processes such as the Acquisition Review Board meetings, the Logistics Review Board meetings, that dealt with acquisitions activities and logistic support systems development.

The Logistics Review Board and the Acquisition Review Board members were mostly flag officers and senior captains in the Navy Material Command, in which the Fleet Hospital Project Office was a resident activity.

Paul Stillwell: Were these primarily line officers?

Admiral Wilson: Primarily line officers, some Supply Corps officers. Eventually the fleet hospital project came under the chief of the Supply Systems Command, and of course we were under constant scrutiny there for the acquisition process.

One of the good things that happened to us was in a publication that's put out for the internal consumption of the supply department there. The authors write about such things as management problems and solutions. They discuss acquisition strategies and pitfalls. One little note in the paper spoke of the fleet hospital as having assumed a position in acquisition category II. This article said the program fulfilled its requirements and stated it had become one of the best managed projects in the system. That was kind of a morale boost for us. It gave us heart that we had done the right thing to go through all the hard wickets. The worst thing that can happen to you is to get near the end of a project and have someone in a position to influence things say, "Ah, you failed to go through this wicket. Therefore your project is null and void, can't be funded." You can be kicked out the window, off the shelf or wherever.

Paul Stillwell: Did you have to go through the same kind of wickets that weapon systems did in DSARC?*

---

* DSARC—Defense Systems Acquisitions Review Council.

Admiral Wilson: We did not have to go through DSARC, because the price tag was under one billion dollars. That was the only threshold that we didn't meet. Frankly, I would have had no compunctions about going to a DSARC, because I felt that our requirement and our approach to acquisition were golden. I would have been able to defend it anywhere along the line.

Paul Stillwell: Did the program suffer any setbacks from that year when you had to do it sub rosa?

Admiral Wilson: No, not really. I have no way of knowing whether it progressed any more slowly than it would have had I been more available, but I don't think it did. I don't think it slowed down a bit. Don Hagedorn really kept it moving, and there was no other place for it to move except in his department at that time, so I don't think we lost any time.

Paul Stillwell: Are there any milestones you might cite in this long process it went through?

Admiral Wilson: Oh, yes. There were some very significant milestones. I alluded to one where we got the planning money from CNO. Secondly, where we acquired Don Hagedorn to run the support office and get the logistics underpinning organized. Another was when we finally got a project office together and could get a full-time staff together to make things happen. Another was to move the support office to Alameda and get space for assembly.

Paul Stillwell: The decision also to settle on a tent as your basic unit was a milestone.

Admiral Wilson: Yes, there were a lot of design milestones that we could go on about for hours. What kind of electrical fittings should we have? Should they fit with the Army or should they fit with European standards, or how should they fit with both? What size diesel generators should we have? Where should they be? What kind of waste disposal system should be used? The decisions in the design world are multitudinous, and we went through all these wickets and all these gyrations. That was what the project office was all about, to make those decisions after analysis.

So it worked. By 1980, when Admiral Arentzen left and the antagonism to the program evaporated, it was a lot easier because the project had come along quite nicely. We had passed some of the milestones. We had achieved a degree of certainty and stability and security that the project was going to fly, so we could all be a little more comfortable about working at it.

One of the things that's very difficult to do is to recruit people to an unknown. You can identify people around you whom you would love to have working in the project, but if you can't provide them with the assurance that working on the project is a career-enhancing step, it's difficult to get them to volunteer if they're not convinced in their own minds that this is a worthwhile project. They don't want to work on a loser, so it's difficult.

Paul Stillwell: That's understandable.

Admiral Wilson: Yes, it is, very understandable. I recruited all of our staff members by explaining to them what the program was all about. None of them were told that they were under any duress to come. If they wanted to come, I could use their talents, if I thought they had the talents. I didn't interview many people who didn't have what we needed. The bad ones didn't come forth. We had all good ones.

Paul Stillwell: You described the way Hagedorn caught fire on this. Was that a typical reaction?

Admiral Wilson: Yes, it was. The same thing happened to Tom Christensen, who became our supply officer.* He came over from the Navy Research Lab one afternoon to spend 30 minutes, and we were there for three hours. I described the program to him in detail and where we expected it to go, and he bought off on it very quickly. Ben Bienkowski was

---

* Commander Thomas W. Christensen, SC, USN.

another one.* He was a Medical Service Corps officer who became our medical plans officer. The comptroller, the predecessor to the man who is there now, was a willing recruit. He wanted to change jobs and was anxious to get the job we had for him. The same thing was true with the engineer, Ray Smith. The chief of staff, Don Morton, same thing.† All these people became volunteers to the program after it was explained to them. It was a very healthy kind of staff to have, because nobody had been brought to it kicking and screaming. So the staffing worked out well over time.

Eventually, in 1983, the program received its funding. I had been relieved of the job of project officer by then. My relief was Captain John Swope, a Naval Academy graduate who went into medicine, became an anesthesiologist, and became interested in the fleet hospital soon after its inception.‡ He became the fleet hospital staffer who coordinated the fleet hospital equipment lists in conjunction with specialty adviser groups from all the services. He had an electrical engineering degree and was an electrical engineer. He did a very good job during his tour as the fleet hospital project manager.

From the fleet hospital project I had gone over to the Surgeon General's office to be his resource manager, and then on to be the Deputy Surgeon General until I retired in 1984. With their first acquisition money in 1983, the project went on to procure several hospitals. The inventory rapidly grew. The Fleet Hospital Support Office let a contract for the assembly of all the components out at Alameda, and the hospitals started coming off the line little by little. The first field test and evaluation was done in May of 1987 at Camp Pendleton.

Getting a crew trained is another whole matter. When you design a project like this, you have to identify the kinds of people you need and the numbers, but you also then have to provide a training program for them. We had a full-time training officer and a very large training contract with other parts of the Navy to train the people to operate these hospitals. When we finally fielded it in one of these hospitals, it was the culmination of eight or ten different necessary components coming together, not only the facilities, but the logistic support, the training, the people selection, the coordination with the Seabees, the

---

* Commander Faustyn J. Bienkowski, MSC, USN.
† Captain Donald A. Morton, CEC, USN.
‡ Captain John P. Swope, MC, USN.

plans for the assembly of the job, and all these functions interacting smoothly. It was a very complex operation and finally all came to fruition with this first test and evaluation, which turned out very well. There were a few glitches, but that's why the field test was done. A permanent training unit was established at Camp Pendleton to train crews for the field hospitals.

Paul Stillwell: Did you go to Pendleton to see the results of your efforts?

Admiral Wilson: Yes, I did.

Paul Stillwell: What do you remember from that experience?

Admiral Wilson: Being very impressed. One of the things that impressed me the most was when I looked out and saw this great mass of material, I said to myself, "I'm sure glad I didn't know it was going to be this big and complicated when I started, or I never would have tackled it." [Laughter]

It's possible to accomplish a great deal if you start out with a reasonable logic and basic premise and surround yourself with knowledgeable people who know how to do things. I didn't build the fleet hospital. I had some ideas and assembled a group of people who, together, did know how to build it. That's the way most projects are done. Nobody knows enough to do it all. It takes a lot of people with a lot of talent in various areas and spheres to put together something that works, and that is what happened in the fleet hospital project.

The best part, and the satisfying part, is that it did come together. Fleet hospitals were in the inventory and some deployed when the whistle blew in the Persian Gulf.[*] They were ready to go, fully staffed, and crews trained. The maritime pre-positioning ship carrying a fleet hospital got under way; it was met in the Gulf by the proper people and the site properly prepared. The hospital went up in the allotted time, and when erected, it

---

[*] The United States launched the Desert Shield buildup in Saudi Arabia in the summer and autumn of 1990 in response to the Iraqi invasion of Kuwait. Desert Storm, the war to liberate Kuwait, began in mid-January 1991.

worked. It was worth all the effort.

Paul Stillwell: To what extent was this used in Desert Shield and Desert Storm?

Admiral Wilson: There were three fleet hospitals fielded, 1,500 beds total. They were, of course, out there at the same time the hospital ships were there. The Navy had 3,500 Navy hospital beds in the area or field within a matter of a month.

Paul Stillwell: How did that compare with the other services?

Admiral Wilson: The Army eventually had a lot more beds than we did, but they didn't have them out there early. They had a lot more beds in a backup position in Europe. Ours were the ones that were out there Johnny-on-the-spot with the sophistication. The Army was not terribly well prepared.

Paul Stillwell: Well, one thing that you haven't really talked about was the planning for how you get it from where you store it to where you are going to use it.

Admiral Wilson: During the development of the concept, the issue of the come-as-you-are war, that is, the war that comes on quickly, is supposedly hard fought and over quickly, was the crux of the strategic thinking. With that in mind, we planned, right from the outset, that these units should be pre-positioned somewhere. Everything in the fleet hospital is air transportable in an Air Force C-141 transport. It's all containerized, so it can be readily handled in a container port. I say, "all containerized." Obviously you can't put trucks and big trailers and water tanks and things of that sort in boxes, but everything that's possible has been containerized—all the break-bulk cargo. The idea was to either have it afloat in the MPS, the maritime pre-positioning ships, or to have it deployed somewhere where it could be picked up and reasonably promptly moved to the area of concern.

This prompted a series of efforts having to do with identifying pre-positioning sites, whether we could use buildings of opportunity, where those sites would be, how did we get diplomatic clearance to get them, how are they going to be managed while in storage, who was going to take responsibility for their physical security and their technical updates, and a host of other questions related to pre-positioned facilities. These issues were addressed and worked on for several years.

What happened in the Persian Gulf? There was one 500-bedder afloat, one was brought in from Diego Garcia, and another was brought from Norway to the Persian Gulf. They were available and they used them. Those of us who have talked about it to one another since the Gulf War really felt fulfilled that the fleet hospital did its thing. When we go back to the beginning of the project in 1976 and look at it in 1990, it's a long time to make something like that happen, but it takes time in the government to do anything. It takes time to design all the pieces and parts and make all the logistic support come into being. Of all those things, the design and logistic support are probably the most complicated and the most important.

Paul Stillwell: Well, let me suggest a hypothetical scenario—that there had been terrible casualties in Desert Storm and there had not been a system such as this. There would have been a great hue and cry in the media and in Congress: "Why weren't you ready?" The fact that you had them and they turned out not to be needed never seemed to get much attention.

Admiral Wilson: That's always the way. You know, bad news makes the front page. As a historian, you know that. There's no way you can account for it except it's the way the world is. The Army did get some bad press in Congress. Congress really got after them about being so unprepared. The sad part of it is that anything and everything that the Navy bought was available to everybody else. Congress decreed through the committee system that we should be 90% standard among the services for these deployable medical systems. Ninety percent standard isn't a big problem, because 90% of it is standard anyway. A bed's a bed and a stand is a stand and a sink is a sink. We had good designs that were thoroughly acceptable.

By the way, we had Army and Air Force representatives in the Fleet Hospital Project Office and organization all the time for the sake of letting them know what we were doing, how we were doing it, why we were doing it. Their presence also served as a conduit for their commentary for improving the system as it evolved. So we felt very strongly that this had to be an effort that everybody could benefit from, because the only difference between and among us was the suits we were wearing. So I am really disappointed that the Army didn't do its thing in the proper time and came up embarrassed, because they could have had as much as we had or more.

Paul Stillwell: There are some things that you can procure for this setup and store indefinitely. There are others that have expiration dates: medicines and what-have-you. How do you deal with the perishable part?

Admiral Wilson: There's a program for replacing them annually in a certain number of the units. So there's an adequate number of hospitals that are up and ready on five minutes' notice. That's been thoroughly addressed. There's also an effort that goes into these units to validate the operability of the components, to check the machinery, check the lab machines and make sure they are there and functional. I don't know how much more you can do while waiting for the next war.

The great danger is to neglect it and fail to update it, because pretty soon you have a pile of obsolete rusty junk in the corner that nobody cares about. The biggest hazard is to lose the appropriation that will fund the fleet hospitals' proper maintenance and eventual updating. Right now, the equipments in the hospitals are ten years old. We ought to be starting to think about replacing some of that old stuff with new gear.

Paul Stillwell: While all this was going on, the Navy was also bringing along two new hospital ships, which were conversions from tankers. How did that tie in with your program?

Admiral Wilson: The hospital ship program started somewhere around 1980. Before then we had done a study called "The Alternatives to a Dedicated Hospital Ship." There was a thought pattern that said, "We've got all kinds of containers, and you could put all sorts of things in containers. Why can't we put a hospital in containers and place the containers in a big ship like a carrier or some other large ship?"

So we went through that evolution. We went through the possibilities of could we indeed take a World War II carrier and convert the hangar deck to a hospital? Was it possible to generate the supporting systems? We did a rather decent study that said "no." There was no really logical way to do it, and the principal obstruction was in the area of engineering. It had to do with water, soil chutes, air-conditioning, and access. So the idea was studied but not found feasible.

Around 1980, Dr. John Moxley, who at the time was Assistant Secretary of Defense for Health Affairs, and a very strong proponent of readiness and available medical assets, raised the question of hospital ships. He was not trying to dictate what ships or anything of the sort. He simply raised the question, "Why don't we have some hospital ships?"

He suggested that the United States might be a suitable hull. As we mentioned earlier in this biography, Kit and I had sailed to England on the SS United States, so I had a reasonable appreciation of its characteristics. I went to Norfolk with a group of appropriate and interested people to take a look at the ship, and to determine whether or not there was any possibility in our eyes that the ship could be converted to a hospital ship with any degree of efficiency.

While on that trip we had an interesting little encounter. We were staying overnight at the Norfolk BOQ. When we came down to go to work that morning, I was accosted by a short, stubby individual in a blue boiler suit. He came up to me and said, "Wilson, did you ever get that problem solved in the Guam?"

I said, "I don't know." I had to think for a minute, and finally two things dawned on me. A number of months before, we had been on the West Coast inspecting the medical facilities in the USS Guam, one of the old LPHs. There was a problem in its medical department with a sterilizer. We had identified the problem and had a solution in hand, so I left the ship and forgot the issue. But this gentleman had not. Suddenly it occurred to me that this was Admiral John Bulkeley, head of the Board of Inspection and Survey.[*]

---

[*] Rear Admiral John D. Bulkeley, USN, began serving as president of the Board of Inspection and Survey in 1967, continued after his age-mandated retirement in 1974, and remained until he finally left active duty in 1988.

I said, "Admiral Bulkeley, I don't know whether we fixed that or not." I said, "I was comfortable that we had a solution to the problem in hand when I left the ship, but, to be truthful, I haven't checked back on it."

He said, "Well, you need to do that. That's an important thing."

It had taken me a couple of minutes to realize, first of all, that it was Admiral Bulkeley. Then I was so impressed with the fact that here's a man that visits virtually hundreds of ships every year and that, all of a sudden, he could pick out one ship at one time several months before, remember the nature of the problem, remember my name in connection with that problem, and then recognize me after having seen me perhaps one or perhaps two times in both our lives. He was truly an amazing man.

Anyway, on that trip we did look at the SS United States. It was in a bad state of dishabille, shall we say, like a lady with her hair down, but it was still a structurally sound vessel and all the rest. I took a look at it, thought it over a little bit, and I said, "Gee, I'll bet you a dime I could get 2,000 beds and 25 ORs in that ship." It subsequently turned out that that became the requirement. [Laughter] It came out of the computer that way. I have no way of knowing whether the computer was adjusted or what happened, but suddenly we had a requirement for 2,000 beds and 25 ORs, and that's what we have in the inventory today in those two hospital ships.[*]

Anyway, Jack Moxley impressed on the world that we needed hospital ships to round out support for the operating forces that was currently represented only by the fleet hospitals. The Navy dragged its feet. They dragged their feet so you could see their toe marks in the concrete highway.

Paul Stillwell: Who in the Navy?

Admiral Wilson: OP-04 in particular, Vice Admiral Bill Cowhill.[†] He was a difficult man to deal with. His typical greeting to me was, "What do the goddamn doctors want now?"

---

[*] Two former commercial tankers were converted to hospital ships. The USNS Mercy (T-AH-19) went into service in 1986 and the USNS Comfort (T-AH-20) in 1987. Both arrived in the Persian Gulf in September 1990 as part of the Desert Shield buildup.
[†] Vice Admiral William J. Cowhill, USN, served as Deputy Chief of Naval Operations (Logistics), OP-04, from 20 June 1979 to June 1983.

Finally, the Navy was forced to do something, and they elected to buy two San Clemente-class tankers and convert them. Through the program budget memorandum to the budgeting system, DoD forced the Navy to invest $560 million in the hospital ship program. They bought these ships from their owners and converted them at National Steel and Shipbuilding in San Diego. Incidentally, the conversion costs came in well under $560 million for the two of them. Then they became coastal assets, one for the East Coast and one for the West Coast.

In selling the fleet hospitals to the Navy, we told them that they were force-oriented. We told them that some of the land-based beds were for the Marines and some were for the fleet, and the hospital ships were oriented to the fleet. They bought that, and that was one of the reasons they finally approved the program, for programming purposes. The Navy put it in its program and then took it out at the last minute. That's frequently called the gold-watch maneuver. A service will put an item in the budget and then take it out at the last minute when they know that there's a DoD proponent for that particular line item. They know that no matter what they do with it internally, it will be put back in the program by DoD.

Paul Stillwell: That way they could use their money for something else they want.

Admiral Wilson: No, it's all the same money.

Paul Stillwell: Oh, okay.

Admiral Wilson: There's no more money, but the decision as to how to allocate is taken out of their hands, so therefore they can say to their submariner friends, "I had your request in the program, had it all funded, then those goddamn DoD people did it to us. They changed the money; they took it from you and gave it to him." So the programmer keeps his "points" intact that way.

The other thing that happens comes when they want to do budget cuts. The other side of the gold watch is that somebody says, "Okay, BuMed, you've got to give up $25 million in your '93 budget."

"Really? Okay, I'm going to close Bethesda. That will save me $25 million in one spot, and I can run everything else." Never happen. So DoD takes the money from somewhere else, plugs it into wherever it's needed and Bethesda stays open. These are all programmer tricks.

That's how the hospital ships came into being. They were put there by DoD and, again, the fleet hospital office was involved with the hospital ships, mainly in supplying them with basic equipment listings, which are very difficult to put together. It's time consuming and very difficult. We had compiled them for the fleet hospitals on a department-by-department basis, so we knew what was required, and we gave them the material we had, and they utilized it and it was a lot easier for them.

Personally, I was involved with the hospital ships mostly in subtle ways, not overtly. I wasn't involved in the management of making the Navy do it or anything of that sort. I got involved by insisting that we put a pre-commissioning detail aboard that would supervise the selection and acquisition of the equipments. We would then have somebody aboard who acted like a military construction liaison officer to evaluate the ship from the functional point of view of the medical department, as opposed to a ship driver. I had inputs to it that way, but I was not a driving force in it, other than to represent the agency within the medical department that stated the requirements. I was "Mr. Requirements" and said, "We need hospital ships."

Paul Stillwell: I had a tour of one a couple of years ago in Baltimore and it was both well thought out and well executed. Beautiful ship.

Admiral Wilson: They are beautiful ships. Gorgeous. They are as modern as tomorrow's newspaper.

Paul Stillwell: The advantage they have over the fleet hospital is that it is designed as a system rather than as a bunch of components.

Admiral Wilson: They are designed as whole, intact, and integrated systems rather than components put together to make a hospital. It's a rigid, unitary system, and it's mobile under its own power, and, of course, it's obviously for a different purpose. They are very difficult to move inland, however.

Paul Stillwell: Indeed they are. [Laughter]

Admiral Wilson: So I think we'll have to stop until next time.

Paul Stillwell: I look forward to that one. You have whetted my appetite for the next chapter.

Interview Number 6 with Rear Admiral Almon C. Wilson, Medical Corps, U.S. Navy (Retired)

Place: Bureau of Medicine and Surgery, Washington, D.C.

Date: Monday, 7 June 1993

Interviewer: Paul Stillwell

Paul Stillwell: Admiral, it's great to see you again. We talked before about the fleet hospital program, and you're ready to resume at this point.

Admiral Wilson: Right. After a year in command of the Health Sciences Education and Training Command, I went over to be the first flag officer on the staff of the Commandant of the Marine Corps. At the time, General Robert Barrow was the Commandant.[*] I went to him immediately and said that I was pleased to be on his staff, but I felt that I could do a lot for him if he would permit me to spend a good deal of time on the fleet hospital program, since the fleet hospitals were essentially oriented to the Marines' medical support. He agreed to that.

Fortunately, I was able to get Captain Don Hauler, a Medical Corps officer who had been the medical officer for the Commandant for five years.[†] Plus we were able to get Commander George Harris, Medical Service Corps, who had spent nearly 20 years serving with the Marines.[‡] They really ran the office while I did only the things I had to do from the titular head point of view. I was given great latitude to conduct the affairs of the fleet hospital and to get involved in the hospital ships program.

After a year at Headquarters Marine Corps, I became the project manager for the fleet hospital, a full-time job fraught with many pitfalls we discussed earlier. The program was pretty well along, although it hadn't been funded in 1982. The idea of the fleet hospital, the concepts, and designs were well in hand, the plans for acquisition were in

---

[*] General Robert H. Barrow, USMC, served as Commandant of the Marine Corp from 1979 to 1983.
[†] Captain Donald R. Hauler, MC, USN.
[‡] Commander George S. Harris, MSC, USN.

place, and a good many milestones had been passed. The program underwent very strict scrutiny all the time.

In the fall of 1982, after 18 months as the project manager of the fleet hospital, I was transferred to the Surgeon General's staff in the Pentagon as the resources manager. This was a disappointing job, because there was not really much for me to do. The Surgeon General at the time was J. William Cox, and he didn't have much for me to do. He rather ignored me. His successor, Admiral Lew Seaton, was next in line for the job of Surgeon General. Bill Cox had made me his deputy, and I continued in that job with Lew Seaton.*

Lew Seaton had a rather interesting background in that he went from chief of a clinical service, the eye service at Bethesda, to command of the hospital in Groton, Connecticut, from which he made flag. He then went out to Pearl Harbor as the CinCPacFlt/CinCPac medical officer for a tour, and then returned to Washington in command of the Naval Medical Command, which was a function of a reorganized medical department. It's interesting to note that as the Commander of the Naval Medical Command, Admiral Seaton never had a deputy and did not seem to know how to delegate authority. This proved out when he became the Surgeon General, and for the remaining time when I was the Deputy Surgeon General, I was more or less roundly and soundly ignored, except for attendance at meetings.

During this period of time, I was asked to sit on a variety of committees, most of which had to do with readiness and training and operational concepts and plans. Even though I wasn't a part of the organizations that were holding the committee meetings, I was always invited and did participate. This, I think, was a recognition of the fact that I had been around a long time and had been exposed to the issues they were discussing.

The principal thing I did during this period as the Deputy Surgeon General was to foster and support what was known as the MDAB, the Management Development Advisory Board. This was an effort to create some career paths of significance for the several medical department corps in various jobs and tracks. We did this by identifying all of the skills required in all of the billets in the Navy medical department, from lieutenant commander on up. With those skills requirements we determined the education

---

* Vice Admiral Lewis H. Seaton, MC, USN, served as the Navy's Surgeon General from 1983 to 1987.

requirements to achieve those skills. We then listed the government agencies and organizations that could provide the training and education necessary to provide those skills, and match them up with the jobs. The idea was that when an individual job came open—by appropriate designators attached to an individual's service record indicating his additional professional qualifications—we could better identify people with the necessary skills, background, and education who were ready to take those jobs.

Paul Stillwell: What had existed up to then? Was there no such list of requirements?

Admiral Wilson: There was nothing formal about it. It was managed by the detailers. In each of the communities there were people who headed up various specialties. For example, in the Medical Service Corps there were people who made recommendations on the assignment of optometrists, pharmacists, physiotherapists, chemists, medical technologists, and various laboratory people. The same thing was true in the Medical Corps, where there were surgeons and specialists of various kinds who were consultants to the Surgeon General. They made recommendations to the detail office as to where people should go and when.

Paul Stillwell: So this really was formalizing an informal system.

Admiral Wilson: True. We were trying to establish a management system that had logic and could be tracked back to the realities of practice of medicine in the Navy at the time.

Paul Stillwell: Was this in any way tied in with the DOPMA legislation?[*]

Admiral Wilson: No, it was not. This was purely and simply an effort to define what we needed in terms of experience, skills, education, and training for the various billets throughout the Navy medical department.

---

[*] DOPMA—Defense Officer Personnel Management Act.

Paul Stillwell: How much interaction was there with NMPC?[*] Did it have its own requirements?

Admiral Wilson: NMPC was very cooperative. They were quite willing and did cross-reference our people with what were known as AQDs, additional qualification designators. These indicated that a given individual not only had his basic skills but also had additional training in something. They were enthusiastic and got to the point where a good many billets had been identified as requiring additional qualifying designators. The unfortunate part of it was that after I retired in the fall of 1984, the entire effort was put aside, principally by Lou Mantel, who relieved me.[†] In spite of later efforts to dig up this information to see if it had any current value, it has not as yet been found or at least surfaced as a tool to be evaluated.

Paul Stillwell: So how is it done now—the same way it's always been?

Admiral Wilson: Apparently it's being done the same way it's always been done, more or less by the seat of the pants by the people who know the people involved and not by any more strict definition of requirements. It's unfortunate, because the study was accomplished by talented and experienced people. The effort was wasted, because it was never employed or even tested.

Paul Stillwell: Does this suggest that the people who are being assigned to billets even now are not put in as well as they should be or could be?

Admiral Wilson: I'm not in a position to say that. All I am in a position to say is that the system that we devised and had ready for trial appeared to have a logic that would have helped in the selection of people based on identifiable skills related to a specific billet.

---

[*] NMPC—Naval Military Personnel Command, an organization that existed temporarily in the 1970s and 1980s. It was known before and after as the Bureau of Naval Personnel.
[†] Commodore Lewis Mantel, MC, USN.

Paul Stillwell: There must be some program to train people in these various specialties so that they will be available when needed.

Admiral Wilson: Within each of the corps, there are training opportunities that are offered occasionally. The Navy in general has been quite backward about offering additional educational opportunities to a lot of people. Only in the last 10 or 15 years has there been any effort whatsoever to give medical officers any inkling as to management techniques. It's getting better as time passes, but there was a long time when you grew into command by the seat of your pants and not because you were very well experienced or a particularly well trained manager. Management for commanding officers in the past was sort of an on-the-job training, the kind of thing you learned by observation if you happened to be an executive officer.

Paul Stillwell: Another possibility is the people who had a natural talent for that just moved up because others spotted their potential.

Admiral Wilson: That's true. Nowadays there is a prospective executive officer course and a prospective commanding officer course offered to everybody in the Navy assuming command. It's run by the line community, and medical officers attend it because obviously command problems are similar in any kind of installation. It's a new thing in the past 10 or 15 years. Those who have attended give varying responses as to its value. I'm certain it's of great value to a lot of people. Some who had more experience than others perhaps don't learn as much. However, it does give everyone an even start when they take command, and that, I guess, is worthwhile.

Paul Stillwell: What opportunities are there for individuals who are very good as physicians but don't aspire to be managers or don't have the talent?

Admiral Wilson: There are very good chances for them. I don't know of very many people in my experience in the Navy who were forced out of clinical work into full-time administrative work against their wills. We have a very significant segment of the Medical

Corps that does not wish to get involved with full-time administrative work. As you become more senior, even in a clinical position, the need to have administrative talents increases. As you become more senior, you have to assume more responsibilities, especially organizationally. There are those who achieve captain who virtually refuse to do any administrative work. Most of these folks wind up in smaller installations where there is not as much of an administrative demand. They are very competent clinicians who just don't care to participate in the management world, but who do very good work for the patients. Since they cannot or will not assume more administrative responsibilities, they are kept out of billets that require admin effort. This is simply good management.

Paul Stillwell: Just comparing that to the line community, a line officer would not have an opportunity to operate that way. He would have to assume the administrative responsibility to keep on being promoted.

Admiral Wilson: Absolutely. It's a completely different life. In the medical department, obviously, there are two different tracks for senior medical officers. There's the totally clinical track and the administrative track in the infrastructure which supports clinical operations. Each is important, and it's important that the infrastructure personnel be knowledgeable of the clinical world, because a great many administrative decisions depend on an insight into the clinical requirements for proper decision-making and resource allocation. This is one of the reasons that medical officers have been in command of hospitals for the most part. In recent years a good many Medical Service Corps officers have been placed in command of hospitals. They have served admirably, they are good administrators, with long experience, and they have been carefully selected for command. We've also had some nurses who had command of hospitals, and they served admirably as well.

Paul Stillwell: Were there problems among the Medical Corps officers when Medical Service Corps and Nurse Corps people took these commands?

Admiral Wilson: In various places there have been morale problems. In some places there was outright antipathy, and in other places things have worked very well. It depended in large measure on both groups. If the Medical Service Corps officer or Nurse Corps officer in command was an upright, forthright clinical person or Navy medical administrative person who understood the differences between administration and medical decisions, it worked well. If there were conflicts over decisions or resource allocations or personnel assignments, it caused some trouble. There are always some diehard people, particularly medical officers, who resent the fact that Medical Service Corps officers become their superior officers in terms of command structure.

Paul Stillwell: You can see a counterpart in, say, naval aviation, where the NFOs have moved into command positions over pilots.*

Admiral Wilson: Absolutely. It's the nature of people.

Paul Stillwell: Well, it would also depend on an individual's leadership abilities. A good leader would excel and win the respect of the doctors.

Admiral Wilson: Very true. It's been very variable but predictable based on that very thought pattern. The good ones did well, and the less good ones didn't do as well. Unfortunately, some of the good ones had staffs that were paranoid or antipathetic. Even though they were good personally, there was difficulty because the skipper was an MSC. That's the way it happened.

Congress had a hand in this. When we had a shortage of medical officers, they were adamant that medical officers should do clinical things and be less involved with administration. It was very hard to convince them over the years that certain physicians mature beyond their clinical years in terms of medical administration, and are better off for themselves and particularly for the services if they are assigned to administrative jobs. One of the things that people don't understand about physicians is that physicians can become tired of practice, become bored, and want to do something else. Physicians are not

---

* NFOs—naval flight officers.

prone to admit this, but it does happen. Certain of those people move on into administrative posts with admirable efficiency and aplomb and effectiveness.

Paul Stillwell: Is there a likelihood or a possibility that that individual's skills as a clinical physician would atrophy from not practicing, from not keeping up with medical literature and so forth?

Admiral Wilson: Certainly. When you are a physician and elect to take an administrative route, it is very difficult to maintain your clinical skills at peak levels, depending on your job. Now, there are people who become executive officers or commanding officers in small hospitals who are able to spend a day or so a week or parts of days working in their specialties and maintain their skills to some degree. In larger installations the administrative demands on the command structure are such that it's really impossible from the time point of view.

Paul Stillwell: Well, let's take your case. Here you were, the deputy to the Surgeon General, certainly an administrative job. Did you miss from the psychological point of view not seeing patients?

Admiral Wilson: No, I didn't. I had ceased clinical practice many years before I assumed the job as Deputy Surgeon General. In the late '60s, when I was a senior commander and selected for captain, I asked to go to the war college and was granted that privilege. From that time on, I went on into operational medicine and administrative medicine. I made this decision with full knowledge of the fact that I would be divorcing myself from the clinical world permanently. It was only partly elective, because certain aspects of my health dictated that I no longer operate. It was a relatively easy transition, and I found it enormously satisfying in the sense that having been in the Navy as long as I had and being as well acquainted with it as I was, I was able to provide the wherewithal to provide the younger, more currently trained people with the resources necessary to carry on the practice of medicine in the Navy in a seemly fashion. I derived a great deal of satisfaction out of contributing to that administrative and logistics infrastructure, and that's really what I spent the rest of my career doing.

Paul Stillwell: Well, it's a happy circumstance when a person can find that niche he enjoys.

Admiral Wilson: It is. Over a period of 42 years, I spent 31 years in day-to-day service in uniform. During that time I really had three careers. I started off as a line officer. I thoroughly enjoyed that, and it was a tremendous learning experience. Then I had a period as a medical officer, and I certainly enjoyed that time. Then I had a third career as an administrator and manager, and that, too, was interesting.

It's not usual in one lifetime for one person to have three careers, and to be happy and satisfied in each of them. I feel very fortunate for having had that experience, and I don't know where else besides the military that that can happen to you. CEOs in the civilian world go from company to company, but, by and large, they are doing the same thing in each place. They're developing and marketing products, managing money and resource allocations. That's what we did. So it's been quite a fascinating experience.

Paul Stillwell: Well, you had cast your lot in this particular plane. What were the frustrations, though, that come from working with a Surgeon General who would not let you function effectively?

Admiral Wilson: They were manifold. It was disquieting, to say the least, not to be able to pick up some challenges that I knew were there and needed to be done. But to do a lot of those things you needed the approbation and support of the Surgeon General. It wasn't there. It was futile to attempt.

Paul Stillwell: Well, it turns out that was even the case on this qualification system you worked on.

Admiral Wilson: Yes.

I was extended a couple of times on active duty as a flag officer because of some premature retirements by other flag officers, so I stayed on active duty rather longer than most. Admiral Seaton asked me to stay on for a couple of years, and at the end of one year he said, "Well, this is your year to retire."

I said, "Not really."

But he said, "Oh yes, it is. I remember."

So with the experience I'd had the in previous 18 months, two years, I felt that it was not worthwhile to spend another year of frustration and inaction. So I retired in the fall of 1984. It turned out to be a very happy circumstance.

Paul Stillwell: What can you say about his personality, his working style, and so forth?

Admiral Wilson: Well, Admiral Seaton's working style was very different from a great many successful people. He was prone not to delegate. He had a small group of people in whom he placed great trust. One of them was a captain, Medical Service Corps, who'd been a first class corpsman when Admiral Seaton was a lieutenant in the submarine service. He tended to hold things close to the vest and not really utilize his flag community in particular as an advisory group or a group off which he could bounce ideas.

This, of course, had been the pattern for Admiral Arentzen. Admiral Cox, perhaps, was a little bit more management oriented in using his flags, but not much. The one thing in common with all these Surgeons General: they were all hostage to the budget people. None of the Surgeons General knew enough about the budget process to challenge the people who put the budget together and executed it.

So what the Comptroller said really made a great deal of difference to the SG, perhaps more than anything anybody else said. Now, there were exceptions. Some of the Surgeons General—particularly Admiral Arentzen was very adamant about certain types of expenditures, and so he influenced the allocation of funds perhaps more than some of the others. But I didn't find it to be on a rational basis; I found it to be on a personal attitudinal basis.

Paul Stillwell: Do you think there was a morale problem in the Medical Corps because of this management style by the Surgeon General, not consulting his flags?

Admiral Wilson: Well, there certainly was in the Arentzen administration, and the Cox and Seaton administrations didn't improve it much.

Paul Stillwell: Admiral, back in the mid '80s we were reading very frequently about all the problems in Navy medicine. It became front-page news in the civilian media as well as Navy Times and so forth.* How might you explain those problems from the Navy Medical Corps standpoint?

Admiral Wilson: Well, several things had major impacts on that whole problem. Of course, the first of them was the loss of the draft. Military service, during and after Vietnam, was not something that was uppermost in most people's minds and especially physicians. So the Medical Corps dropped down to about 3,300 medical officers from some number in the mid-4,000s after the draft ended. By 1976 and 1977, we were in dire straits for numbers of medical officers and had to find other ways of providing care, some of which we simply could not provide and had to allocate to the civilian sector through the CHAMPUS program.

The bad name that Navy medicine got came from a variety of sources. A good deal of it was dissatisfaction with the reduced services available; this was especially true in the retired communities and in those areas where vital services such as obstetrics and gynecology were reduced or deleted from the services rendered by some of our smaller hospitals.

Throughout all of this we had a series of Surgeons General who had varying management styles. Admiral Custis became the Surgeon General in 1973, and he brought with him a very strong personality and a good personality. He was well liked and he had a great following. He could talk to people, he was believable, and he was as honest as the

---

* See Captain Arthur M. Smith, MC, USNR, "Are We Losing Confidence in Navy Medicine?" U.S. Naval Institute Proceedings, May 1986, pages 120-131.

day is long. He knew how to delegate authority and how to support his subordinates' efforts in major management areas.

After Admiral Custis came Admiral Arentzen, who came really ill-equipped to be a Surgeon General. In the first place, he did not have his clinical tickets. He did not have his boards, he was not certified by any specialty, which had been pretty much a universal requirement for SGs in the past. While it doesn't necessarily imply that you're a better manager to have your clinical boards and such, it means a great deal to the practicing community, who put great store by such things as a matter of clinical achievement. After all, when you're running a clinical operation like the Navy medical department, those credentials assume importance to the medical officer community.

Admiral Arentzen also was not terribly well versed in the operational part of the Navy, the fleet in particular, although he'd had service on ships a time or two. His management style was very much one of an authoritarian type of regimen. He ruled by edict. He had a small group of people, many of whom were junior, who acted as sort of a kitchen cabinet. He had the reputation of delving down into organizations and asking junior people their opinions about various ongoing issues and actions within those departments. It almost—in fact, it did—resemble a spy system. He had a private number on which certain of these people called him from the field. This became well known.

He had a particularly interesting person in a Captain Jim Quinn, who was a medical officer who had served in Portsmouth when Admiral Arentzen had command of that hospital. When he went to San Diego in command, he took Jim Quinn with him, and when he came to Washington as Surgeon General he took him to the bureau. Jim Quinn became his right-hand man in spite of any other assistants he had. He became a close confidant of the Surgeon General to the exclusion of all flag officers and many other senior people in the system.

Admiral Arentzen could not delegate routine things to his senior people, and that became a source of irritation. He did not deal well with the line. He was apparently uncomfortable with it, to say the least, and he would frequently send a representative to a line meeting rather than go himself. When he did appear, he was very quiet and not terribly articulate in defending his positions. He had some very fixed ideas about certain things, and I heard him say one time in response to a request for some money from one of his commanding officers, "That's just poor management. He doesn't need that money and I'm not going to underwrite mismanagement." To my certain knowledge, there was nothing mismanaged. It was quite the reverse.

In addition to such attitudes, he had great favorites among some of the corps, particularly the Medical Service Corps and the Medical Corps, and everybody knew it. Morale in the field was really at a low ebb. Some of his flag officers approved his style of management, and some of his senior captains did and fell in with his mode of operations. One such admiral took me to lunch one day and asked me to bury the hatchet with the Surgeon General, with whom I disagreed on many items. I said, "Well, I don't have a hatchet to bury. I believe in the chain of command. I believe in educating your juniors, training them to do more in the next level of endeavor that they are about to go to. I think they need the opportunity to make decisions, to make mistakes, and be corrected. They need a place in the sun so when they leave at the end of the day they can say, 'I have accomplished something of value.' If those are bad things that the Surgeon General doesn't deal with and is criticizing me for, just tell him that I'm sorry, but that's the way the Navy is put together."

In addition, Admiral Arentzen was not at all prone to use the collective advice of his flag officers. Some of them, whom he had convinced that his mode of management was appropriate, were listened to. A number of them were roundly and soundly ignored. Even though they worked in the bureau, they were not in some cases even asked about the major decisions in their area of responsibility. In general, Admiral Arentzen was an autocrat. Of course, that style of management just doesn't work well in an organization of the size and the diversity of the medical department, so morale was extremely low. Recruiting was not good.

Paul Stillwell: Well, if people feel they don't have the authority or can't control their destiny, that would do terrible things for morale.

Admiral Wilson: Oh, it was very distressing.

Paul Stillwell: No job satisfaction.

Admiral Wilson: None. Unfortunately, the other services were aware of Admiral Arentzen's mode of doing business, and I spent a lot of time glossing over some of the actions he had taken when I was questioned by the other service members. Although I never did apologize for him, I almost had to at times for some things that were so offbeat.

Paul Stillwell: Do you remember any examples?

Admiral Wilson: None that I haven't mentioned.

Admiral Arentzen was succeeded by J. William Cox, who was an internist and cardiologist, who again had virtually no experience with the line community. He'd had one tour as an internist in Subic Bay, and then came back to a clinical job in Philadelphia, and eventually he set up the Health Sciences Education and Training Command. Prior to that he had had a job in the bureau running the training section. When it became obvious that we needed to concentrate our education and training efforts in one place, he was elected to set up the Health Sciences Education and Training Command, and he did a good job. It was well organized, practical, and effective. He garnered for himself a group of people who were knowledgeable about education and very productive. From that command he made flag, and eventually went out to San Diego and commanded the hospital. He returned to the bureau as the head of the professional division, the human resources division, it was called. From there he was selected as Surgeon General.

He had two major problems. He didn't know much about the Navy and how it operates, thinks, or the way it does business, and how to deal with it. He had a personal ego that was unfortunately large and a factor. He was prone to pontificate about issues, items, and actions with which he had had very little experience. He never gave me much trouble, because most of the time that he was Surgeon General, I was out of the bureau. I did become his deputy just before he left, but by and large, I was out in other jobs either in the Health Sciences Education and Training Command or at the Marine Corps Headquarters or running the fleet hospital project. He did not have any major impact on issues that I was dealing with at the time. He was very supportive of both the fleet hospital project and the hospital ship program, which I was working on at the time. He was supportive of the HSETC effort, because he had set up that command and wanted to see it run well.

During this time there was an episode out at the naval hospital at Bethesda. It all started when a former CNO, Admiral Carney, was taken out there to be treated for some sort of emergent clinical problem.* The story I heard was that he was told at the emergency room that they couldn't take him. They were too busy, so he should go to Walter Reed.† He had a son who was a retired Marine brigadier general, and the brigadier general called the Surgeon General.‡ A great deal of criticism erupted around that particular issue.

The hospital had been inspected by the committee on accreditation of hospitals of the American Medical Association and had been put on probation. The commanding officer at the time was Admiral Joe Horgan, and he apparently had not picked up the loose ends to take them off probation.§ Well, when this was discovered, CNO got in the act, and an investigation of the medical department's operation came about. Well, it resulted in a reorganization of the Bureau of Medicine and Surgery. It was during this reorganization effort that Admiral Cox lost some of his credibility with CNO.

Admiral Bill Small was the VCNO at the time, and he assumed a major role in defining the ultimate structure of the reorganized Bureau of Medicine and Surgery.** It was reorganized so that there no longer was a bureau, but there was a Navy Medical Command. Admiral Cox was criticized quite severely for not having better and more inventive ideas about this reorganization, and he eventually retired early.

I stayed as the Deputy Surgeon General for approximately a year and then retired. Vice Admiral Seaton stayed and finished his tour. He was very severely criticized for some inaction related to the operation of a clinic for captains and admirals out in San Diego. At the time there was great criticism over equality of treatment for everybody. They had discontinued sick officers' quarters, so all the patients on any given ward were mixed officer and enlisted, female, etc. The VCNO became quite perturbed after Seaton

---

* Admiral Robert B. Carney, USN, served as Chief of Naval Operations from 17 August 1953 to 17 August 1955.
† Walter Reed Army Medical Center in Washington, D.C.
‡ Brigadier General Robert B. Carney, Jr., USMC (Ret.).
§ Rear Admiral Joseph T. Horgan, MC, USN.
** Admiral William N. Small, USN.

was told to shut that clinic down, and it didn't happen as quickly as the VCNO thought it should have. Admiral Seaton was more or less in the doghouse for that situation.

I retired in the fall of 1984. He finished out his tour through 1987 and then retired. A lot of the problems in the '80s were due in large measure to the personalities and the management styles of the Surgeons General. They had problems dealing with some of the aspects of medical department operations. They had a lot of problems with the line and understanding and communicating effectively with them. As a result, morale was low, recruiting was way behind schedule, and the department was really in rather sad shape. This, of course, all came out in the various publications, and the Navy Medical Department was really at a low point in its history. We had an unfortunate problem related to some deaths in the cardiac service at Bethesda, which caused a great wave of antipathy toward the department for seeming dereliction of control over clinical matters.

The department had a lot of housecleaning to do, and a lot of clinical stature rebuilding to do. Fortunately, the next Surgeon General who came on the scene after my retirement was Admiral Jim Zimble, and he was exactly the right man for the job.[*] He was well thought of and an able clinician—board-certified obstetrician and gynecologist. He had a pleasant manner with people and a very effective management style. He had a marvelous sense of humor, understood the line, and he had experience as a submarine medical officer working with them. He was very well accepted.

Paul Stillwell: We used the term during a break that he was a "breath of fresh air."

Admiral Wilson: He certainly was. We'd had a period of 11 years where there wasn't much to brag about. Then he came along and did a great job.

In October of 1983, as we mentioned in a previous interview, there was a bombing in Beirut. Well over 200 Marines were killed, and a large number were injured. Most of the injured were transferred to Central Europe in the air medical evacuation system.

As a preamble to the congressional direction to have an investigation, Senator Tower had the Senate Armed Services Committee convene on Monday, the day after the

---

[*] Vice Admiral James A. Zimble, MC, USN, served as the Navy's Surgeon General from 1987 to 1991.

Beirut bombing.* That morning, we received a call at the Surgeon General's office, asking that the Surgeon General come over to testify before this committee. The SG was out of town, so I went. CNO's office told me that we were required to be there by 11:30. So I duly hopped in a car and went over to the hearing room. When I walked in, I was met by an aide, who directed me to the one vacant seat of three at a table in the hearing room. In the left chair was Major General Bernie Trainor of the Marine Corps.† In the middle chair was Caspar Weinberger, the Secretary of Defense, and I was directed to sit in the third chair, to Caspar Weinberger's right.‡

Cap Weinberger leaned over to me and said, "Why in the hell didn't we use those Israeli hospitals?" I told him that we had no political arrangement to do that, but it didn't make any difference, because we had the worldwide system of evacuation to take care of such instances. I told him that we had a surgical team offshore in one of the amphibious vessels, we had the air-evac system, and that this was a worldwide system that would function no matter what was on the beach adjacent to the difficulties. That if it had happened on the east or west coast of Africa or some other coast in an underdeveloped country, we would have acted in the same fashion. He took that aboard, and when he was asked why, he repeated virtually verbatim what I just mentioned here.

The participants were seated at a U-shaped table with Senator Tower at the head of it, of course. On my right was Senator Ted Kennedy, who sat there during the questioning, apparently doodling on a pad of paper.§ As the questioning went around the table to the various members of the committee, he continued to sit there and doodle, seemingly disinterested. When it came his turn, he suddenly became not only active but bombastic and highly critical of the fact that we had not used the Israeli hospitals. He ranted and raved and went on in loud tones and very critical content about the way the management of the casualties had been conducted and that he was not satisfied. With that, he turned it off and started to doodle again. It was obvious that he had made a statement for the record of the Armed Services Committee of the Senate at the time. I thought that was a very

---

* Senator John G. Tower (Republican-Texas).
† Major General Bernard E. Trainor, USMC.
‡ Caspar W. Weinberger served as Secretary of Defense from 21 January 1981 to 23 November 1987.
§ Senator Edward M. Kennedy (Democrat-Massachusetts).

revealing episode as far as Ted Kennedy was concerned. The committee did not give any of us any kind of a hard time over this issue. It was a matter of gaining the information as to why we conducted ourselves as we did.

The truth of the matter was that we have worldwide system for dealing with such incidents. We put the system in motion, and it served admirably. But Congress insisted on an investigation, and Admiral Zimble was elected to conduct that investigation.* He did so, and he came back with a very well-thought-out, very well-documented report that pointed out some major difficulties that should be met head-on. The Chief of Naval Operations at the time apparently took umbrage at the ideas and wordage in this report, and Jim Zimble was a sort of persona non grata.† He was assigned to the office of the Assistant Secretary of Defense for Health Affairs, and in that job, he did admirable service. By the time the Surgeon General selections came around, we had a new CNO, and Zimble was selected to be the new Surgeon General.‡ He did a great deal to straighten out the medical department, as I observed from retirement and from many talks with him during those years.

Having retired, I certainly had no further authority but still retained a lively interest in what went on in the medical department. It was with a great sense of pleasure that I was able to see the hospital ships come to fruition, go into service, and eventually deploy in the Gulf War. The fleet hospitals were deployed and found to be of the quality that we had hoped for when they were designed. All in all, I felt a great sense of satisfaction for the things in which I had been involved. I felt particularly fortunate to have been around long enough to see some of the long-term projects we started come into being and function as they were designed. Such opportunity has not happened to a lot of people, and I am appreciative of that experience.

Paul Stillwell: As you came up to the time of retirement, you had really gone a little earlier than you wanted to. Did you feel a pang of regret about taking off the uniform?

---

* Zimble was then a rear admiral, serving as fleet surgeon for Commander in Chief Atlantic Fleet.
† The Chief of Naval Operations in 1983 was Admiral James D. Watkins, USN.
‡ Admiral Carlisle A. H. Trost, USN, was CNO when Admiral Zimble became Surgeon General in 1987.

Admiral Wilson: Yes and no. About six months before I retired, I was beginning to get the feeling that it was time for me to leave. I had been around long enough to see the same problems surface three and four and five times without solution. It occurred to me that I certainly didn't have any fresh new answers to these old problems, and perhaps I should get out of the way and let some new blood have a go at them. So I was retired without any feelings of great loss nor of being pushed out of the service. I must say that after retirement I had the usual feelings of letdown. It's quite like stepping off the sidewalk into the street. One day you're in uniform with a job and office and a secretary and access to a lot of amenities, people are asking your advice, and you're giving opinions. The next day, you're just another retired Navy guy. This, of course, is psychologically quite deflating. As much as I had attempted to prepare myself, I felt this way for some months after retirement. However, through the good offices of my wife and a good home and hobbies, I survived.

About four years after retirement, I was asked to be a consultant with a firm that had a contract to provide a computer-based information system for the military hospital system. Since I've been out of clinical medicine for a long time, and I knew nothing about computers, I was a little reluctant to get involved. But after having done so, I learned that they were more interested in my experience with the acquisition system than with either my clinical or computer experience. So for about the last five years, '88 to '93, I've been consulting with this firm, trying to warn them of and steer them around the pitfalls and potholes in the federal acquisition system as they designed and tested and installed this marvelous hospital information system. The new information system has been shown to provide a great deal more efficiency for our hospital operations.

Working as a consultant has been intellectually very stimulating, because the people involved are very intelligent people. They're dedicated, energetic, and are making things happen and are proud of their products. This, of course, rubs off on you if you feel that you've had even a slight part of that experience. So it's been very satisfying. I tell my friends that it keeps my head from turning into concrete without interfering with my lifestyle.

Paul Stillwell: What's the name of the company?

Admiral Wilson: I work for Burdehsaw Associates, Ltd., in Bethesda. They have assigned me to a corporation headquartered in La Jolla, California, called Scientific Applications International Corporation. SAIC, as it's called, has the contract to provide this computer-based integrated medical information system.

Paul Stillwell: How does the system work?

Admiral Wilson: It uses a variety of modules which deal with specific facets of the hospital. For example, there's a laboratory module, a pharmacy module, an administrative module, a clinical nursing module, a radiology module, a reports-generation module, an outpatient order system. They're working on an in-patient order entry system. It's a series of 12 functionalities that feed into a main computer and utilize a common data base. It is applicable to virtually any size installation, the differences being how many outlying clinics have to feed in and how big the data base is, but it's very flexible.

Paul Stillwell: Is this solely for military hospitals?

Admiral Wilson: It was contracted to be developed, tested, and installed in military installations. I'm sure that the company is going to find a great market for it in the civilian world, once it's all debugged and brought up to date.

Paul Stillwell: Did it have any predecessors in civilian hospitals?

Admiral Wilson: There are other systems in hospitals, but they're not as extensive as this one, and they're not as well integrated, apparently. As I say, I am not an expert in the computer world, and all I know is really hearsay from conversations with our colleagues in the corporation. If they had been able to buy something off the shelf to meet this need, I'm sure they would have done so, but obviously there was not a system of sufficient size and capability to do it. It's apparent from what we are learning that there's going to be enormously improved efficiency from this system. It will not necessarily save money in the sense of fewer dollars, but it will hopefully support more services for the same number of dollars and people, thereby increasing the efficiency in the systems.

Paul Stillwell: Can you give any examples of the efficiency?

Admiral Wilson: In the pharmacy, in some of the installations where they've had these systems on trial, the pharmacy waiting time has been reduced from 30 or 40 minutes to less than five minutes. The other time saver has been in recovering information from files, retrieving laboratory reports, X-ray reports.

Paul Stillwell: Are individual patient records computerized and put in the system?

Admiral Wilson: Yes, they are.

Paul Stillwell: Is there a concern about confidentiality of those records?

Admiral Wilson: Security of the system is a major concern. They're dealing with it, I know.

The other thing about it is that once in place, all the installations can be interconnected electronically, so that transfer of information about a given patient from location to location will be possible and certainly an advantage.

Paul Stillwell: Well, I've seen a few examples just as a consumer. The local Giant pharmacy, for instance, has a system that warns you about drug interactions. It also prints out a sheet that talks about side effects and whatever else the doctor perhaps didn't think to tell you about.

Admiral Wilson: Absolutely. These are the kinds of things that are integral parts of all these systems. That's a big one, the drug interactions.

Paul Stillwell: Well, let's look at it from another perspective. You've been retired here for close to ten years. How are you as a retired officer treated by the Navy medical system?

Admiral Wilson: Oh, beautifully. They are very concerned, they are very responsive. We make every effort not to abuse the system, and the hospital at Bremerton near our home has been extremely helpful to us. Mrs. Wilson and I have both had surgery there and are patients in their specialty outpatient services as necessary. They've been very helpful.

Paul Stillwell: Have you gotten involved with CHAMPUS?

Admiral Wilson: No, we're beyond that now. We're into Medicare and have used Medicare on some occasions. In fact, there's a shortage of internists at the hospital, so we use the services of a private internist.

I'm very satisfied with the way we're being treated, and we've tried never to abuse the system. I am concerned about the new health care reform that is on the horizon at the federal level. I certainly hope that it doesn't limit or decrease the amounts of services available to our current active duty people and retirees. Rightly or wrongly, I feel that when the people enlisted or were commissioned and signed up, there was a tacit but thoroughly understood part of it that said, "We're going to take care of you medically during and after your service." I think to violate that benefit would cause a terribly adverse reaction in the services.

Paul Stillwell: Well, there have been disruptions already in that the system no longer works the way it used to—that you just go to a Navy hospital.

Admiral Wilson: Nothing stays as it was, so we'll just have to wait and see.

Paul Stillwell: Another subject area to bring things up to date on would be your family: your children, grandchildren, your wife.

Admiral Wilson: My wife and I have been married over 48 years now, we have one son, Geoff, who is retired from the Navy as a lieutenant commander and is gainfully employed by the Johns Hopkins Applied Physics Lab near Washington.

He and his wife, Louise, have twin boys, one called Geoffrey, spelled the same as his father, the other one Christopher. The twins graduated from high school this year. Geoffrey is going to Boston University as a psychology major pre-med student, and his brother, Christopher, is going to the Air Force Academy.* Time marches on, the kids grow up, and grandparents grow old.

As for Mrs. Wilson and me, we're living out in the great Northwest, enjoying retirement. Even though our children live here in the East Coast, it's only five or six hours by air, and that's as close as you can be by car in some locales. So we're quite happily retired and feel like we've had a wonderful career and a wonderful time in the service and wouldn't have had it any other way.

Paul Stillwell: Well, certainly that was the major thing in your life, and it's a happy circumstance that it worked out so well.

Admiral Wilson: Indeed.

Paul Stillwell: Well, let me say on behalf of the Naval Institute that I am very grateful for this contribution you've made. We have very few medical officers in our collection. As I listened to you, I was struck by your descriptions all along the way: being a line officer, working as a clinical physician, a surgeon in Vietnam, moving into the administrative side of it, the fleet hospital program. These are things that we just wouldn't have had covered in this kind of depth and candor without you, so I'm very grateful for your contribution.

---

* As of early 2002, Geoffrey had completed his undergraduate education, been commissioned as an ensign in the Medical Corps, USNR, and was partway through his training as a medical officer. After dropping out of the Air Force Academy, Christopher transferred to Embry-Riddle Aviation University, from which he graduated with a major in aeronautical engineering and minor in airlines management. As of early 2002 he was a copilot with Northwest Airlink, a commuter line operating out of Memphis, Tennessee.

Admiral Wilson: Well, it's been my pleasure, and I certainly hope I have been objective and impersonal with all the comments I have made. What I have said are reflections on what I observed and felt as time passed, and that's what I had hoped to record.

Paul Stillwell: Thank you very much.

Admiral Wilson: My pleasure.

Index to the Oral History of
Rear Admiral Almon C. Wilson,
Medical Corps, U.S. Navy (Retired)

Addabbo, Representative Joseph P.
Rear Admiral Harry Etter had a difficult time with Congressman Addabbo because of a BuMed proposal in the 1970s to close the naval hospital at St. Albans, New York, 202-203

Africa
In the early 1970s Wilson and his wife went on a safari to Kenya and Uganda in East Africa, 165-167

Air Force, U.S.
In 1965-66 badly wounded men were evacuated from Vietnam to Clark Air Force Base Hospital in the Philippines, 81, 85, 89-90, 93, 100, 107, 124-125; in January 1966 a B-57 bomber crashed at Danang, South Vietnam, 100; in the mid-1960s Vietnam wounded were staged through the airbase at Yokota, Japan, then to the naval hospital at Yokosuka, 125-127; in the mid-1960s the Military Airlift Command provided flights for service personnel and their dependents, 136; involvement in September 1970 in the Jordanian crisis in the eastern Mediterranean, 162-163; in the early 1970s Admiral Thomas Moorer, Chairman of the Joint Chiefs of Staff, made his trips in a specially configured KC-135 aircraft, 192-195; the Navy's fleet hospitals have been containerized for rapid shipment in Air Force C-141 cargo planes, 250; provided representatives to work with the Navy in the 1970s and 1980s in the development of the fleet hospital program, 251-252

Alcohol
At the San Diego Naval Hospital in the early 1960s Wilson prescribed whiskey for retired senior officers who were patients, 59; served to Navy medical personnel in the mid-1960s when they were serving in or near Danang, South Vietnam, 114; strict drinking-and-driving laws were in place in the early 1970s in the United Kingdom, 165; served at a party in London in 1971 to celebrate the supposed 100th anniversary of the U.S. Navy Medical Department, 173; during a trip to the Middle East in 1973 two bottles of whiskey in Wilson's luggage broke, leaving him with Scotch-soaked clothing, 191; in the mid-1970s the Great Lakes Naval Hospital established a rehabilitation center to treat chronic alcoholics, 223-224

Almy, Lieutenant Commander Gary L., MC, USN
In the mid-1970s was the chief of psychiatry at the Great Lakes Naval Hospital, 208-209

Amphibious Warfare
    In April 1945 the ships of Transport Division 103 put Army troops ashore during an amphibious assault at Legaspi in the Philippines, 18-20; further U.S. amphibious operations in 1945 in the Philippines and Borneo, 22-25

Antisubmarine Warfare
    During World War II naval personnel received antisubmarine training at Miami and Key West, Florida, 10-12

Arentzen, Vice Admiral Willard P., MC, USN
    Served from 1976 to 1980 as the Navy's Surgeon General, 217-218, 230; Wilson's assessment of, 230-233, 267-271; in 1979 took the fleet hospital program away from Wilson, 244, 247

Army, U.S.
    In April 1945 the ships of Transport Division 103 put soldiers ashore during an amphibious assault at Legaspi in the Philippines, 18-20, 24-25; in the mid-1960s Army medical facilities in South Vietnam shared supplies with the Navy, 84-85; in the mid-1960s Army hospitals in Yokohama, Japan, and San Antonio, Texas, specialized in treating burn patients, 131; in the late 1970s the Army lab at Natick, Massachusetts, provided a new type of tent for use in the Navy's the fleet hospital program to develop transportable medical facilities, 241; not as well prepared medically as the Navy was during the 1990 Desert Shield buildup, 250-251; provided representatives to work with the Navy in the 1970s and 1980s in the development of the fleet hospital program, 251-252

Asbury Park, New Jersey
    Served as a training site in 1944 for midshipmen in the V-12 reserve officer program, 3-5, 8

Australian Army
    Provided troops in the summer of 1945 for amphibious operations in Borneo, 22-24

Ballenger, Captain Felix P., MC, USN
    As commanding officer of the Yokosuka, Japan, Naval Hospital in the mid-1960s, initiated a unit for treating burn patients, 131-132; Wilson's assessment of, 134, 199

Barrow, General Robert H., USMC
    Around 1980, during his tenure as Commandant of the Marine Corps, he supported the fleet hospital program to develop transportable medical facilities, 258

Beaver, Captain John F., CEC, USN
    In the early 1970s, while serving as naval district civil engineer in New Orleans, forwarded a directive for the construction of an unnecessarily large hospital in the city because of political pressure from Congressman F. Edward Hebert, 182

Beirut, Lebanon
In 1970 Wilson visited the city and got a sense of local sentiment about the United States, 157; medical aspects of the October 1983 bombing of the Marine barracks in Beirut, 164, 273-274; congressional investigation after the disaster, 273-275

Bolivia
In the 1970s the U.S. Navy sent a medical team to Bolivia to aid in a people-to-people health program, 183-187; Bolivian naval forces in that era were sparse, 185

Borneo
Site of amphibious assault by Australian soldiers in 1945, 22-24

Bremerton, Washington, Naval Hospital
In 1952-53 treated men who had been wounded in the Korean War, 39-40

Brown, Vice Admiral Robert B., MC, USN
In 1966, as the Navy's Surgeon General, received a briefing on medical conditions in the Vietnam War, 122, 198; brief description of his career and attributes, 197-198

Budgetary Considerations
As Secretary of Defense in 1972, Melvin Laird asked the Navy to come up with the cost of modernizing its medical and dental facilities, and the money was later forthcoming, 176-179, 187-188; impact of cost increases on military construction programs, 180; maneuvers used in getting budget money approved in the early 1980s for hospital ship conversion, 255-257

Bulkeley, Rear Admiral John D., USN (Ret.) (USNA, 1933)
As head of the Board of Inspection and Survey around 1980, he demonstrated to Wilson a remarkable memory for details, 253-254

Bureau of Medicine and Surgery, Washington, D.C.
In the mid-1960s made plans to build new naval hospitals in several locations, 64-65; in 1971 members of the staff held a party in London to celebrate the supposed 100th anniversary of the U.S. Navy Medical Department, 172-173; work in the early 1970s in planning for the design, construction, and upgrading of naval hospitals, 175-183, 187-188; in the 1970s the Navy sent a medical team to Bolivia to aid in a people-to-people health program, 183-187; operated as an old-boy network until the mid-1970s, when a new Surgeon General introduced modern management, 195-197; value of having physicians as commanding officers of naval hospitals and Surgeons General, 199-200; Rear Admiral Harry Etter had a difficult time with Congressman Joseph Addabbo because of a BuMed proposal in the 1970s to close the naval hospital at St. Albans, New York, 202-203; difficulties in the 1970s with the end of the draft and resulting lower availability of physicians in uniform, 204-205; management style in the late 1970s by the Surgeon General, Vice Admiral Willard Arentzen, 230-233, 267-271; attempts in the late 1970s to get the BuMed and the rest of Navy medicine into the Planning, Programming, and Budgeting System, 232-233;

development of the fleet hospital program from 1976 onward, 234-252; outfitting in the 1980s of two tankers converted to be hospital ships, 252-257; in the early 1980s Wilson fostered the Management Development Advisory Board to chart career paths and educational requirements for people in the Navy's medical department, 259-262; changing patterns have developed in the Navy medical community as Medical Service Corps and dental officers have been able to achieve command, 263-264; balance between clinical work and administrative work as doctors become more senior, 264-266; Navy medicine got a black eye in the mid-1980s because of a variety of problems, 268-273

Bureau of Ships
During and after World War II a huge supply of shipboard equipment and parts was stored at the naval supply depot in Scotia, New York, 35-37

Camp Pendleton, Oceanside, California
Provided training in the mid-1960s for Navy medical personnel who were going to care for Marine Corps units in Vietnam, 70-71

Carney, Admiral Robert B., USN (Ret.) (USNA, 1916)
Former Chief of Naval Operations who, in the early 1980s, was turned away from medical treatment at Bethesda Naval Hospital, 272

CHAMPUS
The Civilian Health and Medical Program of the Uniformed Services was established to provide medical care at a time when the Navy no longer had as many doctors in uniform as before, 205

Chelsea, Massachusetts, Naval Hospital
In the mid-1960s served the medical needs of the Navy population in the Boston area, 63-69; brief history of the hospital, 63-64; in the mid-1960s BuMed made plans for a new hospital at Chelsea, but it was never built, 64-66; in 1974 the hospital closed as part of a general draw-down in facilities, 66

Chicago, Illinois
During World War II was a hospitable city for young midshipmen on liberty, 9-10

China
Shortly after the end of World War II the high-speed transport Liddle (APD-60) visited Tientsin, 31-32

Chu Lai, South Vietnam
Was the site of a medical facility in 1965-66 that treated Marines wounded in combat, 88-89, 91-93, 98, 103, 107-108, 117

Clark Air Force Base, Philippines
In 1965-66 badly wounded men were evacuated from Vietnam to the Clark Air Force Base Hospital, 81, 85, 89-90, 93, 100, 107, 124-125

Classified Information
In 1944 radar was considered to be highly classified at the naval training center in Miami, Florida, 10-11

Cofer, USS (APD-62)
High-speed transport that was involved in amphibious operations in 1945 in the Philippine Islands, 17-19

Colbert, USS (APA-145)
In 1945, right after the end of World War II, operated out of Port Arthur, Manchuria, and on 17 September 1945 hit a floating mine, 28, 30

Commercial Ships
In the mid-1960s dunnage from ships that delivered cargo to Danang, South Vietnam, was used to improve conditions at the local Navy hospital, 94-95

Communications
In the early 1970s, when he traveled by Air Force KC-135, Admiral Thomas Moorer, Chairman of the Joint Chiefs of Staff, had a sophisticated communication capability, 194

Computers
In the early 1970s, the Bureau of Medicine and Surgery obtained computers and a programmer to aid the process of facilities planning, 179-180; in the mid-1970s Commander Robert White developed a computer program to predict casualties in the event of combat, 235; in the late 1980s and early 1990s Wilson worked for a company that provided a computer-based information system for military hospitals, 276-278

Congress, U.S.
In the early 1970s the city of New Orleans was programmed to receive an unnecessarily large new naval hospital as the result of Representative F. Edward Hebert's political clout, 181-183; Rear Admiral Harry Etter had a difficult time with Congressman Joseph Addabbo because of a BuMed proposal in the 1970s to close the naval hospital at St. Albans, New York, 202-203; criticized the Army for not being well prepared medically for the 1990-91 operations in the Persian Gulf, 251; conducted an investigation in the aftermath of the October 1983 bombing of the Marine barracks in Beirut, Lebanon, 273-275

Cowan, Rear Admiral John S., MC, USN
In the mid-1960s, as top medical officer for the Pacific Command, convened conferences with medical representatives from throughout the theater to discuss the treatment of Vietnam War casualties, 123-124

Cowhill, Vice Admiral William J., USN
Around 1980, as DCNO (Logistics), proved difficult to deal with in connection with supplying the Navy with hospital ships, 254-255

Cox, Vice Admiral J. William, MC, USN
Served from 1980 to 1983 as the Navy's Surgeon General, 244, 259; career background, 271; Wilson's assessment of, 271-272

Custis, Vice Admiral Donald L., MC, USN
Did an excellent job from 1973 to 1976 as the Navy's Surgeon General, particularly in instituting modern management, 195-196, 199-202, 268-269; in 1974 supported Wilson's handling of a racial problem at the Great Lakes Naval Hospital, 210-211

Danang, South Vietnam
In the mid-1960s was the site of the headquarters of the Third Marine Division and its affiliated medical facility, 72-121; in October 1965 was attacked by the Viet Cong, 79-80, 86-87; Wilson's military concerns while serving as commanding officer of the Danang hospital, 95-98; in January 1966 Naval Support Activity Danang opened a hospital, 100

Davis, Vice Admiral George M., MC, USN
Assessment of this officer who served from 1969 to 1973 as the Navy's Surgeon General, 198-199

DeForest, Lieutenant Commander Don D., USN
In late 1950 this officer was sent on an urgent mission to sweep mines on the east coast of Korea, 40

Discipline
Procedures followed in the mid-1970s for dealing with various cases at the Great Lakes Naval Hospital, 219-221

Drugs
Prior use of by recruits who entered the Great Lakes Naval Training Center in the mid-1970s, 222-223

Eccles, Rear Admiral Henry E., USN (Ret.) (USNA, 1922)
For many years after his retirement in 1952, taught logistics at the Naval War College, 150-152

Education
In the early 1940s, through the V-12 program, Union College in Schenectady, New York, provided education and Navy officer training, 2-4; influx of veterans as students at colleges and universities following World War II, 37-39; in the mid-1960s Sophia University in Tokyo had programs for foreign students, 71; Wilson and his family studied at Sophia University, 137-138; in the late 1960s, Wilson earned a master's degree in international affairs from George Washington University, 147-149; in the early 1980s Wilson fostered the Management Development Advisory Board to chart career paths and educational requirements for people in the Navy's medical department, 259-262

Egypt
In the early 1970s the U.S. Navy ran a medical research unit in Egypt in order to study tropical diseases, 155-156

Eske, Captain Louis H., MC, USNR
In September 1970 joined the Sixth Fleet staff, even though the fleet commander, Vice Admiral Isaac Kidd, did not want a senior medical officer, 163-164; did an excellent job of planning that enabled the fleet to be prepared for the 1983 bombing of the Marine barracks in Beirut, Lebanon, 164; in the mid-1970s served as the medical contingency planning officer in BuMed, 235

Etter, Rear Admiral Harry S., MC, USN
In the early 1970s, while stationed in the Bureau of Medicine and Surgery, was slow to recognize the value of computers for facilities planning, 179; had a difficult time with Congressman Joseph Addabbo because of a proposal in the 1970s to close the naval hospital at St. Albans, New York, 202-203

Families of Servicemen
Interactions with neighbors in the mid-1960s when the Wilson family lived in Belmont, Massachusetts, near Boston, 67-69; when Wilson was serving in Vietnam in the mid-1960s his wife and son lived on the Japanese economy and studied in Tokyo, 71; in the mid-1960s Wilson's family had the opportunity to do some traveling and sightseeing in the Far East, 136-137; in the mid-1960s Wilson's family lived on the Japanese economy and studied at Sophia University in Tokyo, 137-138, 140-142

Farrell, Major General Walter Greatsinger, USMC (Ret.)
As a patient at the San Diego Naval Hospital in the early 1960s, had a great fund of sea stories, 59-61

Fitness Reports
Evaluation of medical officers who served in 1965-66 with the Third Medical Battalion in South Vietnam, 102-103

Fleet Hospital Program
    Began in 1976 and progressed from there as a means of developing transportable field hospital facilities that could be set up when and where needed, 234-251; around 1979 established a Fleet Hospital Support Office at Port Hueneme, California, later moved to Alameda, 239, 243; testing of various transportable structures, 240-241; in 1981 BuMed established the Fleet Hospital Project Office, 242; in 1990 fleet hospitals deployed to the Persian Gulf region as part of Operation Desert Shield, 249-251

Food
    In the summer of 1945 Navy chow on board the high-speed transport Liddle (APD-60) was a great boon to Army men who had been fighting ashore for a long time, 25; rations fed to Marines during the Vietnam War had the effect of causing constipation, 99-100; standing rib roast was featured at a party in London in 1971 to celebrate the supposed 100th anniversary of the U.S. Navy Medical Department, 173

Gaffney, Lieutenant Commander William S., USNR
    Reserve officer who commanded a ship in the early 1950s as a break from his normal work as a forest ranger, 46-47

Gibb, Lieutenant Thomas W., Jr., CEC, USN
    In the mid-1970s became involved with the fleet hospital program to develop transportable medical facilities, 234

Giordano, Captain Andrew A., SC, USN
    In the mid-1970s supported the fleet hospital program to develop transportable medical facilities, 237-238

Goff, USS (DD-247)
    Old four-stack destroyer that was used in 1944-45 for antisubmarine warfare training at Key West, Florida, 11-12; ship-handling characteristics, 12

Gordon, Commander Charles Vance, USN
    In the years shortly after World War II he was executive officer of the advisory group that aided the South Korean Navy, 42-43

Gordon, Commander Charles Vance, Jr., MSC, USN
    In the mid-1970s developed computer models to deal with medical contingency operations, 235-236

Great Britain
    In the early 1970s Naval Activities, United Kingdom, a U.S. Navy command, was involved in logistic support of activities in the area, 155; work of the medical dispensary, 155; in the early 1970s U.S. Navy personnel attended a "Save the Children Ball" at Thurso, Scotland, 165; supply of medical care to service personnel and their dependents involved various clinics, 168-169; in 1971 members of the

Naval Activities, United Kingdom staff held a party in London to celebrate the supposed 100th anniversary of the U.S. Navy medical department, 172-173

Great Lakes, Illinois, Naval Hospital
When Wilson reported in 1974, the commanding officer's billet had just been downgraded from rear admiral to captain, 205; in the early 1970s the CNO, Admiral Elmo Zumwalt, pushed racial awareness training through UPWARD seminars and produced unfortunate consequences at Great Lakes, 207-216; reorganization in the mid-1970s of the enlisted structure at the hospital, 216-217; disciplinary procedures for dealing with the hospital staff, 219-221; increasing turnover of hospital staff to keep people from stagnating, 221; cooperative ventures with other health-care providers in the area, 221-222; in the mid-1970s established a rehabilitation center to treat chronic alcoholics, 223-224; Wilson's methods for administering the hospital and staff, 224-227; huge set of quarters for the hospital commanding officer, 227-228

Great Lakes, Illinois, Naval Training Center
In the early 1970s experienced a number of unpleasant racial incidents, 206; the Recruit Training Command received new enlisted personnel that came from a wide variety of backgrounds, 218-219; drug use in the background of recruits, 222-223

Greece
Athens was a way-station in 1970 for delivery of high-priority cargo to the Sixth Fleet in the eastern Mediterranean, 162-163; in the early 1970s, Admiral Elmo Zumwalt, the Chief of Naval Operations, strongly pushed to have U.S. Navy ships home-ported in Athens, 170-171

Green Cove Springs, Florida
Site for the mothballing of Navy ships shortly after the end of World War II, 34

Grinstead, Rear Admiral Eugene A., Jr., SC, USN
As Chief of the Supply Corps in the late 1970s provided support to the fleet hospital program to develop transportable medical facilities, 239

Guam, USS (LPH-9)
Amphibious assault ship that was the subject of an InSurv inspection around 1980, 253-254

Gulf War
In 1990 fleet hospitals were deployed to the Persian Gulf region as part of the Desert Shield buildup, 249-251

Gunnery-Naval
Provided in 1945 by cruisers to support amphibious operations in the Philippines, 22

Hackleback, USS (SS-295)
New submarine that late in World War II provided training services for antisubmarine ships, 11

Hagedorn, Captain Lawrence D., SC, USN (Ret.)
In the late 1970s became part of the team running the fleet hospital program to develop transportable medical facilities, 239-240, 242, 244, 246

Hauser, Lieutenant Commander Roger G., MC, USN
Navy doctor who did a superb job in the mid-1960s in providing medical services to Marines wounded in Vietnam, 104-106, 128

Heaton, Lieutenant Harley L., MSC, USN
In the mid-1960s was involved in the planning for a possible new naval hospital at Chelsea, Massachusetts, 64-65

Hebert, Representative F. Edward
In the early 1970s the city of New Orleans was programmed to receive an unnecessarily large new naval hospital as the result of Hebert's political clout as a congressman, 181-183

Helicopters
In 1965-66 were used for the evacuation of combat wounded in Vietnam and the delivery of medical teams, 81-83, 89, 98-99, 103-104, 108; transfer of patients in the mid-1960s from Yokota, Japan, to the naval hospital at Yokosuka, 125-126

Hospital Corpsmen
Training in the mid-1960s at Camp Pendleton, California, to prepare for duty in Vietnam, 71; duty at Danang, South Vietnam, 87, 101-102; went into action with the Marines in Vietnam, 88-89, 110-111; stopped at the hospital in Yokosuka, Japan, in the mid-1960s before going to Vietnam, 124

Hospitals
In 1952-53 Bremerton Naval Hospital treated men who had been wounded in the Korean War, 39-40; in 1959-61 the small station hospital at Subic Bay in the Philippines handled a variety of medical cases, 48-58; in the early 1960s San Diego Naval Hospital treated a variety of patients, including retired senior officers, 58-62; in the mid-1960s Chelsea Naval Hospital served the medical needs of the Navy population in the Boston area, 63-69; in the mid-1960s the Bureau of Medicine and Surgery (BuMed) made plans to build new naval hospitals in several locations, 64-65; closing of several naval hospitals in the early 1970s, 65-66; in 1965-66 the Third Medical Battalion facility at Danang, South Vietnam, treated both combat wounds and the usual assortment of illnesses and injuries, 76-121; badly wounded men were evacuated from Vietnam to other medical facilities, 81, 85, 89-90, 93, 100, 106; the naval hospital at Yokosuka, Japan, expanded its capacity greatly in the mid-

1960s to handle casualties from the Vietnam War and treated other kinds of patients as well, 124-136, 138-139; work of the Bureau of Medicine and Surgery in the early 1970s in planning for the design, construction, and upgrading of naval hospitals, 175-183, 187-188; in the early 1970s the city of New Orleans was programmed to receive an unnecessarily large new naval hospital as the result of Representative F. Edward Hebert's political clout, 181-183; value of having physicians as commanding officers of naval hospitals and Surgeons General, 199-200; Rear Admiral Harry Etter had a difficult time with Congressman Joseph Addabbo because of a BuMed proposal in the 1970s to close the naval hospital at St. Albans, New York, 202-203; issues in the mid-1970s at the Great Lakes Naval Hospital included racial awareness training, among other things, 205-229; the fleet hospital program began in 1976 and progressed from there as a means of developing transportable field hospital facilities that could be set up when and where needed, 234-251

Hospital Ships
Used in the Vietnam War, 79, 105-106, 108; outfitting in the 1980s of two tankers converted to be hospital ships, 252-257; the mothballed commercial passenger liner United States was considered around 1980 for possible conversion to a Navy hospital ship, 253-254

Idi Amin
In January 1971 this dictator seized power in Uganda, 166-167

Inchon, Korea
Shortly after World War II the high-speed transport Liddle (APD-60) was part of a convoy that delivered troops to Inchon from Okinawa, 26-28

Inspection and Survey, Board of (InSurv)
The amphibious assault ship Guam (LPH-9) was the subject of an InSurv inspection around 1980, 253-254

Intelligence
When Marines were wounded in Vietnam in the mid-1960s the medical personnel at Danang notified the intelligence section of the Third Marine Division headquarters, 83

Iran
Visited in 1973 by Admiral Thomas Moorer, Chairman of the Joint Chiefs of Staff, 190-191

Ireland
In the early 1970s the U.S. Navy made arrangements with local medical facilities in London to treat service personnel stationed there, 168-169; hostilities between Protestants and Catholics, 168-169

Italy
In the early 1970s shellfish in Italy carried hepatitis to humans, 169

Japan
In the early 1950s Sasebo served as a support base for U.S. Navy ships operating in the Far East, 43-44; in the mid-1960s the naval hospital at Yokosuka had a heavy patient load because of battle casualties from Vietnam and the treatment of other medical problems, 124-136, 138-139; in the mid-1960s Wilson's family lived on the Japanese economy and studied at Sophia University in Tokyo, 137-138, 140-142

Japanese Army
During U.S. amphibious landings in the Philippines in the spring of 1945, fired at the incoming U.S. ships, 19-20; in 1945 fired upon Australian troops as they landed in Borneo, 23

Japanese Maritime Self-Defense Force
In the late 1960s Captain Matsuo Matsui was a student at the U.S. Naval War College, later became a vice admiral, 143-144

Japanese Navy
In December 1944 a kamikaze suicide plane inflicted heavy damage on the high-speed transport Liddle (APD-60), which was operating in the Philippines, 12-13; in 1945, right after the end of World War II, Americans sought souvenirs on board a captured Japanese midget submarine at Inchon, Korea, 27

Jordan
Was involved in a crisis in September 1970s when Palestinian commandos captured commercial airliners, 162

KC-135 Stratotanker
In the early 1970s Admiral Thomas Moorer, Chairman of the Joint Chiefs of Staff, made his trips in a specially configured Air Force KC-135 aircraft, 192-195

Kamikazes
In December 1944 a Japanese suicide plane inflicted heavy damage on the high-speed transport Liddle (APD-60), which was operating in the Philippines, 12-13

Kennedy, Senator Edward M.
Was involved in a congressional investigation following the October 1983 bombing of the Marine barracks in Beirut, Lebanon, 274-275

Kennedy, Lieutenant Commander William D. USNR (USNA, 1928)
Resigned after graduation from the Naval Academy, then returned to active duty for World War II, 17; had wartime command of the high-speed transport Liddle (APD-60), 17, 20-22, 29; personal characteristics, 20-22

Kenya
  In the early 1970s this was one of the countries Wilson and his wife visited during a safari trip in East Africa, 165, 167

Key West, Florida
  In 1944-45 was the site of Navy antisubmarine warfare training, 11-12

Kidd, Vice Admiral Isaac C., Jr., USN (USNA, 1942)
  As Commander Sixth Fleet in September 1970, reluctantly accepted a senior medical officer for his staff and then developed a fast friendship with him, 162-164

Korea
  Shortly after World War II the high-speed transport Liddle (APD-60) was part of a convoy that delivered troops to Inchon from Okinawa, 26-28; in late 1953 ships of Mine Squadron Three patrolled off the coast of South Korea and conducted minesweeping exercises, 41-42, 44

Korean Navy
  In the years following World War II the South Korean Navy received ships and fuel from the United States, 42-43

Korean War
  Top-notch Naval Reserve doctors served on active duty during the war, 39-40; U.S. minesweeping operations in 1950 on the east coast of Korea, 40

Kuwait
  Visited in 1973 by Admiral Thomas Moorer, Chairman of the Joint Chiefs of Staff, 191-192

Laird, Melvin R.
  As Secretary of Defense in 1972, asked the Navy to come up with the cost of modernizing its medical and dental facilities, and the money was subsequently forthcoming, 176-179, 187-188

Landis, Captain Cary E., USN
  In the early 1970s was involved in the program to home-port U.S. Navy ships in Athens, Greece, 171

Leave and Liberty
  During World War II Chicago was a hospitable city for young midshipmen on liberty, 9-10

Lebanon
  In 1970 Wilson visited Beirut and got a sense of local sentiment about the United States, 157; medical aspects of the October 1983 bombing of the Marine barracks in Beirut, 164, 273-274; congressional investigation after the disaster, 273-275

Liddle, USS (APD-60)
High-speed amphibious transport that in early 1945 was repaired at San Francisco after being damaged by a kamikaze in the Philippines, 12-14; post-repair sea trials, 15-16; wartime deployment in 1945 to the Western Pacific, 17-25; the ship operated as part of Transport Division 103, 17-18; in April 1945 put Army troops ashore during an amphibious assault at Legaspi in the Philippines, 18-20; in 1945 conducted further amphibious operations in the Philippines and Borneo, 22-25; appendectomy on board for an Australian soldier, 25-26; postwar activities in the Western Pacific included the transportation of personnel, 26-31; difficulties in riding through typhoons, 28-31; visit to Tientsin, China, 31-32; return to the United States for inactivation and decommissioning in June 1946 at Green Cove Springs, Florida, 32-33

London, England
In 1971 members of the U.S. Naval Activities United Kingdom staff held a party in London to celebrate the supposed 100th anniversary of the U.S. Navy Medical Department, 172-173

Lowery, Rear Admiral Clinton H., MC, USN
In 1979-80 was briefly in charge of the fleet hospital program to develop transportable medical facilities but did not actively pursue it, 244

Mahin, Rear Admiral Harry Paul, MC, USN
Got sidetracked from command in the early 1970s because the CNO, Admiral Elmo Zumwalt, heard a negative comment about him, 215

Mainstay, USS (AM-261)
Minesweeper that in the mid-1950s operated in the Far East, 44-45

Marine Corps, U.S.
Landing at Danang, Vietnam in March 1965, 70; mid-1960s training exercises at Camp Pendleton provided useful background for Wilson before he headed to Vietnam, 70-71; in 1965 Okinawa served as a way station for Marines and Navy medical personnel en route to Vietnam, 72; Danang served as headquarters for the Third Marine Division during its fighting in the northern part of South Vietnam, 72-76; in 1965-66 the Third Medical Battalion at Danang and nearby areas treated combat casualties and the usual assortment of illnesses and injuries, 76-121; badly wounded men were evacuated from Vietnam to medical facilities in other countries, 81, 85, 89-90, 93, 100, 124-125; Lieutenant General Lewis Walt, commanding general of the III Marine Amphibious Force in the mid-1960s, was concerned about the welfare of his Marines, 84, 91-94; in December 1965 launched an offensive operation in Vietnam called Harvest Moon, 87-89, 91, 98-99; provision for handling the bodies of Marines killed in Vietnam, 107; the naval hospital at Yokosuka, Japan, expanded its capacity greatly in the mid-1960s to handle Marine casualties from the Vietnam War, 124-136; a number of gunnery sergeants who were promoted to

platoon leaders suffered ulcers because of the additional stress, 130-131; medical aspects of the October 1983 bombing of the Marine barracks in Beirut, Lebanon, 164, 273-274

Matson Navigation Company
In early 1945 Matson's shipyard in San Francisco repaired battle damage to the Navy high-speed transport Liddle (APD-60), 12-14

Medical Problems
In the summer of 1945 the ship's doctor performed an appendectomy on board the high-speed transport Liddle (APD-60), 25-26; cases of malaria were treated in the early 1950s at Bremerton Naval Hospital, 39; food poisoning in the mid-1950s in Mine Squadron Three, 44; several appendicitis cases in the same period, 44-45; in 1959-61 the small station hospital at Subic Bay handled a variety of medical cases, 48-58; in the early 1960s the San Diego Naval Hospital treated a variety of patients, including retired senior officers, 58-62; in the mid-1960s the Third Medical Battalion at Danang, South Vietnam, treated combat casualties and the usual assortment of illnesses and injuries, 76-121; badly wounded men were evacuated from Vietnam to other medical facilities, 81, 85, 89-90, 106, 124-125; the naval hospital at Yokosuka, Japan, expanded its capacity greatly in the mid-1960s to handle casualties from the Vietnam War and to treat other medical problems, 124-136, 138-139; a number of gunnery sergeants who were promoted to platoon leaders suffered ulcers because of the additional stress, 130-131; in the early 1970s the U.S. Navy ran a medical research unit in Egypt in order to study tropical diseases, 155-156; in the early 1970s shellfish in Italy carried hepatitis to humans, 169; value of having physicians as commanding officers of naval hospitals and Surgeons General, 199-200; in the mid-1970s Wilson had a pre-cancerous condition on one kidney, 217

Miami, Florida, Naval Training Center
During World War II naval personnel received antisubmarine training at Miami, 10-11

Military Airlift Command
In the mid-1960s the Military Airlift Command provided flights for service personnel and their dependents, 136

Military Construction Liaison Officers
Role in the early 1970s in ensuring that the designs for new hospital facilities were satisfactory from a medical standpoint, 177-180

Mine Squadron Three
In late 1950 performed minesweeping operations on the east coast of Korea, 40; in late 1953 ships of the squadron patrolled off the coast of South Korea and conducted minesweeping exercises, 41-42, 44; ship crew members had a variety of medical problems, 44-45

Mine Warfare
In the period right after the end of World War II floating mines posed a hazard in the Yellow Sea, 26, 28, 31; the attack transport Colbert (APA-145) hit a floating mine, 30; U.S. minesweeping operations in 1950 on the east coast of Korea, 40; in late 1953 ships of Mine Squadron Three patrolled off the coast of South Korea and conducted minesweeping exercises, 41-42, 44

Minter, Vice Admiral Charles S., Jr., USN (USNA, 1937)
In the early 1970s, as Deputy Chief of Naval Operations (Logistics), reluctantly agreed to a large new naval hospital in New Orleans because of the political clout of Congressman F. Edward Hebert, 182-183

Moorer, Admiral Thomas H., USN (USNA, 1933)
From 1972 to 1974, while he was Chairman of the Joint Chiefs of Staff, had Wilson as his personal physician, 189-195; 1973 trip to the Middle East, 190-191, made his trips in a specially configured KC-135 aircraft, 192-195; personality of, 193-194

Moxley, Dr. John
Around 1980, as Assistant Secretary of Defense for Health Affairs, pushed for the Navy to obtain hospital ships, 253-254

Murray, Captain Dermot A., MC, USN
After service as an anesthesiologist, in the early 1970s he was director of the planning division of the Navy's Bureau of Medicine and Surgery, 175

Naval Activities, United Kingdom
In the early 1970s was involved in logistic support of U.S. Navy activities in the area, 155; work of the medical dispensary, 155; in the early 1970s U.S. Navy personnel attended a "Save the Children Ball" at Thurso, Scotland, 165; supply of medical care to service personnel and their dependents involved various clinics, 168-169; in 1971 members of the staff held a party in London to celebrate the supposed 100th anniversary of the U.S. Navy medical department, 172-173

Naval Facilities Engineering Command
Role in the early 1970s in planning and designing naval hospitals in various places, 176-180; in the mid-1970s and beyond was involved in the fleet hospital program to develop transportable health care facilities, 237, 239, 243

Naval Forces Europe, U.S.
In the early 1970s was a far-flung command, and Wilson visited many of the activities to get a sense of their activities, 153-160; staff included a number of officers who did not have promising careers ahead of them, 159-160; the staff wore civilian clothes in London to keep a low profile, 161

Naval Reserve
   In World War II young men received both college education and naval training as part of the V-12 program, 2-10; top-notch reserve doctors served on active duty during the Korean War, 39-40

Naval War College, Newport, Rhode Island
   In the late 1960s Wilson was a rare exception as a Navy medical officer assigned to attend the war college, 139; one of the great side benefits of the school is making contacts that will be useful in future years, 142-143; contact with foreign students, 143-144; the curriculum in the late 1960s was useful but not as demanding as it became in the 1970s, 144-148, 150-151; discussion in the late 1960s at the Naval War College about U.S. nuclear strategy vis-à-vis the Soviet Union, 145; visiting speakers were useful, 149-150; war games, 152; value of war college teaching when Wilson took a subsequent job in London, 154

Navy League
   In the mid-1970s the local chapter in the Chicago area got involved with the Great Lakes Naval Training Center, 228-229

New Orleans, Louisiana
   In the early 1970s the city was programmed to receive an unnecessarily large new naval hospital as the result of the political clout of Congressman F. Edward Hebert, 181-183

Norris, Rear Admiral Frank T., MC, USN
   In the late 1950s headed the professional division in the Navy's Bureau of Medicine and Surgery, 47; in the late 1960s corresponded with Wilson about the possibility of Wilson being assigned to the Naval War College, 139; in 1969 arranged for Wilson to be assigned to the staff of Commander in Chief Naval Forces Europe, 153; asked Wilson to check on conditions in Morocco, 159; in 1970 arranged to assign Captain Louis Eske as Sixth Fleet medical officer, 163; negotiations in the early 1970s with Wilson to transfer him from London to Washington, 174

Northwestern University, Evanston, Illinois
   During World War II was the site of midshipman training for young men in the V-12 officer program, 5-10

Nuclear Weapons
   Discussion in the late 1960s at the Naval War College about U.S. nuclear strategy vis-à-vis the Soviet Union, 145

Okinawa
   In 1965 served as a way station for Marines and Navy medical personnel en route to Vietnam, 72-73

Olongapo, Philippines
  The town became raunchy in the period around 1960, after the U.S. Navy gave up control of it, 48

O'Neil, Rear Admiral Warren H., USN (USNA, 1945)
  In the mid-1970s was in command of the large naval complex at Great Lakes, Illinois, 206, 211, 228

Parsons, Captain William Seavey, USN (USNA, 1928)
  In 1945, right after the conclusion of World War II, commanded Transport Division 103 in the Western Pacific, 27

Pay and Allowances
  Pay of $50.00 per month in the early 1940s for seamen training to be officers through the V-12 program, 3, 9-10; before the ship's serviceman rating was created enlisted men who worked as tailors received extra pay, 4; the Navy has to pay bonuses to retain medical officers on active duty, 203-204

Pendleton, Camp
  See: Camp Pendleton, Oceanside, California

Penn, Commander Buddie Joe, USN
  In 1974 was part of an Inspector General team that went to the Great Lakes Naval Hospital to investigate problems with a racial awareness seminar facilitator, 210

Perloff, Lieutenant Milton M., USNR
  Officer who had shipboard duty in World War II and then taught in the midshipman school at Northwestern University, 5-6

Persian Gulf
  See: Gulf War; Iran; Kuwait

Philippine Islands
  In December 1944 a kamikaze suicide plane inflicted heavy damage on the high-speed transport Liddle (APD-60), which was involved in the Battle of Ormoc Bay, 12-13; condition of Subic Bay in 1945, 18; in April 1945 the ships of Transport Division 103 put ashore Army troops during an amphibious assault at Legaspi, 18-20; further 1945 amphibious operations, 21, 24; in 1959-61 the small station hospital at Subic Bay handled a variety of medical problems, 48-58; in 1965-66 badly wounded men were evacuated from Vietnam to the Clark Air Force Base Hospital, 81, 85, 89-90, 93, 100, 107, 124-125; in the mid-1960s, the top medical officer for the Pacific Command, Rear Admiral John S. Cowan convened annual conferences with medical representatives from throughout the theater at Baguio to discuss the treatment of Vietnam War casualties, 123-124

Phillips, Captain George L., USN (USNA, 1925)
In the mid-1950s commanded Mine Squadron Three, which was based in Sasebo, Japan, 43-44

Planning
In the mid-1960s the Bureau of Medicine and Surgery (BuMed) made plans to build new naval hospitals in several locations, 64-65; Sixth fleet medical planning enabled it to have necessary offshore resources in October 1983 when terrorists bombed the Marine barracks at Beirut, Lebanon, 164, 168; work of the Bureau of Medicine and Surgery in the early 1970s in planning for the design, construction, and upgrading of naval hospitals, 175-183, 187-188; response of BuMed when Secretary of Defense Robert McNamara introduced the Planning, Programming, and Budgeting System in the early 1960s, 197; attempts in the late 1970s to get the BuMed and the rest of Navy medicine into the Planning, Programming, and Budgeting System, 232-233; the fleet hospital program began in 1976 and progressed from there as a means of planning and developing transportable field hospital facilities that could be set up when and where needed, 234-251

Quinn, Captain James J., MC, USN
Served in the late 1970s in the Bureau of Medicine and Surgery and kept the Surgeon General, Vice Admiral Willard Arentzen, well informed, 230-231, 269

Racial Issues
In the late 1960s and early 1970s the Great Lakes Naval Training Center experienced unpleasant racial incidents, 206; in the early 1970s the CNO, Admiral Elmo Zumwalt, pushed racial awareness training through UPWARD seminars, 207-216

Radar
In 1944 was considered to be highly classified at the naval training center in Miami, Florida, 10-11; in 1945 the junior officers on board the high-speed transport Liddle (APD-60) were inexperienced in the use of radar, 15-16

Rockets
In 1945 U.S. LCI(R)s were used for shore bombardment during amphibious assaults in Borneo, 23

San Diego Naval Hospital
In the early 1960s treated a variety of patients, including retired senior officers, 58-62

San Francisco, California
In early 1945 the Matson shipyard in San Francisco repaired battle damage to the high-speed transport Liddle (APD-60), 12-14; during World War II it was a bustling city, particularly on the waterfront, 16

Sasebo, Japan
In the early 1950s served as a support base for U.S. Navy ships operating in the Far East, 43-44

Scotia, New York, Naval Supply Depot
In 1946, right after World War II, had huge stocks of a wide variety of shipboard equipment and parts, 34-37; postwar changes, 37

Scotland
In the early 1970s U.S. Navy personnel attended a "Save the Children Ball" at Thurso, 165; Holy Loch was the base for ballistic missile submarines, 168

Seabees
In October 1965 the Viet Cong attacked the Seabee compound at Danang, South Vietnam, 79-80; supervised the framing of hospital tents at Danang, 87; in the early 1970s built a pontoon barge to support a U.S. Navy medical facility in Bolivia, 183-184; in the early 1980s provided support for the fleet hospital program to develop transportable medical facilities, 244, 248-249

Seaton, Vice Admiral Lewis H., MC, USN
From 1983 to 1987 served as the Navy's Surgeon General, 259, 266-267, 272-273; career background, 259

Shore Bombardment
In 1945 U.S. LCI(R)s fired rockets ashore during amphibious assaults in Borneo, 23

Sixth Fleet, U.S.
Involvement in September 1970 in the Jordanian crisis in the eastern Mediterranean, 162; in 1970 Wilson suggested the fleet staff needed a more senior medical officer than a lieutenant and started a process by which BuMed supplied a captain, 162-164; Sixth fleet medical planning enabled it to have necessary offshore resources in October 1983 when terrorists bombed the Marine barracks at Beirut, Lebanon, 164, 168; operations in the early 1970s involved political tensions, 167-168; in the early 1970s, Admiral Elmo Zumwalt, the Chief of Naval Operations, strongly pushed to have U.S. Navy ships home-ported in Greece, 170-171

Skelly, Lieutenant Robert S., MSC, USN
Officer who in the mid-1960s was aggressive in supporting the Third Medical Battalion at Danang, South Vietnam, 94-95

Small, Admiral William N., USN (USNA, 1948)
In the early 1980s, as Vice Chief of Naval Operations, had a role in reorganizing the Bureau of Medicine and Surgery as the Naval Medical Command after perceiving a number of shortcomings, 272-273

Soviet Union
In 1969, after graduating from Sophia University in Tokyo, Geoffrey Wilson traveled to the United States via the Soviet Union, including a trip on the trans-Siberian Railroad, 141-142; discussion in the late 1960s at the Naval War College about U.S. nuclear strategy vis-à-vis the Soviet Union, 145

Sparks, Captain Henry A., MC, USN
In the early 1970s was in charge of the U.S. Navy medical research unit in Egypt, 155-156

Stein, Colonel Ignatius J., MC, USAF
Air force doctor who performed valuable service in the mid-1960s when wounded men from Vietnam arrived in the Philippines for further treatment, 85

Stoecklein, Captain Herbert, MC, USN
In 1965, as detailer for BuMed, arranged for Wilson to serve a year in Vietnam, then go to the naval hospital in Yokosuka, Japan, 70

Strange, Captain Robert E., MC, USN
In 1974, as psychiatric consultant to the Surgeon General, went to Great Lakes Naval Hospital to investigate a problem with a racial awareness instructor, 210-211

Subic Bay, Philippines
Condition of in March 1945, shortly after being captured from the Japanese, 18; construction of an airstrip in the 1950s at Cubi Point, 18; in 1959-61 the small station hospital handled a variety of medical problems, 48-58

Swope, Captain John P., MC, USN (USNA, 1958)
In the early 1980s took over as head of the fleet hospital program to develop transportable medical facilities, 248

Third Medical Battalion, Third Marine Division
See: Vietnam War

Tientsin, China
Multinational atmosphere in the city in late 1945, right after World War II ended, 31-32

Tower, Senator John G.
Was involved in a congressional investigation following the October 1983 bombing of the Marine barracks in Beirut, Lebanon, 273-274

Training
During World War II, young men received education and Navy officer training through the V-12 program, 2-10; antisubmarine training during World War II at Key West and Miami, Florida, 10-12; mid-1960s training exercises at Camp Pendleton

provided useful background for Wilson and Navy hospital corpsmen before they headed to Vietnam, 70-71; training of Navy doctors to be effective managers, 200; in the early 1970s the CNO, Admiral Elmo Zumwalt, pushed racial awareness training through UPWARD seminars, 207-216; in the mid-1970s Wilson went to a "charm school" for newly selected rear admirals, 229-230

Transport Division 103
Composition of during the latter part of World War II, 17-18; in April 1945 the ships of the division conducted an amphibious landing at Legaspi in the Philippines, 18-20; further 1945 amphibious operations in the Philippines and Borneo, 22-25

Turco, Lieutenant Commander Ronald F., MSC, USN
In the mid-1970s became involved with the fleet hospital program to develop transportable medical facilities, 234

Turner, Vice Admiral Stansfield, USN (USNA, 1947)
In the early 1970s, as president of the Naval War College, made the curriculum much more demanding than it had been, 148

Uganda
In 1971 Wilson and his wife visited during a safari trip in East Africa and had to escape after dictator Idi Amin seized power in a coup d-état, 166-167

Union College, Schenectady, New York
Wilson's studies there in the early 1940s, 1-4; after World War II Wilson returned to the college to complete his degree and attend medical school, 37-38; huge influx of returning veterans as students after the war, 38

United States, SS
Mothballed commercial passenger liner that was considered around 1980 for possible conversion to a Navy hospital ship, 253-254

UPWARD Seminars
Program in the early 1970s through which the CNO, Admiral Elmo Zumwalt, pushed racial awareness training, 207-216

V-12 Program
During World War II, young men received education and Navy officer training through this program, 2-10

Venereal Disease
Treatment of in the 1959-61 period at the naval hospital at Subic Bay in the Philippines, 56

Vietnam War
Early U.S. involvement included a Marine Corps landing in March 1965 at Danang, 69-70; 1965 training exercises at Camp Pendleton provided useful background for Navy medical personnel on the way to Vietnam, 70-71; in 1965 Okinawa served as a way station for Marines en route to Vietnam, 72-73; as the Third Medical Battalion was established in 1965 near Danang, it was short of needed supplies, 72-73, 76, 84-86, 119-120; description of the Third Marine Division headquarters and affiliated facilities at Danang, 73-76; in 1965-66 the Third Medical Battalion at Danang treated combat casualties and the usual assortment of illnesses and injuries, 76-121; October 1965 Viet Cong attack on Danang, 79-80, 86-87; badly wounded men were delivered from Vietnam to medical facilities in other countries, 81, 85, 89-90, 106, 124-125; helicopters were used for the evacuation of combat wounded within Vietnam and the delivery of medical teams, 81-83, 89, 98-99, 103-104, 108; in December 1965 U.S. Marines launched an offensive operation called Harvest Moon, 87-89, 91, 98-99; Viet Cong use of land mines, 100-101, 111; provision for handling the bodies of Marines killed in Vietnam, 107; rest and recreation facilities, 111; role of psychiatrists in dealing with young Marines who have been in combat, 114-116; those serving in Vietnam itself often had little information about the war as a whole, 116-117; in the mid-1960s, the top medical officer for the Pacific Command, Rear Admiral John S. Cowan convened annual conferences with medical representatives from throughout the theater to discuss the treatment of Vietnam War casualties, 123-124; the Yokosuka Naval Hospital expanded its capacity greatly in the mid-1960s to handle casualties from the Vietnam War, 124-130; a number of Marine Corps gunnery sergeants who were promoted to platoon leaders suffered ulcers because of the additional stress, 130-131

Walt, Lieutenant General Lewis W., USMC
As commanding general of the III Marine Amphibious Force in the mid-1960s was concerned about the welfare of his Marines fighting in Vietnam, 84, 91-94; personal characteristics, 93-94; weekly meetings with battalion commanders, 116

Weather
Shortly after World War II ended the high-speed transport Liddle (APD-60) was buffeted by typhoons in the Western Pacific, 28-31

Weinberger, Caspar W.
As Secretary of Defense, testified before Congress in the wake of the October 1983 bombing of the Marine barracks in Beirut, Lebanon, 274

Wendt, Admiral Waldemar F. A., USN (USNA, 1933)
Positive assessment of this admiral who served from 1968 to 1971 as Commander in Chief Naval Forces Europe, 153, 160-161; involved in the command's social events, 161; supported Wilson's initiatives in various areas, 162-163; had to make adjustments to civilian life in 1971, when he retired from active duty, 170

White, Commander Robert L., MSC, USN
   In the mid-1970s developed a computer program to predict casualties in the event of combat, 235

Wilson, Rear Admiral Almon C., MC, USN (Ret.)
   Boyhood in the 1920s and 1930s in upstate New York, 1-2; parents of, 1-2; siblings of, 1; education of, 1-4, 37-39, 137-138; reserve officer training through the V-12 program resulted in a commission in 1944, 2-10; in 1944-45 took antisubmarine training at Miami and Key West, Florida, 10-12; served as a junior officer in 1945-46 on board the high-speed transport Liddle (APD-60), 12-34; wife of, 12, 14-15, 35, 38, 67-68, 70-71, 137-140, 142, 149, 154, 161, 165, 167, 173-174, 194, 276, 280; worked at Ellis Hospital in Schenectady, New York, when he was a college student, 15; served for a few months in 1946 at the Naval Supply Depot, Scotia, New York, 34-37; returned to civilian life in 1946 and finished his undergraduate studies, 37-38; son Geoffrey, 38, 48, 67, 70-71, 140-142, 154, 280; in 1952 completed his degree from Albany Medical College, 38-39; internship in 1952-53 at the Bremerton Naval Hospital, 39-40; service in 1953-54 as medical officer for Mine Squadron Three in the Far East, 40-46; in the late 1950s worked in a Veterans Administration hospital in Utah, 46-47; served from 1959 to 1961 as a surgeon at the naval hospital at Subic Bay in the Philippines, 48-58; augmentation into the regular Navy, 58; surgery duty from 1961 to 1964 at the San Diego Naval Hospital, 58-62; served in 1964-65 as a surgeon at the Chelsea Naval Hospital near Boston, 63-69; service in 1965-66 as commanding officer of the Third Medical Battalion, the facility in Danang that served Marines fighting in the Vietnam War, 69-121; provided post-tour briefings following his return from Vietnam, 122-124; served from 1966 to 1968 as chief of surgery at the naval hospital in Yokosuka, Japan, 124-141; attendance in 1968-69 as a student at the Naval War College, 142-154; in the late 1960s earned a master's degree from George Washington University, 147-149; from 1969 to 1971 served in London as medical officer on the staff of Commander in Chief Naval Forces Europe, 153-174; in 1971-74 served as deputy director and then director of the BuMed planning division in Washington, 175-188, 195-205; additional duty in 1972-74 as personal physician to Admiral Thomas Moorer, Chairman of the Joint Chiefs of Staff, 189-195; in 1974-76 commanded the naval hospital at Great Lakes, Illinois, 205-229; in the summer of 1976 was selected for flag rank, 217-218; served 1976-79 as assistant chief for material resources in BuMed, 229-244; in the early 1980s ran the fleet hospital program to develop transportable medical facilities, 244-259; in 1982-84 served as head of the BuMed resources division and deputy to the Surgeon General, 259; activities following retirement in 1984 from active naval service, 275-280; grandsons, 280

Wonsan, North Korea
   In late 1950 was the site of U.S. minesweeping and an amphibious landing, 40

Wulfman, Captain William A., MC, USN
   In the mid-1960s served in Vietnam as medical officer for the III Marine Amphibious Force, 84-85

Wygant, Captain Benyaurd B., USN (Ret.) (USNA, 1901)
   During World War II, as commanding officer of the V-12 midshipman school at Northwestern University, provided sound lessons in leadership, 9

Yokosuka, Japan, Naval Hospital
   Expanded its capacity greatly in the mid-1960s to handle casualties from the Vietnam War and also treated patients with other medical problems, 124-136; initiated a facility for treating burn patients, but the result was disappointing, 131-132; in the mid-1960s established an intensive care unit, 133; Japanese employees of, 135-136, 138-139

Yokota, Japan, Air Force Base
   In the mid-1960s Vietnam wounded were staged through the airbase at Yokota, then to the naval hospital at Yokosuka, 125-127

Zimble, Vice Admiral James A., MC, USN
   Did a fine job from 1987 to 1991 while serving as the Navy's Surgeon General, 273; conducted an investigation about the medical aspects connected with the bombing of the Marine barracks at Beirut, Lebanon, in October 1983, 275

Zumwalt, Admiral Elmo R., Jr., USN (USNA, 1943)
   In the early 1970s, as Chief of Naval Operations, strongly pushed to have U.S. Navy ships home-ported in Greece, 170-171; did not follow the chain of command in various personnel initiatives, 172, 215-216; was involved in programs to support South American navies, 186; in the mid-1970s his gatekeeper tried to prevent the Surgeon General, Vice Admiral Donald Custis, from seeing Zumwalt, 201-202; in the early 1970s, as CNO, pushed racial awareness training through UPWARD seminars, 207-216

www.ingramcontent.com/pod-product-compliance
Lightning Source LLC
Chambersburg PA
CBHW080617170426
43209CB00007B/1451